❧ BORN TOO SOON ❧

✺ BORN TOO SOON ✺

The Story of Emily,
Our Premature Baby

Elizabeth Mehren

Doubleday

New York   London   Toronto   Sydney   Auckland

PUBLISHED BY DOUBLEDAY

a division of Bantam Doubleday Dell Publishing Group, Inc.
666 Fifth Avenue, New York, New York 10103

DOUBLEDAY and the portrayal of an anchor
with a dolphin are trademarks of Doubleday,
a division of Bantam Doubleday Dell
Publishing Group, Inc.

Book Design by Dorothy Kline

Library of Congress Cataloging-in-Publication Data

Mehren, Elizabeth.
    Born too soon : the story of a mother and a very small child / by
Elizabeth Mehren. — 1st ed.
        p.   cm.
    1. Mehren, Emily—Health. 2. Infants (Premature)—Massachusetts—
Boston—Biography. 3. Mother and infant. 4. Pregnancy in middle
age. I. Title.
RJ250.M44   1991
362.1'9892'011092—dc20
[B]   90-23851
                                                                       CIP

ISBN 0-385-26279-5

Printed in the United States of America
June 1991
1   3   5   7   9   10   8   6   4   2
First Edition

For Daddy Fox,
for Grandma Jean,
and most of all,
for Emily

Acknowledgments

The deeply personal nature of this story at times made it very difficult to write. But from the very beginning I believed in Emily's spirit. I trusted her courage and recognized that this child of mine had large lessons to teach all of us. My literary agent and friend, Carol Mann, also understood the strength of Emily's message, and encouraged me to write this book. Nancy Evans, then the publisher of Doubleday, gave me confidence and sound professional guidance. I am grateful to her for believing in this book. At Doubleday, I was fortunate enough to work with Casey Fuetsch, a skilled and sensitive editor.

I leaned on many people during the writing process. My friends Joanna Lennon, Elizabeth Campbell, Lane Retallick, Ann Marie Cunningham, and Pat Morrow listened endlessly. My *Los Angeles Times* colleagues Richard Eder, Jean Patman, Mary Rourke, Barbara Saltzman, Carol Powers, Diane Spatz, and the late John Brownell urged me on. Shelby Coffey, the editor of the *Los Angeles Times,* generously gave me time off to write my book. My friend Alexandra Marshall, a gifted novelist, gave me advice on tone and structure.

From the very first moment that I began writing this book, my husband, Fox Butterfield, was completely supportive. His loving reinforcement helped me through many dark moments. I am also thankful to Fox for agreeing to let me write about intimate and sometimes painful moments between us. If the shoe—or in this case, the word processor—had been on the other foot, I'm not at all certain that I would have been as accommodating.

Finally, I will forever be grateful to the nurses who cared for Emily and gave her comfort.

—E.M.

Child of the pure, unclouded brow
And dreaming eyes of wonder!
Though time be fleet and I and thou
Are half a life asunder,
Thy loving smile will surely hail
The love-gift of a fairy tale.
        —Lewis Carroll
            Through the Looking-Glass

For reasons of privacy many of the names in this book have been changed. But the reader can rest assured that all conversations and events took place as described.

❧ BORN TOO SOON ❧

ONE

For once the plane was scheduled to depart on time. I had made this coast-to-coast trip so often that I had come to expect the runway delays that sometimes kept the plane sitting on the ground for hours. Today the flight attendant assigned in the first-class cabin was a woman I judged to be about my own age, late thirties or early forties. Her dark hair was pulled back in a neat chignon. Her wedding band sparkled with big diamonds, and matching stones glittered in her earlobes. "Right on time," she promised, but she crossed her fingers when she said it. We veterans of the airways knew that you weren't off till you were off.

As usual, I had booked my favorite bulkhead seat. No one in front of me, lots of leg room, and far, far from the dreaded smoking section. I had packed a lot, too much probably, into this quick trip to Los Angeles. So I was genuinely looking forward to the uninterrupted quiet of the long flight across the country. It meant an escape from telephone calls and a respite from any decisions more complicated than what to eat or drink. These days, twenty-four-and-a-half weeks pregnant, my beverage of choice was milk.

Sliding my one light bag into the overhead compartment, I secretly hoped my growing midsection was noticeable. I had worked hard for this pregnancy, and was proud of it. My mother teased me when we shopped for maternity clothes in San Francisco a month or so earlier. "You *want* people to see that you're pregnant," she clucked with some bewilderment and the slightest note of disapproval. She had, after all, raised me with the prideful reminder that she had remained so svelte while carrying me that when she arrived at the hospital to give birth, some of the staff couldn't tell she was pregnant.

My mother was right. I was proud of this pregnancy. I did want to show it off. But to my chagrin, I apparently took after her. For here I was, nearing the six-month mark, and not one person at my office in Los Angeles the day before had said a word. I had even attended a small meeting of senior writers where one woman close to my age had just had a baby and another, several years older, was a month from having one. Pictures of Anne's newborn were passed around and admired, and we all fussed over Sara, the next incipient mother. Everyone at the table was dumbfounded when I piped up and said, "Me, too." I had spent years perfecting the independent career woman archetype. My marriage at age forty was enough of a surprise. But now a baby?

But that same scene, or something very much like it, was probably being played in offices all over the country at that moment. All over America, old ladies like me were frantically playing Beat the Biological Clock.

And so that afternoon on Flight 8, it felt especially comforting to click my seat belt shut. What was normally a routine act, a perfunctory gesture that came with sitting down on an airplane, today felt like a little extra hug for the baby girl who was due in fifteen and a half weeks. As soon as we'd learned her gender, my husband Fox and I had named her Emily. As I closed the belt around my belly, I gave the bulge a brief massage. You're safe, baby Emily, I was telling her with each loving stroke of my hand. You're inside me and you're safe. We're strapped in here together.

Before I was pregnant, this trip would have been routine, too. As an East Coast correspondent for the *Los Angeles Times,* I darted across the country on at least a monthly basis. I traveled so frequently, and often on such short notice, that at home I kept my toothbrush and cosmetics in a little flowered travel case, always ready to be tossed into a suitcase. After almost twenty years of dragging luggage around airports, I had learned to buy clothes based as much on how much they weighed as on what they looked like. I usually carried a small computer, a canvas bag stuffed with books and papers, and that oxymoronic creation of the luggage industry, a "carry-on" bag. (Carried on by whom? A gorilla?) Journalism students often told me they were attracted to the field because it sounded so exciting and romantic. When these aspiring scribes would ask me, wide-eyed, what it took to be a reporter, I would picture myself hauling all that stuff as I stumbled down an airport corridor, and reply, "Strong shoulders."

My travel schedule was such that friends liked to tease that for me, a frequent flyer award would be a week at home, not an excursion to some unpronounceable destination. When they found out I was pregnant with Emily, they playfully asked if I had enrolled her in her own mileage award program.

The truth was quite the opposite. When I learned that our chemically enhanced attempt to become pregnant had been successful, I instantly rearranged my existence. No more jogging. No aerobics. No alcohol, not even a celebratory sip of champagne. No caffeine, and no more midday meals of microwave popcorn while sitting at the word processor. I knew the statistics about first-trimester miscarriages. Many years earlier, I had had one myself. So the fast-paced life stopped immediately. When Fox and I traveled to Boston to spend weekends with Ethan and Sarah, his children by his previous marriage, I took the train, not the shuttle. During our annual Christmas ski vacation, I helped the family get dressed to hit the slopes, then curled up with a book in front of the fireplace. Sarah Ferguson, the wife of Prince Andrew, was skiing at this same stage of pregnancy, as one colleague in Los Angeles snidely reminded me. But, as I snapped back, Sarah Ferguson was fifteen years younger than I was. I'd had plenty of seasons to ski, and I had

lots more ahead. This was my winter to read books and to get
happily fat.

Fox and I had worked hard for this pregnancy. There was no
way we were going to jeopardize it.

Ours was a magical later-in-life love, the kind where, in car-
toon strips, turtle doves hover overhead. We stole kisses in the
kitchen, and slow-danced to golden oldies while the chicken was
broiling. This behavior earned us rebukes from Fox's son, Ethan,
who believed we were too old for such disgusting displays. "Cut
the mushy stuff!" he would order us. In return we appointed Ethan
president-for-life of the family morals squad.

I was thirty-nine when Fox and I met; he was forty-seven. We
had each been married before, he far more recently than I. In the
ten years since my divorce, I had waltzed with some of America's
leading swamp monsters. These men purred lyrical lines that came
to sound distressingly familiar. Comparing notes, close friends and
I began to suspect that these verbal gems had come from some sort
of handbook issued at birth to all modern American men. But time
after time, I fell for this poetic inanity. And falling—as in "falling
in love"—is exactly the right term. I always seemed to land on my
head, as if I had been pushed from a plane without a parachute.
Each excursion into the romantic stratosphere left me bruised and
unhappy, but never seemed to knock any sense into me.

Over the years, my experience with the opposite sex had convinced me that modern science just might be wrong: Maybe the
heart was an organ that could regenerate. For each time mine was
shattered, I foolishly tried again. I wanted a loving partner, badly. I
wanted to share my life with a man I cared about, trusted, respected, and admired. I wanted a family. A lifetime ago, in my first
marriage, I had often threatened to have ten children. Circumstances conspired to prevent that. Now I would settle for one.

Having a child was not merely a condition of my marriage to
Fox; it was an assumption. We decided to marry almost as soon as
we met. Both of us were generals in love's army of the walking
wounded. Fox's divorce had left him a mess. The first time I saw

him, I thought he looked shell-shocked and pale gray, as if he were in urgent need of a transfusion of hope. But his gentle earnestness was a mighty weapon. My past romances had taught me to be, first of all, skeptical and suspicious. I had come to believe that there was not one heterosexual man on earth who had an honest agenda. A man might look nice and act kind and thoughtful on first encounter, but wait until you got him home. When I met Fox my brain told me this man was radioactive, too recently out of a marriage to know what he wanted. Luckily, I ignored my brain. I fell in love with his heart, his soul, and his wonderful intellect.

The truth is that even though neither of us ever expected to find this kind of love, we were both ripe for it. Anyone who speaks with fond nostalgia about swinging singledom is either a pathological liar, a revisionist historian, crazy, or all three. It was awful. Having given up expecting ever to be swept away by Prince Charming, I was now hoping that somewhere on the planet I might at least bump into Mr. Decent. I met Fox at a dinner party. There he was, an honest guy who drove an American car with dog hair in the backseat, and a fellow print journalist at that. He wooed me with no false premises, no empty promises. From him I heard not one of the bad-script lines I had nearly become inured to. Maybe, blessedly, that manual of outrageous lies had never made it to Lancaster, Pennsylvania, the year he was born.

Fox knew how much I wanted a child. It was never a secret; I blurted it out to him on perhaps our second date. A sensible forty-seven-year-old man with two children would have grabbed his Nikes at that point and bolted. But Fox genuinely wanted me to be happy. In some ways we were both dinosaurs—relics who believed that falling in love and having a baby were all of a package. He treasured the idea of a living product of our love. On a less ethereal level, he had talked the question of a baby over with Ethan and Sarah, his children. They were then eleven and eight years old respectively. A baby sounded like a neat idea, they told him. It meant that we would all be one family—that this still-fictional baby would be a biological link between us.

So Fox and I coined a little code. We used it when we signed off on the telephone, when we exchanged notes or letters, and especially when we raised a toast. It became our mantra. "L, M, and B," we would say, for "Love, Marriage, and Babies."

Things proceeded smoothly on the love and marriage front. The babies were another matter. The ticking of my biological clock robbed me of sleep as I worried over each passing month. I panicked and turned to my doctor for help. She prescribed Clomid, a pill that can improve the climate for conception. Its only detraction, she warned, was that it increased the odds for having twins. Fox and I decided we could live with that risk. In fact, we kind of liked the idea of having twins. One-stop shopping, I told myself. We named our mythical twosome Ben and Emily.

Months passed. No Ben, no Emily. I found that Clomid had another downside for me—and, I later learned, for many women. It made me crazy. It exacerbated monthly mood swings to the point where I pogo-sticked from termagant to two-year-old. I screamed, yelled, stomped, and slammed doors. And the things that came out of my mouth! My doctor Jane and I agreed that alternative measures were in order. I signed up for the fertility program at a local hospital.

All this must have seemed especially strange to Fox. Here he already had two healthy kids, attained through conventional means, and with, I am told, relatively little effort. Now his sperm was under scrutiny. (It passed, and with such high marks that one of the staff doctors at the hospital came racing down the hall to show me his top-scoring petri dish. "Elizabeth, look!" she said, barely able to contain her enthusiasm. "Have you ever seen such motility?" I was not sure what motility was, but, not wanting to hurt her feelings, I admired the little mound of glop and agreed that I had never seen anything quite like it.) The doctors told us nothing was wrong with either of us, and that they could find no "reason" that we had been unable to conceive up to that point. Other than the fact that my eggs were old, tired, and probably fat and lazy, there was nothing specific we could pin it on. Like millions of others, we suffered from something called "idiopathic" infertility. I thought it would better be termed idiotic infertility.

And so there began a series of orientation sessions, counseling sessions, training sessions, and a treatment program that would begin with injections of Pergonal, a hormone compound that helps to stimulate ovulation. We would proceed, if necessary, to in vitro fertilization, the space-age technique that yielded what the media inaccurately described as test-tube babies. This was it, the brave new world of reproductive technology. It was more than a little bit creepy to contemplate.

It meant that along with dozens of other desperate women, I got to spend a lot of time in a crowded hospital hallway, waiting for this early morning test or that predawn procedure, sipping gravelly coffee out of cardboard cups. A nervous scan of the room confirmed that we were all engaged in the same tenuous mission. It meant, for each of us, endless blood tests and sonograms with a condom-covered probe. It meant, as I raced across town clutching tiny vials of my husband's vital body fluids, that our love was rapidly bouncing from the bedroom to the laboratory. And it meant, to Fox's horror, that he would be expected to give me injections for five to seven days each month.

He went ashen at this development. Fox had spent three years as a correspondent for the *New York Times* in Vietnam. He had carried wounded colleagues out of a surprise attack in which he had been reported killed. He observed and wrote about horrible, unthinkable atrocities.

But all his time in combat and all his philosophical coolness could not prepare him for the task of sticking a needle in my fanny. Fox reminded me at this juncture that one career he had never considered, not even for one second, was medicine. Still, he bravely endured a training session in which a nurse led him through Pergonal target practice on something called a plastic posterior. It was a shimmery gray slab of a thing, similar in color and texture to a dead whale. Meredith, the chief nurse in the fertility program, tossed it down casually on a paper-covered examining table. I felt my own gluteal muscles tighten in response. I hoped I looked a little more attractive when I assumed the same position.

In certain areas between Fox and me, and probably between any loving couple, the tired old chestnut that opposites attract definitely applies. Whereas I tend to race through any kind of directions and hope later that I have a vague idea of what I am supposed to do, Fox, the perfectionist, studies each syllable of any instruction manual. Whether it's skiing, serving a tennis ball, or shoving a syringe into his wife's behind, he wants to make sure every movement is artful and appropriate. Meredith, a New Yorker propelled by a perennial sense of urgency, grew impatient as Fox stolidly mixed the Pergonal powder with the saline solution, then filled the syringe, tested it for air bubbles, and slowly removed its plastic sheathing. He poised his hand above the plastic posterior and practiced flicking his wrist ("Like a dart!" Meredith commanded. "Like a dart!"). He looked dubious when Meredith assured him that the faster he did this, the less painful it would be for the plastic posterior, and ultimately for me. Finally he was ready, and with grim determination, plunged the needle into the dead whale. He exhaled so loudly that it sounded as if a truck tire had been deflated in the tiny examining room. Only then did I realize that Fox had been holding his breath the entire time.

When it came time to try the shot on the live whale, me, Fox and I engaged in a veritable gavotte of postponement. We had been told the injection must be administered in the evening, preferably around eight o'clock. It was a Saturday, we were at our house at the shore in Massachusetts. Ethan and Sarah were with us. We did everything we could think of to delay the inevitable. We played games with the children, then read them an especially long bedtime story. We labored over the kitchen cleanup; suddenly it became imperative to scrub the floor. We read the newspaper, right down to the classified ads. I think I briefly considered cleaning the oven, the ultimate act of domestic masochism.

Finally it was one in the morning. The children were sound asleep. I had taken my beloved bubble bath. I gulped down a giant glass of wine, but forbade Fox the same indulgence. Now of all times, I wanted him to have a steady hand. I plopped down on my stomach on our bed, and out of one eye I watched him turn our bedroom into a home chemistry lab. With assiduous attention to each step in the process, Fox prepared for the big moment. Finally he was squeezing the air bubbles from the syringe and swabbing my skin with an alcohol pad. I tried not to grimace as I thought about what was coming next. "I love you!" Fox said feebly as at last he administered the injection.

It didn't hurt a bit, not even slightly. He shuddered and accepted congratulations for his courage. We felt a bit giddy, proud of ourselves for surviving this form of contemporary torture, and laughed that this was really modern life, when a guy has to stick two things into his wife for her to get pregnant. Then we faced a dilemma of etiquette and housekeeping that our mothers had never prepared us for: How do we hide the syringes from the kids?

The fact is that neither of us had a great deal of faith in this whole ritual. We knew the statistics, and they weren't great. Amazingly, the average hyperfertile teenager has only about a 20 percent chance of conceiving on any given sexual foray. With this kind of chemical intervention alone, that was the best we could hope for. More realistically, we had about a 15 percent chance of getting pregnant. Fox and I are not gamblers, and it's a good thing. No one with any respect for the odds would hang much hope on this process.

Instead, we were doing it because we felt we should, because good reporters follow a story to its conclusion. It seemed unlikely to either of us that this slender vial of fluid would really result in a breathing, laughing, crying baby. Besides, we had been warned repeatedly that Pergonal seldom produces a pregnancy on the first cycle. If it is to succeed at all, we were told, it usually takes several months. We felt it was another of God's practical jokes when my period was late that month. It had happened six months earlier, with Clomid. The sense of defeat when my period finally came had been unimaginable, and I had poured all my anger and frustration onto Fox. This month, this first Pergonal cycle, I postponed having a pregnancy test because I didn't think I could endure that trampoline of expectation and disappointment.

But thriftiness, the legacy of my Scottish ancestors, prevailed when I found myself admiring a certain outfit at the Ann Taylor store across the street from my office. It was pale aqua; it had a short, straight skirt; and at about four hundred dollars, it was ridiculously overpriced. It made no sense to spend that kind of money if I was going to be ballooning up with a baby. On the other hand, if, as I suspected, I was not pregnant, I could console myself through consumer therapy. I was already planning what shoes I would buy to go with my new outfit when, at Meredith's urging, I finally took the test. Late that afternoon, I steeled myself for the worst and called for the results. I remember how Meredith's voice softened. "Congratulations, Elizabeth," she said. "You're pregnant."

I was at my office in New York, and I burst into tears. One of my colleagues, thinking I must have just gotten horrible news, rushed to comfort me. Too overcome to speak, I scribbled the words on a pad on my desk: "I'm pregnant!" Debbie threw her arms around me and cried, too.

An entirely uneventful pregnancy ensued. Fox was present when, at nine and a half weeks of gestation, I underwent chorionic villi sampling to examine the chromosomal structure of the fetus. This was the newest in antenatal testing, a process in which a slender catheter is inserted vaginally into the uterus to retrieve minute fragments of villi, the tissue that becomes the placenta. Unlike amniocentesis, which has been used successfully for several decades, CVS involves no puncturing of the uterus with a needle. Because it is performed at such an early stage of the pregnancy, CVS theoretically reduces the trauma of termination if the results are chromosomally undesirable. We had been warned, however, that the risks of miscarriage associated with CVS are higher than with amniocentesis. Genetics counselors had also alerted us that the test could not be performed if there were any signs of cramping or contractions, or if I had experienced any first-trimester bleeding. I was lucky in that respect. For me, the entire process took about fifteen minutes, and that included changing my clothes. I felt charmed. I could not help but think that this was another good omen.

Before I underwent the procedure, my trio of feminist physicians had also advised me not to be put off when the CVS specialist walked into the room. Dr. Matson had worked as a model, even in medical school, they told me. She was bright, accomplished, an expert at administering CVS—and disconcertingly beautiful. Cindy, one of my doctors, had done her residency with Dr. Matson. "Walk down the hall with her and you disappear into the wall," Cindy remembered. "It's like you're not even there."

As it happened, Dr. Matson's pulchritude was exceeded only by her efficiency and well-rehearsed lack of affect. She was all business. No time for small talk, not even when she ran a cart of instruments into my foot. Fox, meanwhile, was uncertain how to react. He was no dope himself, obviously, and he had been sufficiently pummeled by years of contact with feminists to have attained at least a reasonably raised level of consciousness. He knew that beauty and brains were not incompatible. But Fox had not had Cindy's pre-CVS warning. I could not remember seeing him so taken aback in the presence of a female professional before.

He was further stunned by the truly remarkable marvels of modern medicine. Clear as day, the accompanying sonogram revealed a tiny object bouncing from one corner of the screen to another. It looked like it was gymnastics hour in the womb. "That's your baby," Dr. Matson told him. Ruth, the nurse, pointed to little flipperlike appendages—arms and legs, she promised. In just moments, Dr. Matson had retrieved the appropriate quantity of fluid and villi. The procedure was painless and amazingly quick. Since Fox's last child had been born in Hong Kong, with a nurse sitting on the mother's stomach to help facilitate labor, this process seemed too twentieth-century to believe.

Because I was terrified of the outcome, Fox made the phone call two days later that told us the baby's chromosomes were normal. The fringe benefit of the phone call was that we got to learn the baby's gender. "I am pleased to inform you that on or about July 8, you will be the mother of Emily Butterfield," Fox said when he called at my office that afternoon. He had adopted a tone of mock formality, but his voice was bursting with pride and happiness. When we completed the twelfth week of the pregnancy, we breathed another huge sigh of relief. The risk of miscarriage diminishes significantly after the first trimester. All the indicators were positive so far. After working this hard to get this pregnancy we weren't about to take it for granted, but now we felt we could relax a little and actually enjoy it. Things looked good, my doctors told me.

Ethan and Sarah were quick to catch on to the joyous spirit of the pregnancy as well. We followed the baby's progress in pictures, each week studying the photographs in *A Child Is Born,* a book that chronicles gestation from inside the womb. It was Sarah who took one look at the pictures of a seven-week-old fetus and squealed, "Ewww, E.T.!" Emily hadn't even been born yet, and as far as her brother and sister were concerned, she already had her nickname for life.

Emily began kicking at exactly eighteen weeks of gestation, right when the books say the kicking should start. It was a Sunday evening, and Fox and I were sprawled out on the couch reading the newspaper. I felt something strange, like a butterfly spanning its wings. Instinctively I clutched my lower abdomen, and told Fox I was having a muscle spasm. "That's the baby," he said. From his tone he should have added, "you moron." Fox was the veteran of two pregnancies, so in some matters he knew much more than I. "She's kicking," he said.

At seventeen weeks, the doctor who read her sonogram lapsed into raptures over her long femurs, her thigh bones. Great, I thought, she's got those wonderful long Butterfield legs, not the short, fat things I'm cursed with. That's how easy this pregnancy had been. I could worry over relatively unimportant things, like the contours of her thighs, not whether she had legs at all. The seventeen-week sonogram was another of those hurdles, like making it past twelve weeks, after which miscarriage is less likely to occur.

Because chorionic villi sampling is performed at such an early stage in the gestation, the procedure cannot detect gross anatomical deformities. Emily's sonogram once again showed a normally developing fetus.

By far the majority of patients treated by Jane Gerstner, my primary obstetrician, and her two partners, Cindy Rubin and Sandy Baumgartner, were working women like me. Many, I noticed when I sat in the waiting room, were in that chronological never-never land known as "over thirty-five." We fell under the lovely medical umbrella of "geriatric" pregnancies. As long as the pregnancies were proceeding smoothly, the three doctors saw no reason why women in this age group could not conduct normal lives. They encouraged their patients to continue working. There were the practical considerations of maintaining one's paycheck and not exhausting sick leave early on. Equally important, the doctors told me, was the fact that pregnancy was not in itself a career. Obsessing over it, treating it like a chronic disease, and making it the entire center of one's existence, seemed neurotic, they reasoned. Work was not only a diversion, it was a way to define oneself as someone other than a full-time pregnant person. Obviously, they urged good sense and cautioned against exhaustion. They were always available to answer questions and offer advice.

The doctors gave the green light to air travel once I passed into the second trimester. Still, before scheduling this trip in my twenty-fourth week, I checked to make sure it was all right. No problem, they said. Jane even told me she had once authorized one of her older patients to fly to Sweden in her thirty-seventh week. Another patient was in her thirty-fifth week when she flew to Japan to make a speech. Both women delivered normal, full-term infants.

Congenital superstition and a lingering fear that things might not go right kept me from advertising my pregnancy. Some of my colleagues in New York knew I was pregnant, but most showed no interest. The few people in L.A. that I did tell understood my concerns and were happily sworn to secrecy. So for almost six months I had made excuses to cover my absences at the monthly

senior writers' meetings I was expected to attend. It was amazing
how many urgent assignments and last-minute scheduling conflicts
I could concoct.

But as I sailed into my sixth month of pregnancy, it seemed
safe to go. I was eager at this point to share my condition with
friends on the West Coast. Like most first-time pregnant ladies, I
was proud of my accomplishment. Talk about a pushy mother:
Emily hadn't even been born yet, and already I wanted to show her
off.

I stayed with my old friends Ruth and Scott, whose little boy,
Eric, was three years old. Ruth and Scott lived near UCLA, but one
of Eric's very first possessions was an orange-and-black wall pen-
nant that read, "Princeton, Class of 2007." Scott, a partner in a big
Los Angeles law firm, joked that Eric could go to any college he
wanted, but "I'll pay for Princeton." It was easy, and not a bit
arrogant, for us to think and talk like that. Our lives had been
marked by success. Hard work had led to professional achievement
and material comfort. Like so many in our generation, we operated
on a quiet philosophy of entitlement. Life seemed so certain for us
that we could mentally coast through eighteen years and laugh
about what university our children would choose. We could exchange imaginary horror stories about how we would finance their
educations. We never paused for a moment to ponder the possibility
that this might not happen.

After dinner, Eric's nanny from El Salvador, Vilma, placed
her hand on my belly and offered incantations in Spanish. We
toasted with apple juice and looked forward to the time when Eric
and Emily would play together. "Maybe they will marry," Vilma
mused.

So now, flying home with my twenty-four-and-a-half-week-
old baby inside me, I settled in to read *Emperor of the Air,* a
collection of short stories by Ethan Canin, a young author I was
scheduled to interview. I would be in New York in time to have a
late dinner with Fox. I had barely been gone three days, but I
missed him. I took out my trusty Walkman and earphones, the

signal of the experienced traveler to the stranger in the next seat that no, I do not want to talk to you. The tape I had brought with me contained horn concertos by Mozart. They were wonderfully symmetrical, almost mathematical in the way they diverted me. Between Mozart and the book, I felt Emily and I had been transported. I ordered a glass of milk from the flight attendant and immersed myself in my book. Emily had taken a rest, too, it seemed. For a change she was not break-dancing in my belly. I decided it must be nap time, and gave her another soft pat. When I closed my eyes I could picture her as a baby, not as a fetus inside me. I could see her lying on her tummy in a crib, sleeping on a blanket decorated with little bunnies. I love you, sweet bunny girl, I thought, and idly stroked my belly.

I know we were more than halfway across the country because more than three hours had passed. I had dutifully eaten the tasteless airline meal, even the papery potatoes. I was two-thirds through my book, and about to start reading the story called "American Beauty." I folded the book jacket in to mark the page. It was Auden who wrote that tragedy and suffering take place in the midst of life's most mundane moments, "while someone else is eating or opening a window." I stood up, and my life changed irrevocably.

The back of my dress was soaking wet. The seat cover was flooded. I had felt nothing, not even a trickle or the slightest discomfort, and yet fluid had been pouring out of me. It was clear, warm, and odorless. No biology class had prepared me for this; no healthy-pregnancy book had warned of this possibility. Yet I knew instantly what had happened. The amniotic sac had ruptured.

We were thirty-seven thousand feet in the air. Somewhere over Ohio, or maybe it was West Virginia by then, my blissful, carefree pregnancy had come to an end.

TWO

First of all, stay calm. While my heart was running marathons, I kept repeating that to myself. Stay calm, don't panic.

Don't panic? What a joke. I was terrified.

In my darkest nightmares, I have always been afraid that in a true emergency, my vocal cords would freeze. This nightmare image had been with me since early childhood. Someone would jump out from behind a bush. Someone would break into the house when I was alone. Someone would be killed before my eyes. Some terrible, unthinkable fright would take place. I would open my mouth to speak, to shriek, to scream, and nothing would emerge.

Seven miles in the sky, this is not far from what happened. My brain seemed to be screaming at eleven million different frequencies, but it was all noisy gibberish. None of it made sense. And no sound came out of my mouth.

For one wild moment I thought about storming the cockpit and demanding that the pilot land the plane instantly, anywhere. No, not anywhere. I would tell him to find the nearest big city, and get there in a hurry. I thought about asking the flight attendant if she knew a good hospital in West Virginia, the state we must have been flying over by then. Pennsylvania would be coming up soon! They had good medical facilities in Pennsylvania, didn't they?

Abruptly, a relatively reasonable brain wave flashed through. Quick calculations showed it would be at least an hour before I could get to any hospital, anywhere. I looked at my watch and realized that in less than an hour, I would be in New York. If we landed in an unfamiliar city, my husband would not be there, nor my doctors. It would be late at night by the time I would be able to contact Fox. The chances of him getting a plane to meet me were remote. He could drive all night, but still I would not see him before morning. I wanted him there with me. I was very, very frightened, and I desperately needed his strength.

The flight attendant was dumbfounded when I told her what was happening. She said she was embarrassed because she hadn't noticed that I was pregnant. But quickly she regained her composure. Put your feet up, she told me, not that either of us thought that would do much good at this point. Was I having any cramping? No? Good. No bleeding? Even better. Maybe this wasn't as serious as it seemed.

She agreed it was best to try to make it to New York. We were not far away now, and in the same situation, she said, she too would want her husband to be there with her. She understood why I wanted to be treated by my own doctors, if possible. She was crouching in the aisle while we spoke, softly. There was some silent compact between us, some unspoken understanding that to bring undue attention to this mess would make it much, much worse. She seemed to understand that if people were pointing and staring I would only feel more self-conscious, more tense. Without offering any empty words of comfort, because we both knew it probably would not be all right, she urged me to try to stay as calm as possible. If things changed, she said, she would make other plans. Meanwhile, she arranged to have a wheelchair waiting at the airport gate in New York.

The flight attendant offered to call for an ambulance, but through some bizarre act of prescience, I had already engaged a driver who was supposed to be waiting at the airport to drive me to the city. I had never done this before, but two and a half days earlier, when he drove me to JFK, the driver asked idly if I needed a return ride. I was using a car service, which was cheaper than a cab. It seemed like a minor luxury, and a sensible one, since I knew I would be coming in around nine o'clock at night.

For once, I was traveling light. I had no computer, no ridiculously overpacked garment bag, just a small bag that really did fit in the overhead storage bin. I could not call Jane from the airplane. Physicians have answering services, and even in emergencies they receive the information from the service, then call the patient back. The in-flight telephones on board the plane could only make outgoing calls. I phoned her the minute I got to the airport. She told me to go straight to the hospital and said she would alert them of my arrival. I called Fox, and tried not to fall apart completely when the answering machine picked up in his absence.

"This is very important," I told the tape. "My water broke. On the plane. It ruptured on the plane." I was fighting to keep my voice steady, and hoped that what I was saying made some sense. "I may be about to have the baby, right now. I'm on my way to the hospital. I'll be in the labor and delivery area. Please meet me there as soon as possible. I love you."

The hospital guard looked dubious when I said I was headed for labor and delivery. He eyed my too-small stomach suspiciously. "You can't go up there unless you're having a baby," he said. I was in no mood to talk about it. "I don't want to have this baby right now, but that's what's happening," I said. I barged right past him.

A Dr. Crane examined me. She was tall and elegant, with close-cropped hair and penetrating green eyes. They stared right at me as she confirmed the diagnosis I had made myself seven miles above the earth. There was some fluid left, she told me, but very, very little. Most likely this was the result of a low-grade infection, something I would not even have known I had. It might be a case of poor membranes. It probably had nothing to do with the airplane. "These things happen when women get up and walk across the room in their own apartments," she said.

The only thing to do was watch and wait. My body would make more fluid, but with the membranes ruptured, it would continue to seep slowly out. In short, the sac had turned into a sieve. It was possible, however, that the fluid production might outpace the fluid reduction. Some women in this situation had managed to keep their babies inside them for several weeks. Dr. Crane and her colleagues even held out the very slim possibility that I would be able to come close to completing the pregnancy, although I would not be permitted to leave my hospital bed.

More likely, they predicted, the baby would be born within the next two or three days. This was the ordinary course of this extraordinary development. On Friday, Emily would enter her twenty-fifth week of gestation. Yes, they said, many babies did survive at this stage. Some didn't. It was impossible to predict.

We could only watch and wait, Dr. Crane told me. And hope.

Fox arrived, carrying a bouquet of purple tulips he had bought at the corner deli near our apartment. By then I was in the position I would assume for the duration of the pregnancy, however long that might be, with my feet raised over my head. It did not take a genius to figure out that what we were trying to do was to give gravity a chance. My amniotic sac was a leaky bucket, and we were trying to find the angle where the leaks would be least damaging.

A soft brown wrapping, like a stretched-out Ace bandage, was wound loosely around my belly. It held in place a metal gauge that monitored Emily's heart rate. On a stand next to my head, right beside the plastic pail that held the purple tulips, the numbers flashed in red on a meter. Each time her heart rate dipped or rose, it beeped. Fox could not take his eyes off it. He stared at it, hypnotized. The numbers seemed to hover in the range of 140 beats per minute. As an athlete who had played team sports competitively his entire life, he thought this figure seemed very fast. I remembered that before I was pregnant, when we tested our heart rates during aerobic classes, 140 to 160 beats per minute was what we strove for at maximum exertion. "Why is her heart going so quickly?" Fox asked the nurse. She explained that fetuses and small infants work much harder than an adult; that for a child Emily's size, 140 beats per minute represented a normal resting heart rate. We found the bouncing numbers riveting, and more than a little scary. But in a strange way, they were also reassuring. The red numbers were our contact with Emily. As long as they were dancing up and down on the monitor, she was obviously alive.

Fearful situations have always seemed worse to me at night, and now it was very late. We were terrified. We could think of nothing other than the survival of our precious baby daughter. Stress and anxiety are evil, potent forces. They dive-bomb one's sense of reality and gang rape one's physical responses. Everything is out of proportion. Trying to convince myself that it was perfectly normal for my head to be three feet lower than my feet, and that if I just stayed in this ridiculous position long enough, Emily would continue to grow and would be born healthy and on full-term schedule, I fought to keep from losing my grip on things. "I'm scared," I told Fox. "Really scared." He did not move his eyes from Emily's pulsemeter. "Me, too," he said.

Along with my sense of balance and my assumption that life would remain within certain reliable boundaries, I lost my social graces. A kind nurse offered to help me extract my contact lenses, a gravity-defying feat when one's head is pointed toward Patagonia. I remember that she was very patient, and that she had styled her hair in cornrows that formed small circles all over her head. The effect was whimsical, like high-fashion phrenology. She told me she wore contacts herself, and once we had squeezed mine out of my eyeballs, she found some hydrogen peroxide and helped store them in their case. In the madness of the moment, she was calm and sensible, yet I never thought to say thank you. I was too numb with fear.

Literally and metaphorically, I felt I was standing on my head, like Father William in *Through the Looking-Glass*. My father had eschewed traditional fairy tales when I was a small child, and read to me instead the complete works of the two men he felt captured the wisdom and absurdity of the universe, Lewis Carroll and James Thurber. I had waist-length blond hair until I was sixteen, and grew up in a pre-blue-jeans era when little girls actually wore things like pinafores. An orthodox Freudian could probably ascribe large portions of my future problems, possibly even the predicament I now found myself in, to excessive identification with Lewis Carroll's Alice. Covering the comings and goings of Washington, New York, San Francisco, and Los Angeles in my work as a newspaper reporter, I often was reminded of the Mad Hatter's tea party. When Alice arrived to take her place at one of the numerous empty seats at the tea table, the hatter blocked her, crying, "No room! No room!" It seemed as apt a description as any, certainly, for the workings of official Washington, where bureaucrats could think of a million variations per hour on the "no room, no room" theme to try to ward off an inquisitive reporter. Over the years in all those cities, I had on many occasions had face-to-face interviews with people who seemed like latter-day incarnations of the Duchess or the Dodo, operating on precisely the same doctrine of illogic. I thought of all the so-called information officers (I preferred to think of them as misinformation officers) who could only have modeled their behavior on the grinning Cheshire cat or the hookah-smoking caterpillar. "Say what you mean, and mean what you say!" said Tweedledum, or was it one of the legion of editors I had had over the years? Now here I was again, plummeting down the rabbit hole and watching any semblance of normalcy or predictability spin away. "Curiouser and curiouser" was what Alice remarked when she lost her footing and fell to the center of the earth. Just then, I was feeling pretty much curiouser and curiouser myself.

Through some quirk of an unusually generous fate, I was allowed to spend that first night, a Wednesday, in a room where there were other beds, but no other patients. I fell asleep dreading the possibility that the empty beds would soon be filled with women delivering happy, healthy, full-term babies. If I had to live through someone else's labor, I knew I would have to be transferred to the psychiatric unit. Of course, I harbored no ill feelings toward pregnant women I did not even know. But my own state was so precarious that I was not certain I could survive, much less celebrate, the good fortune of strangers.

I mentioned this to Jane, my primary obstetrician, when she came to examine me early that morning. Jane is a striking-looking woman in her midthirties, with masses of thick, curly hair. Her clothes tend toward the flamboyant—today, I noticed, she was carrying her gold lamé trenchcoat—and in a display of personal embellishment I found particularly laudable in a woman with three children, a husband, and a busy medical practice, she always managed to have a perfect manicure. Folding her arms in front of her, Jane stood beside me and offered her most knowledgeable medical assessment of what was going on.

"Oy," she said.

Jane repeated much of what Dr. Crane had told me the night before. It was all a waiting game now, she said. We could only hope for the best. I interrupted to ask her the questions that had been eating at me since I had stood up over Ohio. "Did this happen because I took that airplane trip? Did I bring this on by flying to California?"

Jane shook her head. "Probably not," she said. "I doubt it. But we'll never know for certain."

Laboratory cultures sent out the night before might reveal whether I had an infection, the most likely cause of a ruptured amniotic sac. But not every infection cultured, Jane cautioned. Some were so obscure as to defy identification. She went through the same litany of possible explanations I had heard from Dr. Crane. But Jane added one more. Possibly I was just unlucky.

She agreed that it would be inadvisable for me to share that room with a woman, or women, in any stage of labor. "The object here is to reduce tension and try to stay calm," she said. She said she would look into having me moved to more commodious surroundings. Jane's eyes, too, kept drifting toward the flashing red pulsemeter that displayed Emily's still-steady heartbeat. "That's a good sign," she said. I knew Jane well enough to respect her for the fact that she was trying to offer me cause for optimism wherever we could find it. Probably that was her intention, too, when she told me about a cousin of her husband's who had a baby at Emily's stage—twenty-four-and-a-half weeks—at home, in the toilet. I grimaced, but didn't know how to stop Jane and tell her that such stories only made me more anxious. I didn't want to hear about babies born at home, early, in the toilet. I wanted happy endings, even if they were fictional. I wanted to hear about amniotic sacs miraculously repairing themselves and replenishing themselves with rich fluids for the baby to float in. I wanted a real *National Enquirer* headline: "Nine-pound baby born to mother with no fluid!" But Jane was too honest to appease me with fables. Her husband's cousin's baby, a little girl, was almost three now, Jane continued. "She wears very thick glasses, and she's a little slow," she said. "But otherwise, she's fine."

A "little slow?" I wondered what that meant. I was trying hard not to think about the list of awful consequences I knew could result from an extremely premature birth. Somewhere in the back of my brain, I had almost persuaded myself that if I didn't think about it, it wouldn't happen.

Jane's gaze settled on the beige, hospital-issued pail that held the purple tulips. "Fox brought you those?" she asked. I nodded yes. "They're really nice," she said. She gave me a smile, more brave than convincing, and quietly left the room.

At midmorning a new nurse arrived. She explained that she was assigned to cover the entire room, but since no one else was there, she would basically be available to act as my private nurse. Her name was Marcie, and she was thirty-nine, almost my age. Marcie was a nonstop talker, but because she was also witty, smart, and interesting, this quality was a diversion for me, not an annoyance. At that moment I knew I would welcome anything that distracted me from the horrendous realities at hand. I was too nervous to read, too panicky to concentrate even on daytime TV. In real life, Marcie's uninterrupted patter would have made me crazy.

Now it was oddly comforting. It relieved me of the obligation to think, or even to pretend to think.

Marcie began by filling me in on hospital politics, a subject she felt I should know something about since she hoped I would be there for quite some time. She was a contract employee, not a staff nurse. This meant she worked largely on call. But since good nurses were in short supply, that call was fairly constant. There was major friction between her and many of the staff nurses, Marcie said. She had a habit of speaking her mind, of telling her superiors where to get off whenever she didn't like something. Unfortunately for Marcie, this was not a rare occurrence. In a big city hospital, rules are written in something more solid than stone. In an environment where employees and patients alike soon learned that they were expected to behave like cows, and follow along with the herd, Marcie's attitude had earned her a reputation as a troublemaker.

Personally, I have always admired firebrands. I think of Lucy Van Pelt, of the "Peanuts" comic strip, who once decreed that "It is better to have crabbed and fussed in vain than never to have crabbed at all." I confided to Marcie that I was worried about what would happen when they needed the space in this room, and told her I was afraid they would move me to some mass-birthing area. She agreed that this would be disastrous, and said she would look into trying to avert it.

In the meantime, she amused me with endless and graphic details of her affair with a pitcher for the Boston Red Sox. In the Butterfield household, the Red Sox are a sacred institution. From the day spring training begins until the day the baseball season ends, no one is allowed to speak to Fox while he is reading the sports section of the *Boston Globe*. We are expected to share outrage or excitement over particularly poor or wise player trades. Along with global politics, and what the kids are studying in school, we discuss baseball strategy at the dinner table. Fox's boyhood dream was to play professional baseball, and even today, one of his most coveted photographs shows him on the field at Fenway Park, albeit in a suit with a notebook in his hand. So I knew Fox would relish every morsel of Marcie's story. As she talked to me, she fiddled with dark, tight curls that fell halfway down her back. She knew perfectly well that she was doing me a service when she regaled me with descriptions of rendezvous in hotel rooms from Torrance to Toronto. She was taking my mind off my own terrible troubles, and sometimes, she was even making me laugh.

At my insistence, Fox had gone to work that day. He called several times, and arrived at the hospital just before six o'clock.

"Guess who *she* had an affair with!" I greeted him. Fox listened to the abbreviated version and studied Marcie carefully as she spoke. She was tall and thin and fiery. I could see that Fox's respect for the pitcher on his favorite team had just risen considerably.

But Marcie was just as concerned about the fact that for all our yammering, I had boycotted the revolting, rubbery chicken that had been sent to me as dinner. All day long, she had been offering me encouragement. Emily's signs were so stable that she felt certain I would be able to keep her inside me for a few weeks. "After you've been here a week or so, we'll get someone to come in and wash your hair," Marcie said. I hadn't allowed myself to think about this complication; dirty hair seemed unimportant in the face of the larger issue of Emily's life. But now Marcie was holding this simple act of vanity out as a quiet kind of incentive. We both agreed that if I did end up staying in for a while, and we hoped that would be the case, it would be great if Marcie could take care of me more often. "But you have to eat!" she roared, as if she were reprimanding a small child. Now the two of them, Fox and Marcie, ganged up on me and insisted that I put some of that putrid poultry in my belly. Tension kills my appetite anyway, and at that moment, the last thing I felt like eating was something that looked and tasted like building insulation.

Hospitals do funny things to people. Bovine behavior is one common and often automatic side effect. Orders are orders, rules are rules. You do what they tell you to do because there's no percentage in not doing it, and because in most cases you are too weak to protest anyway. I remembered reading a study that concluded that by the time one reached adulthood, the parameters of patient behavior were well understood. "Good" patients were thought to receive better treatment than problem cases—those who rejected the strictures of the patient role. The corollary was an assumption that the behavior of good patients would be rewarded with more attentive physician intervention, and that these good patients would therefore get better sooner. Being a good patient, by the way, means being a passive patient. It means doing whatever they tell you to do, following orders, not questioning authority.

But even good little patients are sometimes known to rebel. Another frequent symptom of the hospitalized human is regression. At that moment, I had made it back to about age three. Lying there in the famous reverse swan dive position, I knew I sounded like a defiant preschooler when I started to bargain about dinner. "I'll eat this if . . ." I heard myself say, and for a moment, I wasn't sure what outrageous demand I was about to issue. If you promise that it will make Emily big and strong and healthy? If you guarantee that we'll walk out of this hospital with our beautiful baby girl? If you'll find some magic cement to seal up my sac and let Emily go back to where she was supposed to be at this point? That was what I wanted to say, all of it. But I knew it was ridiculous. Marcie was not the enemy, and Fox was Emily's father. I smiled, and decided on something less guilt-inducing. "I'll eat this if you'll bring me some frozen yogurt."

Fox looked stricken. Since childhood, I had been famous, or more likely infamous, in my family for making Golden Fleece demands. "Elizabeth," Fox groaned, "where in the world am I going to get frozen yogurt around here?" Marcie told him about a neighborhood grocery store, then excused herself. It was time for her dinner break. Another nurse, vastly less friendly, popped in to make sure I was alive. She vanished so quickly we were not sure we had seen her at all. Fox remarked that he was glad Marcie was on the case. She was smart and funny and presumably was also adept at running interference with a hospital administration that was already testing his patience.

"I've paid for a private room for you," he said. "But they say you can't be in a private room, that you need to be watched every minute and they can't provide that kind of care in a private room."

I feared for a moment that I might start to moo, that maybe now was when I would begin to turn into a cow, or a Stepford Patient, like all the rest of them.

When Marcie reappeared, she had her hand behind her back. "Here's the good news," she said, and handed me a dish of frozen yogurt from the hospital cafeteria. "I hope you like strawberry." The bad news was that Marcie had learned I was about to be moved out of this room and into the prenatal ward, where five or six other high-risk pregnant women were staying. "It's awful in there," Marcie said. "They call it an intensive care unit, but really it's just a group ward. I tried to talk them out of it, but I lost. They told me I was interfering."

She promised to come check on me, and wished me luck. I gathered from her tone and demeanor that I would probably need it.

Marcie's warnings proved correct. With Fox at my side, my bed was wheeled down the hall to a room where thin sheets separated a roomful of women in various stages of pregnancy. It was after eight o'clock at night. One woman was on the telephone, loudly arguing with someone I took to be a family member. Another was visiting with her mother, or maybe it was her mother-in-law. Every other woman in the ward could hear every single word of their conversation. Another woman was listening to talk radio, and still another, the woman whose bed was closest to mine, had a television turned to something that sounded like it must be "Wheel of Fortune," in Spanish. Finally, there was a woman somewhere in the room who was moaning without letup. She was the one I felt sorry for.

"This isn't going to work," I told Fox. "I can't stay here. This place is going to make me nuts."

Fox was silent. His face was rigid, the way he gets when he prepares to do battle. Twenty years of living in Communist countries and in the Third World had hardened him to dealing with pinheads who view rule enforcement as a form of power.

• • •

He returned with a hatchet-faced nurse whose hat had more badges and ribbons than anyone else's. Uh-oh, I thought, Nurse Ratched is here. "I'm the supervisor," she announced, as if anyone could have taken her for anything else. This woman was the supervisor wherever she went. Out spewed the official version of exactly what Marcie had told me. I had to be there because I had to be watched constantly. (Well, if that was the case, I wondered, why did I have to keep ringing for the nurse?) All of us high-risk moms were in this thing together, the supervisor said, gesturing to my fellow patients. There was a supportive spirit here. (Was she deaf? Or did she really believe that "Wheel of Fortune" was a calming influence?) I would like it here, she declared. It sounded more like an order than a prophesy. I expected her to add, "We have ways of making you like it here." I was unconvinced, but I also knew I had no choice.

"What part of Nazi Germany do you suppose she went to nursing school in?" Fox asked.

"Call Jane at home," I pleaded. "This isn't going to work."

At ten o'clock, Nurse Ratched returned to tell Fox he had to leave. The woman on the telephone had finally concluded her call, and the mother, or mother-in-law, of the other patient had been thrown out along with Fox. The talk radio was a little bit quieter; maybe they called it whisper radio. But the poor moaner was still in pain or great grief or whatever state of discomfort had brought her to this level of despair. And the "Wheel of Fortune" was still going strong.

I rang for the nurse. Ten minutes later, one of Ratched's deputies appeared. Ah yes, constant care, I thought. Good thing I wasn't bleeding to death. "Please," I began. "You've got to ask that woman to turn her television down."

From the other side of the curtain, the "Wheel of Fortune" lady shot back before she had been directly addressed.

"I'm allowed to watch television if I want," she boomed. "It relaxes me. Anyway, it's very quiet. Nobody else can hear it."

"It relaxes her?" I repeated in amazement. "What about the rest of us?"

"Nobody else has complained," the nurse replied. It sounded like a line that was issued in the bureaucratic training corps.

I tried appealing to the nurse's emotions—a futile effort, since she obviously had none. "Listen, I'm in here because I'm about to have a baby who's fifteen weeks early," I said. "I'm trying hard to stave off incipient labor. It's really important that I stay calm and get as much rest as possible. Could you please ask her just to turn it down a little?"

Eventually a compromise was reached. She turned it down fractionally and I fumbled on my nightstand to find my trusty Walkman and my sole Mozart tape. Even through the soaring horn concertos, I could hear the Spanish-speaking Vanna White dub shrieking over the "Wheel's" latest mountain of material marvels.

I must have fallen asleep, and sometime, certainly not before eleven o'clock, when I know I was wide awake, she must have turned off the "Wheel of Fortune." I awoke at about five, consumed by fear and a paralyzing sense of aloneness. It was not the first time since I had arrived at the hospital that the magnitude of the crisis had hit me. But it was the first time I had given in to it. I began to weep uncontrollably.

"Nurse!" the "Wheel of Fortune" lady yelled. "Tell her to stop crying. She's keeping me awake."

The nurse gave me a stern look.

"Stop crying," she said. "You're keeping the others awake."

Fox arrived early in the morning. His attempt to get me moved had been unsuccessful. Even Jane and her colleagues had to swallow the hospital's we-have-to-keep-her-under-constant-watch position. By now my neighbor had switched to Spanish soap operas, and I asked Fox if they realized that "watch" referred to television. He was too grim and single-minded to laugh at that moment. He had a new plan. When Fox and I had signed up for the infertility treatment program, we had had several counseling sessions with the program's resident psychologist. The fertility shrink, as I took to calling her, was a nationally known psychologist named Dr. Katherine Patterson. Initially Fox balked at the prospect of talking over our problems with anybody outside the family. Fox descends from generations of old New Englanders who don't talk to anybody about much of anything of a personal nature, certainly not their problems. His mother's family, the Eatons, arrived around the time of the *Mayflower*. Finding Massachusetts too tame, they soon resettled in the wilds of Nova Scotia. The Butterfields came slightly later, in 1636. In an incident recorded in the annals of Chelmsford, Massachusetts, one Butterfield forebear, a tailor named Sam, was captured by Indians, scalped, and forced to serve as the prisoner of an Indian squaw before escaping seven years later. A second Butterfield ancestor was scalped near Fort Ticonderoga during the French and Indian War. He, too, survived. A third, an ardent supporter of the Revolution named James Butterfield, enlisted in the 7th Massachusetts Regiment the day after the battles of Lexington and Concord. While patrolling as a scout in the woods of central New York, near Cooperstown, James was captured by Indians, scalped, and led off to prison on an island in the St. Lawrence. James managed not only to survive, but to escape in the middle of winter and make his way down the edge of Lake Champlain. If there were to be a joint family crest for these two hardy lines, it would probably read "We Go It Alone."

Not that my precursors were any less tough or independent. My father's family migrated across the Rockies and the Sierra to arrive in California around the time of the Gold Rush. They settled in Placerville, then known as Hangtown because that village in the foothills of the Sierra had the tree best suited for executions. My father's family never made a cent off gold, but one inventive female ancestor was said to have earned a comfortable living by running a restaurant with, as they were discreetly called in those days, "rooms" upstairs for the gentlemen customers and the lady friend of their choice. Both of my mother's parents arrived in San Francisco from Scotland around the turn of the century. My grandmother was such a hearty soul that she slept through the Great Quake of 1906. She was a teenager then, still living at home not far from Mission Dolores. After the huge earthquake, her father beat on her bedroom door to tell her she had to get up. She demanded to know why. "Because," he responded, "the city's on fire." Meanwhile, in the next room, two of her brothers were engaged in a furious fistfight on the floor, one accusing the other of having pushed him out of bed.

Like the Eatons and the Butterfields, neither my mother's nor my father's families would ever have dreamed of asking anyone for help. Malingering was not tolerated. "How long have you had these symptoms?" a doctor might have asked any of them on either side. It could have been cancer or a hangnail, and the answer would have been the same: "Oh, about five years." Luckily for me, however, I was born into a post-World War II California that fancied itself to be a kind of psychotherapeutic nirvana. Just about the time that the first Flower Children sprouted up in San Francisco, so did the notion that therapy, the ubiquitous word for almost any kind of mental health assistance, was at least as beneficial as fluoride in the drinking water, and as basic to daily existence as brushing one's teeth.

To the horror of my chromosomally stoic relatives, I availed myself liberally of these benefits. I knew there were bad therapists out there, and I also knew there were good ones. I knew it often helped to have an intermediary in a discussion between men and women. I knew that sometimes a good therapist could serve as a kind of tour guide, suggesting that one realign one's mental map in order to better appreciate life's scenery.

Though his brain told him all therapists were poseurs, Fox actually liked and respected Kate, as we called the fertility shrink. After I had become pregnant we had seen her several times to discuss issues we might anticipate with the arrival of a child at our late ages and in our relatively young marriage. Now Fox was proposing to ask Kate to run interference against the hospital's administrative minotaurs. He had already put a call in to her office, and as soon as he could speak to her, he would ask her if she didn't think my mental health was at stake in this situation. He smiled. Stubbornness runs in my family, but tenacity is one of Fox's major virtues.

Between Kate, Fox, Jane, Sandy, and Cindy, something must have worked. By ten o'clock, there was Kate, looking very official in a white doctor's jacket I had never seen her wear before, helping to escort me and Fox from the labor area on the second floor to my new private room on the fifth floor. We all laughed at the irony when we saw the plaque outside announcing that the room had been donated by the *New York Times,* Fox's employer for the last twenty years. At last we were getting something back for all those years of blood, sweat, and tears. But did it have to be under these circumstances?

While Fox went out to stretch his legs and pick up a sandwich, Kate stayed in the room to talk for a few minutes. In fact, there was a very important issue she wanted to address. "Have you thought about how you'll feel if the fetus dies?" she asked. "It's a very real possibility." From the first time we had met her, Kate had shown this kind of directness. It was one of the qualities that had made us like and trust her. I knew that her reference to the child inside me as a fetus was a warning not to do any bonding, not to have any genuine expectations one way or the other. It was her way of encouraging detachment. "Have you thought about what you might do?" she asked.

They were big questions, questions that deserved not to be avoided. Though they had never denied that the outcome might be bad, the doctors and nurses had, for the most part, stressed happy thoughts. Don't dwell on the negative, they seemed to be saying. When I visualized, I still saw Emily as a baby. I pictured her on her bunny blanket in her crib, in the high chair that has come down through many generations in Fox's family, with a small shovel and pail, playing in the sand at our house by the sea. No, I hadn't allowed myself to picture her dead. I knew that if she did die, I would feel deep, deep sadness and immeasurable grief. What would I do? I had no idea.

Kate's conversation was sobering, and it was also necessary. No woman who is carrying a baby wants to consider the awful eventuality of the child's death. It is against nature.

Maybe in an earlier era, when couples had many children and

infant death was a common occurrence, it was less devastating to live beyond one's own child. Maybe those pioneer women whose prairie journals I had read for so many years had taken the loss of their children in stride. Maybe the hearts of the mothers of the tiny babies buried in ancient New England cemeteries did not shatter when their infants died in childbirth. But I doubt it. On the scale of the unthinkable, the death of one's child is off the scale.

Fox helped me eat lunch, which was still a chore because of the angle at which I was resting. He pulled the one chair in the room up close to my bed, and then extracted from a brown paper bag a sandwich the size of South Dakota. If we had to be in this terrible situation, Fox said, one of the strengths was that there was a great yuppie deli two blocks from the hospital. "Smoked turkey and Brie," he said between mouthfuls. "Want some?"

Just then Marcie bopped in, bringing with her a tiny, hand-painted wooden clown, the kind that hangs on the edge of a child's crib. "I'm leaving on vacation tonight," she said. "Puerto Rico!" she sang in the manner of Chita Rivera in *West Side Story*. She handed me the little toy. "I wanted you to have this." She had written her home telephone number on a scrap of paper. "Please call me if anything happens," she said. She told me her mother and grandmother were praying for me and Fox and Emily. "I'll pray, too," she promised.

Flowers had begun to arrive from family and friends. A few brave souls tried telephoning, but in my try-to-stay-calm mind frame, I was avoiding speaking to people. Each time I went through the story of what had happened, or what was happening, I grew more anxious. So it fell to Fox to recite the events of the last two days. Our friends and family had besieged him with telephone calls, he said, not without some annoyance. One friend from California had called at 2:30 the previous morning. The West Coast friends kept him busy all night, and the East Coast friends began telephoning at seven in the morning. They meant well, and we appreciated their outpouring of love and support. But the consequence was that Fox had gotten even less sleep than I had.

He mentioned that he had talked to his ex-wife. In the drama of the past day and a half, it had slipped my mind that we were scheduled to have custody of Ethan and Sarah for the coming weekend. They were very excited about it. They had visited us in Manhattan before, and they loved the stimulation of New York.

Poor Fox. The stress was awful for both of us, but he was the buffer to the outside world. Both of us were crumbling. Any doubt about that was erased several hours later when an enormous nurse named Shirley barged into the room and announced, "I'm sorry, sir, but hospital regulations forbid anyone to sleep on the floor." I awoke in protest. "What do you mean, sleep on the floor?" Then, from my south-of-the-border position, I saw Fox curled in a ball alongside my bed.

Shirley was new to nursing, a second career for her. She was meticulous about each step, but she was also excruciatingly slow. Changing the connections on the IV tubes seemed to take forever —or maybe I was just horribly jumpy and impatient. She told me she was on duty until eleven, and then she couldn't wait to take herself out to the fish restaurant around the corner for a huge platter of fried clams. Fried clams? I decided it was better not to think about it.

Looking more exhausted than I had ever seen him, Fox left at about ten. The nursing shift changed at eleven, and Roberta, the night nurse, stopped in to introduce herself. She was Filipino, and was at once gentle and efficient. She checked all my vital signs, and decided that one of the IV tubes needed to be relocated. Before administering the mild sleep medication my doctors had prescribed, she summoned a doctor to reattach the IV tube. Dr. Lopez, the resident who responded to her call, looked to be about twenty-five. She also looked harried and frazzled, and informed me she had been working for two and a half days straight. "But don't worry," she told me as she searched my hand for a new vein. "I'm an ace at this. Best IV inserter in the building."

I told Dr. Lopez that I was feeling woozy, and had strange aches in my abdomen. Could labor be preparing to set in?

"Gas pains," the young doctor insisted, and watched as I took the tablet that would help me sleep. "Don't worry about it. Go to sleep."

Moments later, Sandy Baumgartner, one of the partners in Jane's obstetrical practice, stopped in to see me. Are the pains getting stronger? she asked. I told her they were mild, but still alarming. She concurred with Dr. Lopez's assessment.

"Gas pains," she said. "They're too low to be labor."

Labor pains, said Sandy, "wrap around from behind." What I was describing was probably the result of lying in one position for several days and of stupidly eating dried fruit that afternoon. She saw no reason for me to call Fox. I'd probably just wake him up, and would only worry him unnecessarily.

At two o'clock I rang for Roberta. I was writhing on the bed. The pains had grown far worse. I had no experience in this matter, but I was certain these were not gas pains and that the discomfort I was feeling was not because I had eaten dried fruit.

Roberta scolded me for moving around so much. "You're supposed to be lying still," she said. "In one place."

I begged her to call Dr. Lopez. She told me the doctor was busy, and urged me to try to get back to sleep. If the pains persisted, she would notify the doctor.

"I'm in labor," I kept telling Roberta. "I'm certain of it." By 2:45, she was convinced. Finally, she agreed and called for Dr. Lopez. With a "what is it now?" expression added to her exhaustion, Dr. Lopez blasted back into my room. After one quick look, she announced, as if she had just made an amazing discovery, "You're in labor!"

While Roberta called for an orderly to help escort me to the second-floor labor and delivery area, I reached for the telephone to call Fox. I wanted him to get to the hospital as quickly as possible. At that hour of the night, with very little traffic and an endless supply of cabs on Columbus Avenue, it shouldn't have taken him more than fifteen minutes, tops. But no one answered at our apartment. In the best of times Fox is plagued by insomnia. Sometimes, despite my opposition, he takes middle-of-the-night walks around the block. He also has an annoying habit of disconnecting the telephone before he falls asleep so he won't be awakened by its ring. Could he have felt so confident that nothing would happen tonight that he had unplugged the phone? Or was he out for a late-night stroll? I left a message on the answering machine.

To me it sounded as if I were screaming. I was trying to speak while also groaning in pain. "Fox, if you're there, please come to the phone," I said. "I'm in labor. This is it. The baby is about to be born. Please, please get over here as quickly as possible."

Just to be certain, I dialed the telephone one more time after I had hung up. Again, the machine answered. Again, I felt I was shrieking.

"Me again. It's really serious. Please hurry over here."

The orderly arrived with a wheelchair and looked perplexed when I refused to sit in it. "I'm in labor. I can't sit up," I said. "You're going to have to wheel me down there in a bed."

Once again bureaucracy intervened. "I'm not allowed to take this bed to that floor," he said.

"Well, get another bed," I yelled, surprised that I could still muster that much energy.

He returned with another one, and he and Rebecca rolled me onto it. As he banged and thudded his way down the hall, I imagined that in private life this guy must have a passion for bumper cars.

On the second floor, I was wheeled back to the dreaded pre-natal ICU. One of the awful night nurses actually took that opportunity to gloat about what had happened. "You see," she said, arms crossed in front of her. "This is why you needed to stay here." Her voice was full of smug, I-told-you-so satisfaction. "You needed to be watched."

But the other nurses seemed to have metamorphosed into sisters of mercy in this moment of crisis. Dr. Baumgartner was on her way, one nurse assured me. She stood by me and asked me to describe the pains. I was in the advanced stages of labor, she told me. It would all be over soon. I asked for the telephone and tried to reach Fox. Once again, there was no response. I left another message. I thought my voice sounded feebler, but also more desperate.

I looked up and Sandy Baumgartner was standing over me. She had on a crisp silk blouse and a navy blue pantsuit. For a woman who could not have had more than four hours of sleep, she looked remarkably rested. "Where's Fox?" she demanded. I explained that I had tried to reach him, and had no idea where he was. "Well, can you get hold of your psychologist?" The urgency in her voice upset me.

"Sandy, she lives in Connecticut," I said. "Or maybe it's New Jersey. I don't know. I can't call Kate now." Sandy had another idea. "Call a friend," she said. "Get someone to go to your apartment and try to rouse Fox. You've got to get him here."

By now it was almost four in the morning. The labor had progressed in intensity. I had never felt pain like this before. But more than the pain, I felt fear. What would happen to Emily? I could focus on nothing else.

"Think of someone to call," Sandy urged. "There must be someone."

I punched the number of my friend Ann Marie. In four years of friendship we had nursed each other through innumerable crises, mostly about jobs and men. But this was a big one, calling her at four in the morning and asking her to go wake my husband. She lived about twenty blocks north of our apartment. I calculated that if she was lucky and got a cab quickly, she could be there within ten minutes.

But Ann Marie's message machine answered. Oh, God, I thought, please let her be there. Please let her be screening her phone calls.

"Ann Marie, this is Elizabeth. I'm in labor, and I really need help. I need you to go over to our apartment and try to wake Fox up. If you get this message, can you please—"

A sleepy voice interrupted my entreaty. I told her I was sorry to be calling her at that hour, but I really needed a favor, the biggest I would ever ask of her. What a lucky person I am to have a friend like Ann Marie. Without hesitation she agreed to rush over to West Seventieth Street, right away.

The pain had ascended to a new level still. "It's the baby's head, isn't it?" I asked Sandy. She looked grim, and nodded her head yes. In preparation for the delivery, she had changed to her hospital scrubs. We were still in the prenatal ICU when I motioned for her to lean close to me. What I had to say to her was very important. I wanted to make sure she understood.

"Sandy, please, no heroics," I said. "If this baby is not meant to live, let's not force her." All the fear, the terrible dread and anxiety and panic, were culminating in this moment. My baby's life was at stake. I was terrified that she was too small to survive outside my body. I was just as frightened that she would live, but in an unconscionably compromised fashion. How could I ask this child to live a partial existence? How could I sentence her to an eternity of pain and suffering? How could I consign her to a lifetime of medical limbo? I wanted Emily to feel the joy of life, not merely the burden of it. I wanted her to be that burbling baby on the bunny blanket. I wanted her to be the child in the high chair, the little girl on the beach with the pail and shovel.

Sandy's voice was expressionless. "I don't think you're going to have to worry about heroics," she said. "I don't think she's going to make it."

So that was why she wanted Fox, or Kate, or someone else who knew and cared about me, to be there. She thought the birth process would kill this tiny child, and she didn't want me to endure her death alone.

They were pushing the bed down the hall now. I assumed we were headed for the delivery room. "I'll tell you what's going to happen," Sandy said. "You're going to give me two big pushes. Two big pushes. And then it will all be over."

A cluster of strangers—doctors, I assumed—were standing in the corner of the delivery room. It was a large room with bright lights and a big clock on the wall. Even without my contact lenses I could see that it was 5:25 in the morning.

I felt someone take my hand. "Breathe," urged a heather-soft Irish brogue. The voice belonged to Siobhan, a nurse-midwife who told me she came from Dublin. She had a pixie face and a comforting presence. I hoped she wouldn't leave.

"I don't know how to breathe!" I said. "I never got as far as labor lessons."

She told me to pull in from as deep in my chest as I could manage, and to use the outgoing breath to help push the baby out. It sounded reasonable enough.

I looked up to see Sandy approaching me with a large syringe. I was too involved with the breathing, with trying to bring this child into the world as gently as possible, to feel the injection.

Emily was born at 5:35. She burst out with enormous momentum, like a rocket leaving the launchpad. My brain was growing numb, but I remember thinking that this is how giant pandas are born. They don't linger in the birth process, they don't inch their way into the world. They just blast forth. This was how Emily had chosen to make her entrance, not with a whimper but a bang.

The cry that was filling the room was no whimper either. It was a loud, lusty noise, a cry of protest at having been born too soon. It sounded far bigger than the tiny person who had just been born.

"Sandy, she's crying," I said. It seemed impossible. Hadn't they told me she would be dead?

The injection Sandy had given me was a massive dose of Demerol. If, as she had projected, Emily was to be stillborn, she wanted me to be as unaware as possible. Moments before the drug took hold and knocked me out completely, I heard Sandy reply. "Yes, she's crying," she said. I looked up to see Sandy's eyes round with astonishment. "And she's big!" Sandy's voice suggested she was at least as surprised as I was.

Fox was sitting next to me, his hand gently cupped over mine, when I awoke several hours later. He leaned over the bed so his face could be close to mine. He looked drawn; I thought he must be worrying about how to tell me the bad news. Surely Emily was dead, and he was struggling with how to break it to me. I felt so terribly sorry, sorry for him, sorry for me, and sorrier still for Emily, who would never know her father. I wanted her to know that her daddy loved her very much. I wanted Fox to have heard the hearty cry of his brave little girl. It hurt me beyond measure to think he never would.

He was stroking my hair, something my parents used to do when I was a very little girl. Finally he spoke. "I've just been upstairs," he said. I wondered where "upstairs" was. I was groggy, and felt very empty, as if a gigantic truck had rolled across my lower torso. I was disoriented, but figured I must be in some recovery area. All these hospital spaces looked alike, warrens and caverns splashed with paint the color of mushroom soup. I tried to focus on what Fox was saying, but my brain was playing hide-and-seek, trying to protect me from the awful information it feared was coming. It occurred to me in the midst of these jumbled thoughts that I had no idea what time it was. For a moment, that troubled me. If this was the moment that my worst fears would be confirmed, that I would learn that my child was dead, I wanted to remember everything. I wanted to record every detail. I wanted to know precisely what time it was, just where I was, what Fox was wearing, and every single word he told me.

"There's a little girl up there," he said slowly. He took a short breath.

"There's a little girl up there, and she's ours."

I began to weep, and noticed that Fox was crying, too. If there was a baby up there, wherever "up there" was, then she must be alive.

"She has a big tear in the corner of one eye," Fox told me. He took his finger and gently removed a tear from the corner of my own eye. "Right there," he said.

He wrapped his arms around me, so that our cheeks were touching and his words were tumbling straight into my ear.

"She's alive," he said. "She's beautiful. She's ours."

THREE

Our moment of quiet celebration was short-lived. As if on cue, a stranger emerged from behind the thin curtain around my bed. He was a small man with wavy, graying hair. He wore a goatee, also speckled black and white. His build was compact, and he radiated the kind of nonstop energy that suggested he might begin performing jumping jacks at any moment. The intensity I detected in his deep brown eyes implied he would expect us to join him. I judged him to be in his late forties—about Fox's age.

He introduced himself. "I'm Dr. Friedman, your daughter's neonatologist." These were new terms, *your daughter, neonatologist.* I was proud of the first one, scared of the second. My brain was coming into focus a little bit clearer now; probably the Demerol was wearing off. I realized that this man had just identified himself as Emily's doctor. This felt odd because until now, I had never laid eyes on Dr. Friedman. This was a modern pregnancy, which meant I had started reading books on the subject almost the day I learned we had conceived. I read books on every aspect of pregnancy, how to eat when pregnant, how to exercise when pregnant, how to relax when pregnant. I read the books on how to prepare for childbirth and how to get ready for child-rearing. All the books made a point of stressing the importance of selecting a pediatrician prior to the baby's birth. Friends had described to me the process of interviewing pediatricians, making sure that they felt comfortable with the person who would play such an important role in their child's early years. But Fox and I had never gotten that far. Just like the childbirth classes, where I might have learned how to breathe during delivery, we had missed that part of the pregnancy. So now, instead of choosing a doctor for our baby, we had been assigned one.

Over the years, Fox and I had each interviewed thousands of people in a wide range of circumstances and situations. In covering disasters, we had talked to people in their most vulnerable moments, as they watched their lives explode before them. We had learned that the difference between a good interview and a so-so or lousy one was in establishing some kind of rapport with the subject. We had to find the person's pulse, and swiftly. We considered ourselves fairly quick studies, or I know I did, anyway.

Now I levelled my antennae at Dr. Friedman. If he was not masterminding Emily's life lottery, he was at least calling out the numbers as they fell. We had to trust him; we had no choice. We had to believe in his competence. This felt strange because we had no information on which to base that confidence. None of our friends had referred us to Dr. Friedman, obviously, so we couldn't rely on personal recommendations. We didn't even know where he had gone to medical school, or how long he had worked at this hospital, or where he had worked before. Surely we would have asked those questions had we been able to conduct the famous prebirth interview with him. Was he married? Did he have children of his own? Did he believe in aggressive medical intervention, or was he a laissez-faire physician? He had an impressive title—director of the hospital's neonatal intensive care unit. But that was all we knew about him. It seemed to me that one of my prerogatives as an adult was to choose the people who had direct and important involvement in my life. I had not been "issued" a dentist, an accountant, a lawyer, or, in my days of heavy commuting in Los Angeles, an auto mechanic. I chose all those people. Fox and I were scrupulous in our choices of the professionals we worked with, so it was unnerving to cede our precious baby daughter to this complete stranger.

Dr. Friedman's practiced, smooth manner and obvious intelligence helped allay some of our doubts. Clearly he had been through this bedside debriefing many times before. He was accustomed to dealing with women a few hours out of delivery. He had heard the panicked barrage of questions—How big is she? How are her lungs? How is her heart? How are her reflexes? What is her prognosis? Doctor, is our baby going to live?—from hundreds, maybe thousands of other new mothers. He had seen fathers like Fox, stunned, frightened, and frustrated by their horrible feelings of helplessness.

There was no opportunity for us to confer with each other, but married people learn to speak without words. An exchange of glances between Fox and me confirmed that we really wanted to like this man. We wanted to be able to think of Emily's neonatologist with trust and admiration. Neonatology was a new field, not even certified as a specialty by the American Medical Association until 1975. I had met just one neonatologist in my whole life, and that was ten years earlier, while covering a conference on children's health. I had long since forgotten the doctor's name. But I remembered him telling me he had chosen neonatology because of something his grandfather had told him in his youth. The grandfather loved to garden, and was particularly proud of his roses. "Every bud deserves the chance to blossom," the old man used to tell his grandson.

I hoped Dr. Friedman felt that same way. I hoped he would be honest with us, and straightforward, and able to mollify some of our fears. Fox and I hoped we could have an easy, comfortable working relationship. We hoped that in his hands, our tiny rosebud Emily would have her chance to blossom.

Dr. Friedman explained that he had taken Fox up to the ninth floor nursery. So that was where "upstairs" was. He referred to it as K9, which made it sound like it was intended for stray dogs, not babies. This was the part of the hospital where low birth weight and sick babies were taken. In discussing the neonatal intensive care unit, Dr. Friedman used the hospital shorthand, NICU. He pronounced each letter separately, so that it sounded rather like a child's game—"and I see you." Some people in the hospital, I later learned, called it the Nickyou, as if it were a military installation in Alaska.

Fox and I had just had a baby, a normal event. But in the process, all three of us had been catapulted into an odd and unknown universe where the natives spoke their own language, a tongue called Acronymic. They had their own strange customs and their own quaint costumes. Medicine was the prevailing form of government: What the textbooks taught was the law of the land. Science and technology were the religion here, and the doctors were the keepers of the temple, that much was absolutely clear. The rules were based equally on luck and uncertainty.

In slow, steady tones punctuated with quick, reflexive smiles, Dr. Friedman talked about our daughter. First, the key information: her birth weight. Even through the blur of Demerol, I remembered that Sandy Baumgartner, my obstetrician, had told me in the delivery room that Emily was "big." Now I learned she weighed 760 grams: one pound, eleven ounces. I thought that at some time over the years, I must have bought a head of lettuce that weighed that much. I suspected that the date book I habitually hauled around in my purse weighed substantially more.

"She's very, very small," Dr. Friedman said. But Emily was not the smallest baby ever to have been born. She was not the smallest baby he had ever worked with, and she was certainly not too small to survive. Tinier babies had made it. For her term of gestation, Emily was actually rather large, Dr. Friedman said. And Sandy was right, compared to what everyone had been expecting, Emily was big. The fancy equipment, the sophisticated sonograms used before her birth had misjudged her size in utero. They had underestimated her weight by a full three ounces. The difference was critical. Ten grams is less than a teaspoon. But each ten grams was like ten pounds to a baby Emily's size.

I caught myself smiling as I thought of my three-hour-old

daughter, already proving to the doctors that their wisdom might not be infallible. First she had surprised them by surviving the birth at all. Then she had fooled them with what I was already thinking of as her mighty girth. When I had pondered the qualities I would hope for in my child as I carried her in my womb, I always came back to curiosity, courage, kindness, compassion, and a healthy dose of defiance. I remembered the old story about the woman who spent her entire pregnancy in a rocking chair, end-lessly repeating to herself the phrase, "I want my son to be polite, I want my son to be polite." The pregnancy lasted so long that eventually the woman died. When the doctors opened her up, they found two very old babies, each with long, gray beards, one saying to the other, "After you," "No, after you." In Emily I hoped for a child who would sometimes question authority, and other times cause authority to question itself. Instead of "After you," perhaps she would declare, "Sez who?" So I applauded her for these early acts of polite rebellion. That's my girl, I thought.

Her three extra ounces were definitely a blessing. But Dr. Friedman emphasized that she was still so small that no one could make any realistic predictions. The one guarantee was that there were no guarantees. What we would soon discover as the parents of a preterm infant was that the course made a roller coaster look smooth. The road home for Emily was straight uphill.

At any moment, any day, a preterm child's so-called normal course of development could reverse to the horrific. These tiny babies have a naughty habit of forgetting to breathe. They turn blue in an instant. Wildly irregular heartbeats, called bradycardias, are a constant threat. Infections pounce when least expected. On small, small children, their effects can be ravaging. Many prema-ture infants are blind, or suffer grave visual impairment. Some are deaf. Epilepsy, cerebral palsy, mental retardation, and developmen-tal disabilities that affect movement and learning are common. Because their labor does tend to be rushed, as Emily's was, many premature infants experience severe cranial bleeding. This bleeding in their brains can doom them to a life that is a neurological nightmare.

Technology saves them, in other words. It allows these infants to survive far younger and far smaller than ever was possible before. But these dazzling advances in scientific equipment and expertise may also condemn them to lives of grief and suffering. It is a dichotomy that neither parent nor pediatrician is properly equipped to address.

Probably the most familiar and most common risk to premature infants results from inadequate lung development. Hyaline membrane disease became part of the national medical vocabulary when it killed Patrick Bouvier Kennedy, the infant son of President Kennedy and his wife Jacqueline. Often the preterm child lacks the ability to produce sufficient surfactant, a fatty substance that lines the lungs' air sacs. The condition is known variously as hyaline membrane disease or as respiratory distress syndrome, RDS in the argot of neonatology. Although surfactant production begins in the twenty-second week of gestation, most babies do not manufacture enough surfactant to ensure proper breathing until the thirty-fifth week. Treatment of RDS has improved dramatically in recent years. But respiratory disorders remain a serious and often fatal problem for very tiny babies.

Emily's lungs, not much bigger than tea bags, seemed on initial examination to be remarkably clear of respiratory trouble, Dr. Friedman told us. This was a minor miracle because the more premature a baby is, the more likely it is that he or she will develop hyaline membrane disease or RDS. Almost every baby who weighs under 1,000 grams at birth will display some signs of this condition. Only time and a healthy surge of surfactant can cure RDS. The serious respiratory problems that sometimes set in for these small babies two or three days after birth are known by another acronym, PIP, for pulmonary insufficiency of the premature. This would be one of the conditions the doctors would be watching for in Emily's first few days. We had some cause for cautious optimism, at least on the respiratory front. The cry I had heard from Emily in the delivery room had been unstimulated. She simply shrieked at the sudden change in light and temperature and presumably, at the indignity of being thrust too soon out of her warm, cushiony envi-

ronment. That in itself was another good sign. Many preterm infants need to be "reminded" to breathe. But Emily had done so on
her own. Now she was getting help from an endotracheal tube,
which provided a steady flow of oxygen. Equally important, Dr.
Friedman said, it meant she did not have to use up precious energy
—that is, calories—by breathing unassisted.

Emily seemed alert, Dr. Friedman said. This was another positive indication. Her eyes were still closed, but she was kicking and
pounding and responding to touch. This would suggest that at least
some part of her neurological network was functioning.

I shuddered to think just how much she had already been
touched. Three hours into the world, and our baby had been in-
vaded by probes, monitors, measuring devices, and needles to sam-
ple her blood. It could only feel miserable to have an endotracheal
tube shoved down such a tiny windpipe. It was troubling to think
that her first memories of the world would not involve the security
of her mother's breast, or the solace of her father's arms, but the
discomfort of all this manipulation.

"Twenty-five weeks is very young," Dr. Friedman said, and
smiled. It was a quick flash of a grin, a gesture that seemed more
reflexive than sincere. "But we've had lots of babies that age," he
went on, "and many of them do fine."

Dr. Friedman said it was lucky that Emily had managed to
stay inside me as long as she had. Constant improvements in technology meant that the threshold for survival for these little babies
kept dropping. Just a decade or two earlier, a baby Emily's size and
gestational age would have had only the slimmest chances of living.
Even today, a small hospital that lacked resident experts or state-of-
the-art equipment probably could not offer Emily the same odds of
survival as this big-city hospital with its well-trained staff and ultra-
modern machinery. The changes were happening so fast they were
outpacing social ethics. In many states, including New York, where
Emily was born, twenty-four weeks of gestation is the cutoff point
for legal abortions. Yet Emily, just one day into her twenty-fifth
week, was alive and apparently quite viable. In some ways, the very
fact that she had survived the birth process seemed to lend some

support to the arguments of those who opposed second-trimester abortions in cases where abnormalities had been discovered through amniocentesis. But the people who made those arguments contended further that once a chromosomally defective child was born, medical science could find a "cure" for the condition. That certainly had not been the case for premature infants suffering from serious neurological or respiratory disorders, or for those babies born with partial hearts or other vital organs. For Emily, we would just have to wait and see.

It was fortunate that she was female. No one knows why, but boys born as early as Emily fare far worse. Boys who are "very premature," the description used for babies born in the twenty-fifth to thirtieth weeks of gestation, are much more likely to have serious lung problems than their female counterparts. Fewer of them survive. Among the girls, the hardiest of all these very premature infants are black females. Again, for reasons no one understands, they claim the highest survival statistics of all.

Right now, Emily's survival odds were not terrific. Her condition was considered "very guarded." At best, Dr. Friedman was willing to offer 50-50 odds during this first, extremely critical forty-eight-hour period. Those numbers were discouraging. If I thought my plane had a 50 percent chance of falling out of the sky, would I even consider boarding it? Of course not. If I thought a potential investment had a 50 percent possibility of failing, would I put in as much as a dime? No way. But years of doing verbal combat in the California psychobabble zone had convinced me there really was something to that battered old adage about the glass being half empty or half full. Emily was alive. That was 100 percent better than not being alive. She had all her parts, and none of them appeared to be seriously malfunctioning. Dr. Friedman said she was alert. I decided for the moment to ignore the 50 percent that was against Emily and accept the 50 percent that was in her favor as a wonderful statistical probability. This process is known, I believe, as creative self-deception.

Emily would be watched closely in these first forty-eight hours, Dr. Friedman said. It was impossible to chart out any kind of masterplan, because the course of development for these preterm infants is simply too unpredictable. For now, all her vital signs would be observed carefully and constantly. He warned us that she would probably lose some weight; all babies do after birth—full-term and premature infants alike. But we shouldn't panic, because unless there were unforeseen difficulties, she would be ready to be fed soon. He urged me to have a nurse instruct me in the use of a breast pump. If I chose not to express my own milk, they would be willing to put Emily on a formula diet once she was ready to be fed, Dr. Friedman said. But his own bias was toward mother's milk. All the studies indicated that the long-term health benefits of mother's milk could not be duplicated in a man-made formula. Nature knew what she was doing when she invented lactation.

Almost with every sentence, Dr. Friedman stressed the precarious nature of Emily's condition. We could not think about the future, he seemed to be saying. We had to think about this morning. Anything could happen between now and tomorrow. We had to reorganize our expectations to think of life in terms of five-minute chunks.

Only a few hours had passed since we had landed in this strange new world. I hadn't fully grasped the rules yet. I thought I could be forgiven some of my earthly ways. In any case, I wasn't sure I wanted to part with my wide-eyed optimism.

So I spilled out the question I had been wanting to ask almost since the moment Dr. Friedman had poked his gray-bearded face through the curtain. I was careful to preface my query with "if she lives," and "if she does all right," but Dr. Friedman interrupted me. He was accustomed to hearing this question from mothers in this situation. He could tell them a hundred times that nothing was certain, nothing could be predicted, and still they would demand the same information. "You want to know when you can take her home, right?" For once the smile that beamed on and off like a traffic light actually looked real. "If all goes well, you can probably figure on taking her home sometime around her due date, or maybe a little before." I could see that he was trying to calculate that date, quickly adding fifteen weeks to March 26. "July 8," I told him. I almost assaulted him with it, that's how fast I blurted it out. It had been inscribed on my brain since the day I had watched Jane Gerstner spin her pregnancy calculation wheel and inform me when my child was due. For many months, it had seemed very far away. But it was an easy date to remember. It was Fox's birthday, too.

July 8 still seemed obscenely far into the future. It wasn't even Easter yet, and this baby who was due after the Fourth of July was already among us. I felt a surge of anger on Emily's behalf. This was not the way this pregnancy was supposed to turn out.

For once, I was completely out of my league. All my inventiveness and assertiveness were useless. Lying there listening to Dr. Friedman, trying hard to assimilate every word he said about Emily, I had a hard time suppressing the words that were screaming in my brain: There's nothing you can do. There's not one single thing you can do about this, any of it.

"For many years, these premature infants were not allowed to go home until they weighed at least five pounds," he said. "Now, if they're healthy—if all else goes well—we'll release them to the parents when they make it to four pounds. If Emily's course is normal, that might be sometime toward the end of June. Meanwhile, you should probably plan on spending a lot of time right here between now and then."

"If all goes well," I said.

"Right," said Dr. Friedman, and then, of course, he smiled. "If all goes well."

He was about to leave when Fox stopped him with a request of his own.

"Tell Elizabeth about Emily's state of mind," he said.

"She's pounding and kicking," said Dr. Friedman. "I think she's angry."

This was the best news I had heard yet. Our daughter was a fighter.

Dr. Friedman vanished as nimbly as he had appeared. I told Fox I felt he had a leprechaunlike quality. Leprechauns seemed like friendly enough fellows, and didn't they live among four-leaf clovers, the traditional symbols of good luck? It seemed like a good omen. We decided to take our positive auspices wherever we could find them.

The amount of information Dr. Friedman had imparted was numbing, but there were still many questions he hadn't answered. I began to bombard my beleaguered husband.

"Fox, what does she look like?"

"Well, to begin with," he replied, "she's bright red."

Emily was so florid, Fox continued, that when he first saw her, he was certain she was not his daughter. So far as he knew, there were no red genes anywhere on his family tree. But the residents and nurses on duty assured him this was not abnormal. Premature infants often come out looking like lobsters who have lingered too long in the pot. Give her a day or two, they told him, and she would look peachy.

"She has lots of blond hair," he said. This surprised me, because in the brief glimpse of our child that I had caught in the delivery room, her hair had seemed dark, like her father's. But before I could challenge him, I stopped myself, feeling stupid. Of course her hair had looked dark. It was covered with goop from the birth canal.

Emily was on her back, Fox said, splayed out on a warming table, with her knees bent like a frog.

"Elizabeth, you won't believe that place," Fox said. "It looks like a baby farm."

A series of nurseries opened off a hallway that ran the length of K9, Fox said. Each room was lined with plastic boxes containing babies at various stages of development. Many were on respirators, and almost all were in boxes with lids to maintain the temperature control their tiny bodies demanded. Most of the very small babies were intubated; that is, they had tubes plunged down their throats to spare them the effort of breathing. As a result, the ward was devoid of the crying sounds found in most hospital nurseries.

"And the place is completely public," he went on. True, entry was restricted to parents, grandparents, clergy, and hospital staff.

But once admitted to K9, a parent gave up all illusions of intimacy with his or her newborn child. Along with the stern warning that no children or other nonessential relatives would be permitted to see the babies, Fox said there should have been a sign declaring "Check your privacy at the door." While he was admiring Emily, Fox said, several parents of other children leaned over the warming table to size up this latest arrival. They never even introduced themselves, Fox said, and no doctors or nurses made any attempt to shoo them away. Apparently this was the protocol on K9.

The mention of other parents jolted me back to an issue I had completely forgotten.

"Omigod, Fox, we're supposed to take Ethan and Sarah this weekend."

I had visions of them stranded at LaGuardia, telephoning the apartment and getting the answering machine I had encountered earlier. But Fox had headed off such a disaster by telephoning the kids immediately after Ann Marie had awakened him. He had fallen into such a deep sleep after leaving the hospital the night before that he never even heard the telephone ring. It took Ann Marie, pounding on the apartment door and yelling at him to wake up because his baby was about to be born, to jolt him out of his slumber.

There he was in his undershorts, and she, a glamorous red-head, was wearing a trench coat she had hastily thrown over her silk pajamas. If I hadn't felt so perplexed and hurt by his absence at a time when I needed him so, it might have sounded comical.

Still in their plastic pitcher, the lavender tulips were waiting for me on the bedside table when they wheeled me back to the *New York Times* suite. I was grateful to be out of the labor and delivery area, a part of the hospital that hadn't brought me much luck, and I was pleased to be three floors closer to Emily. The best news of all was that when I was ready, I would be permitted to walk.

When I was ready? I nearly bolted out of the bed. This must have been quite a sight—a woman who hadn't showered or combed her hair in three and a half days, garbed in the standard hospital-issue unisex nightgown, dragging an IV pole like a shepherd's staff. Halfway down the hall, I became aware of the cold, perpetually grimy-looking linoleum under my feet and realized I was barefoot.

"You might want these," a nurse, Donna, said as she handed me a pair of green foam rubber slippers. Then she helped me rig a second unisex nightgown to cover my back. In my haste to visit Emily, it hadn't occurred to me that the nightgowns were open in the back and that, of course, I was wearing nothing underneath.

Standing nearby, Fox watched me with some amusement. He had long since learned not to stand in my way when an idea or, worse, a plan of action, overtook me. Once he had remarked that my favorite Russian novel must be Dostoyevski's *The Possessed.*

This element of my character could be downright unattractive. Fox quickly learned that the best way to get me to do something was to tell me it couldn't be done. But that same obstinance meant that I did not willingly part with points of view. One reason Fox and I probably found ourselves attracted to each other was that he, too, tended to set goals and then plug and plug until he attained them. But whereas I was brash and often impulsive in flinging myself into a particular project, Fox was steady and meticulous. Upstairs in K9, our daughter was going to need every bit of those traits from both of us.

The ninth floor, as it turned out, was the hospital's equivalent of land fill. Some years earlier, the space had been reclaimed from its existence as a storage area and converted to the neonatological unit. From the street it was almost invisible, for it was not actually a full floor. Presumably this half space had never been intended to operate as a full-service facility. It housed only the neonatological nursery, a unit with an average population of about twenty-five babies, and a small laboratory that processed samples and specimens from that unit. None of the doctors had their offices in this area, or even in this building. K9 was clearly a haphazard effort,

one of those construction plans that starts out as a temporary compromise and ends up as at least a semipermanent solution.

The large piece of glass that separated the hallway from the
K9 reception area had chicken coop wire running through it, and
the panoramic view it afforded began with the dingy, cardboard-
box-strewn hall, and ended with the cluttered desk and file cabinets
that filled the small receiving zone. The heavy swinging door, two-
thirds wood and one-third glass and chicken wire, was kept locked
at all times. A sign on the door warned that only parents and
grandparents of the patients in K9 were welcome. We rang the
buzzer alongside the door, then noticed through the chicken coop
picture window that no one was sitting at the receptionist's desk.
We waited a minute or so, then rang again. Still no response.
Finally, on our third attempt, a door we had not noticed opened
and a person we took to be a nurse stuck her head out at us.

"Yes?" she said. Her tone was impatient, and not remotely
inviting.

What a charming couple we must have made: I, in my jury-
rigged high-fashion hospital nightie and matching IV pole; Fox in
the same Banana Republic khakis and sport shirt he had been
wearing for the last three days; both of us dazed and frightened by
what was happening to us and our daughter. Did this nurse think
we had arrived to pose for a layout on fun things to do at the
hospital? Or that maybe we were part of a scavenger hunt or a
scenic tour? Perhaps we were the termite inspectors?

Fox got his voice before I found my tongue. It was probably
just as well.

"We're here to see our daughter," he said. "Emily Butterfield."

"Butterfield?" the nurse repeated. "Butterfield?"

"Look, I was just up here an hour or so ago," Fox said. "She
was born this morning. She's in the intensive care area."

"Butterfield?" the nurse said again, but buzzed us in anyway.

The receptionist's desk was still empty. There was no one
around to instruct us in K9 rules and regulations. "You'll need to
wear gowns," the nurse said over her shoulder as she headed down

the hallway. Without looking at us, she pointed at a small room a few feet from the reception area. "You can get them in there."

The family room, as I later learned this dismal little chamber was called, was no more than ten feet by ten feet. Five or six metal lockers along one wall made me feel as if I were back in high school. They were banged and bent and dented, just like high school, but they had no locks. A green plastic couch took up most of the far wall, and several large brown plastic chairs filled the remaining two walls. Above two of the chairs I was horrified to see a sign designating that space as the room's smoking area. It was obvious that the smoke from one cigarette would fill the entire room; if more than one person was smoking, the air would make me nostalgic for Los Angeles in September, the smoggiest month of the year. I couldn't think of anything more incongruous with the goals of a hospital, ostensibly a haven of health, much less with a unit devoted to the care of small babies with undeveloped lungs. A pay phone hung on the wall above the couch, too high for anyone to use while sitting and public enough so that every conversation would be megaphoned to anyone else in the room. In another corner, a set of shelves housed stacks of pale pink and yellow gowns, standard attire here on K9. A large hamper stood beside it to accommodate used gowns.

Fox slipped on a yellow gown and handed me a pink one. The gowns had cuffs made of cotton knit material, like T-shirts, and for a moment we were stumped on how to slip the sleeve over the IV needle and tube. With no one to advise us, we improvised. Somehow, I got the thing over my arm.

A porcelain sink occupied most of the small L-shaped area between the family room and the receptionist's desk. Its big metal faucets looked like the horns of a stainless steel moose. A large sign above the sink gave instructions on how to wash before entering the nurseries. We were to wash to our elbows, the sign said, and we were to scrub our hands and nails carefully. We could use the pink hospital-approved liquid soap in the dispenser beside the sign or, if we preferred, we could opt for something called an EZ Scrub, available in a second dispenser that also hung on the wall. This handy little package contained a presoaped surgical scrub brush and sponge with its very own little red plastic pick to clean one's nails. Its label revealed that it was "terminally sterilized" by "gamma irradiation." We were not sure we wanted to be terminally sterilized by gamma irradiation, but gamely EZ-Scrubbed our hands, nails, forearms, and elbows anyway.

Fox led the way as we headed down the hall. On the right, the door to the staff lounge was open, and we heard laughter and animated conversation as we passed by. There was a large, walk-in storage area next door, and opposite this, across the hall on the left, a room crammed with unused isolettes and other equipment. On both sides of the corridor, all the other rooms contained babies, lined up in rows in little clear plastic boxes. It was hot and steamy. Bright lights, much like the kind used to stimulate plant growth, glared ferociously. Fox was right. The place did feel hydroponic.

The NICU—I was already starting to think in the lingo—was the last room on the right. Rows of isolettes rimmed the perimeter of this small, brightly lit area. In the center of the room, four isolettes formed a rectangular island, as if these little plastic boxcars had decided to park together. Emily was in the closest of these center-of-the-room isolettes. I knew it was her because she was so pink and tiny.

Every mother gazes in wonderment at the marvel that is her child. Each thinks hers is the most beautiful ever to have been born. Each looks upon her child for the first time and sees a miracle.

I was no exception. My child was smaller than the doll I had played with in nursery school. She was already attached to a spiderweb of tubes and pipes and monitors. Her eyes were fused shut and her hands were clenched in tight, tense fists. Her ears were miniature seashells, delicate and perfectly formed. Her feet were less than two inches long. I thought she was the most magnificent baby I had ever seen.

I could not take my eyes off her. I wanted to memorize every single cell. I was consumed by a new emotion, a mother's pure, unquestioning love for her child. I was gripped by the strength of this feeling. It was mesmerizing to look at Emily.

Other mothers of very premature infants have since told me that they, too, were amazed at how quickly their eyes and brains adjusted to this eerie world of diminutive humans. It is true that with my very first glance at Emily I saw a remarkably small person. But within seconds, I saw not an unnaturally small baby, but my baby. And she was beautiful.

Someone less biased would have seen a child whose skin was so thin it was translucent. Many of her veins were visible, although muted, as if they were being seen through a scrim. Premature babies lack sufficient levels of keratin, the protein that keeps adults and full-term babies' bodies flexible and watertight. So the preterm child's skin looks brittle and tears easily. An objective viewer would have judged Emily, like any child born in the twenty-fifth week of gestation, to be painfully scrawny. A full-term infant gains most of its weight, a pound or more each week, in the final four weeks of gestation. So the very premature baby boasts none of the soft baby fat that makes full-term kids look so robust and healthy. As a consequence, the very premature infant's much-too-bony fingers and toes may seem exceedingly long. Elbows look like sharp corners. The nose may seem jagged, and the chin, with no fat to cushion it, may look far too pointed.

To me, Emily's arms and legs looked long and slender. The truth was, her arms were so thin that the smallest size identification bracelet would have fallen right off her wrist. Instead, the nurses had placed her tag around her thigh. Most newborns I have seen have had meaty little thighs, but Emily's were streamlined. Wrapped around her upper leg, the identification tag was still so loose that with one strong kick it came off entirely.

Premature infants of Emily's gestational age also lack the muscle development of full-term babies. They tend to move their whole bodies at once, without the control of more gestationally advanced infants. They react quickly, and sometimes wildly, to loud noises, bright lights, or sudden movements. Until about the thirtieth week, when muscle tone does begin to develop, their limbs flop about like little rag dolls. They are so flexible that they can easily touch their toes to their ears, a feat that is impossible for a full-term baby. Preterm infants sleep a great deal—about fifteen to twenty-two hours a day, and as they did in the womb, they often sleep in strange, contorted positions. Sometimes they calmly place their feet next to their heads, as if they are about to perform backwards somersaults. Instead, they doze peacefully in this improbable-looking position.

Some very premature infants are born with a fine coating of soft, downy hair, called lanugo, which usually disappears soon after they are born. Emily had just a faint trace of flaxen hair on her shoulders. It looked like golden peach fuzz. The hair on her head was fine, but surprisingly thick. I studied it carefully.

"Fox, how can you say she's blonde?" It looked gingery brown to me, maybe just a shade paler than his own wavy locks. In fact, the more intensely I looked at Emily, the more I thought she resembled her father in every way possible.

"Well, because she is blonde," he said. From our perch outside the plastic box, he gestured to a yellowish fringe.

"Fox," I insisted, and I was startled by the contentiousness in my voice, "this child does not have blond hair."

Now this truly was absurd. Were we going to stand over our newborn child, all one pound, eleven ounces of her, and argue over whether she was blonde or brunette?

"You can touch her if you want."

The voice that offered these words was high and soft. We turned to where it had come from, just a foot or two away from us. We had been so enrapt by Emily that we hadn't seen the young nurse approach. She was in her midtwenties and Filipino, with waist-length hair she had permed and wore pulled off her face with a hair ribbon. She told us her name was Edna, and that she would be Emily's day nurse today and tomorrow. After Dr. Friedman's admonitions against assuming that there would be a tomorrow, I tried not to attach too much significance to Edna's introduction. She was just telling us what her nursing assignment was, I reminded myself, not promising us that Emily would make it through the night.

The isolette was less than three feet long. At either end it contained two round, plastic sheathed openings through which Emily's breathing tubes, heart and respiration monitors were connected to machines. The familiar dancing red numbers showed that her heart was holding steady at between 140 and 160 beats per minute, right where it should be. On the front and back of her isolette there were pairs of portholes, each large enough for one adult hand to slip through. Edna showed us how to unclamp them.

"Are you sure this is all right?" I asked. I worried that opening the porthole would alter the oxygen level inside the isolette. Emily's environment was regulated to a level of about 40 percent oxygen, as compared to 21 percent in normal room air. What if opening the porthole made it drop to 39 percent? I was afraid of introducing strange germs. Emily had no immune system, and would be unable to defend against anything that might attack her. I thought the tiny opening from the porthole might admit the premature infant's counterpart of a burst of cold air. Infants in the NICU need to be watched constantly and from all directions, so only a few of them wear so much as a diaper. If Emily became cold, there was no blanket to pull up for her. I thought she might not want to be disturbed. If she was anything like her father, she would hate to be touched while sleeping.

Edna looked amused. Like Dr. Friedman, she had heard many new mothers express these very same concerns.

"Of course," she said. "These very little babies need to be touched. They like it. It's important for them."

By now Edna was gently stroking Emily. I wanted to try it, too. Edna removed her hand from one porthole, and I guided mine through the other. Emily was lying on her back, in her frog girl position. I ran my finger down an arm as soft as a rose petal. When I got to Emily's hand, it clenched firmly around my finger.

Half of my index finger filled her entire hand. Her grip was strong. This normal reflexive gesture by any healthy child seemed to me like magic. I wanted to cry. Instead, I heard myself talking to my daughter.

"It's me, baby Emily, it's Mom. I love you."

I would happily have stood and let Emily clutch my finger forever. But Fox wanted to touch her, too. Reluctantly, I moved my hand and stepped aside so he could stand directly above Emily. At that moment Edna appeared, pushing a blue plastic chair. I had no idea how long we had been standing there, but a glance at the clock showed we had been in the NICU for more than an hour. Until that moment I had felt no fatigue at all. The excitement of seeing Emily had erased any traces of exhaustion from my sleepless night and early morning delivery. I blessed Edna's sensitivity, for until she produced the chair, I hadn't realized that there weren't any. Apparently, the policy here in the NICU was standing room only.

"Where did you find this?" I asked.

She smiled. "Over there," she said, and pointed to one of the other nurseries. "I stole it. I thought you might be tired. You did just have a baby."

Fox was lovingly caressing Emily's head and whispering sweet fatherly nothings to her. "It's Daddy, Emily. It's Daddy, Daddy loves you." I loved watching them together, father and daughter. But I also felt my eyes drifting to survey the room around us. My focus had been so firmly on Emily that I hadn't had a chance to take in the details of our family's odd new environment.

The room was small, about fifteen feet by twenty-five feet. About two thirds of the ten isolettes were occupied by babies of various sizes, shapes, and colors. At the moment the two warming tables were empty. One baby behind us, I noticed, was lying beneath bright blue lights that had been set up in his isolette. He wore tiny little sunglasses that made him look like a miniature motorcyclist.

"Bili lights," said Edna. Premature babies are prone to developing high levels of bilirubin, a yellow pigment in the blood that can be toxic if it is not purified in the liver. Excess levels of bilirubin can lead to jaundice, which is common in full-term babies as well as preterm infants, or occasionally, more serious conditions. If blood testing reveals that the baby's bilirubin level is too high, the child will probably be treated with several days of phototherapy, or bili lights.

"Almost all of them need phototherapy," Edna said. "Emily will probably have to have it, too." She paused for a moment, then offered this reassurance. "It's not serious. You don't have to worry."

Everything seemed so out of proportion in the NICU. The machines were enormous, bulky, and cumbersome. And they were everywhere. The babies were so dwarfed by comparison that they seemed almost to vanish. Above some isolettes, ropes and cords dangled from IV poles like giant wads of spaghetti. The hoses that were hooked up to endotracheal tubes would have looked equally at home watering the lawn, or maybe putting out a fire. Monitors that sat atop many isolettes looked like they might crush the unsuspecting babies beneath them.

Mostly, the NICU was a very noisy place. The machines gurgled and spat and hissed and spewed and roared. The monitors were all connected to alarms. If the preterm child's underdeveloped nervous system forgot to remind the baby to breathe, the apnea monitor would shriek like the siren on a police car. If the baby's heart rate dropped suddenly, a bradycardia bellowed out news of this development. The monitors were so sensitive that sometimes, if the babies moved abruptly or awkwardly, they could activate the sound system. The beepers and buzzers were at once harsh and shrill. They reminded me of movies I had seen of London during the blitz.

"Cooke," Edna said calmly when one of the alarms began to blast. Without looking, she knew who had set it off. Another nurse rushed to attend to the baby in the far corner of the room.

"False alarm," the other nurse announced.

Edna laughed. "That baby always sets off his buzzers," she said. She was leaning against Emily's isolette. I wondered how she managed to stay so serene in such a chaotic atmosphere. She must have read my mind. "You get used to it," she said.

• • •

It was hard to avoid the feeling that every moment with Emily might be my last. Clearly, if she and I were going to make it through our experience here, I would have to make some kind of a mental leap. I would have to put my trust in these people and their machines. I would have to join their faith. In a funny and distant way it reminded me of studying physics in my freshman year at college. It was a class for non-science majors called Physics 10, and it was also known, because of its notorious lack of intellectual challenge, as Sorority Physics. Four hundred fifty students filled an auditorium in the physical science lab and listened to a world-renowned scientist recount the adventures of a creature called the Physics 10 Squirrel, who was prone to throwing acorns off moving trucks. But starting with the notion of momentum, I never understood the principles. I simply couldn't grasp them. I kept asking why? Or, how can we really know? Finally, in frustration, the professor all but shook me by the shoulders. "You don't have to understand the principles!" he roared. "Just accept them." I took his advice and passed the course with little effort.

Now I was once again in a situation I failed to comprehend. Why had this happened? How had this normal, effortless pregnancy gone so insanely awry? Why were we here? Why must Emily work so hard? How can we really know what she is feeling? How can we know what she will and will not remember?

Much of this was about science and about sound medical experience. But a lot of what was happening to Fox, Emily, and me —and to all the other parents and children thrown into this strange environment—was about faith. We didn't have the option not to believe in these doctors, nurses, and machines. We did not have to understand the principles, as my physics teacher had reproached me so many years before. But we did have to accept them.

"You look tired," Edna said. She was speaking to me, but she might just as well have been addressing Fox. His shoulders were sagging and his eyes had sunk deep into his skull. I had never seen him look so weary.

Edna had written down my room number in the hospital, and she had Fox's phone number at home as well. She promised she would call us if anything changed, and said she would pass the same instructions on to the night nurse, who would relieve her at eight o'clock. "And you can call here any time," she said. "Any time during the day or night." She wrote down the extension on a scrap of paper. "Just ask for whoever is taking care of Baby Mehren."

Baby Mehren? Fox and I traded quizzical looks. Then our eyes fell on the yellow name tag taped to the isolette. In our preoccupation with Emily, we had completely overlooked this matter of nomenclature. But sure enough, she was identified as Emily Mehren. Here was a pitfall of the two-name marriage that we hadn't anticipated. When I had checked into the hospital I had used my own name, which appears on all my insurance records. Therefore, in the myopic view of the hospital's administration, my daughter could not possibly have a different one. Now we understood why the nurse who had buzzed us in several hours earlier had seemed so puzzled. I borrowed Edna's pen and scratched out "Mehren." In its place I wrote the name Fox and I had agreed on months before she was born, the same name Fox had entered on her birth certificate: "Emily Eaton Butterfield."

It was a beautiful name. She was a beautiful baby. I watched her tiny chest heave heavenward with every breath she took. Each gasp of air was a statement of her determination. She was beautiful, yes, and she was very, very brave.

FOUR

Emily did lose weight those first few days. She did go on bilirubin lights. She did wear wraparound sunglasses, and she did look just like a miniature Miami Beach sun worshiper. Early on Sunday morning, her second day of existence, she opened her left eye. It was bright turquoise blue. Her right eye followed a day later. Once Emily figured out how to open her eyes, she didn't want to close them. All the books say newborns have a limited range of vision, and that premature infants see even less. But Emily's eyes pursued objects; they flashed open at the sound of voices. She was still kicking furiously. "Active and alert" was what the nurses kept writing in her daily progress charts.

Her breath sounds continued to be clear bilaterally. Translated, that meant her lungs seemed to be free of respiratory disorders. Though no infection had surfaced in laboratory cultures, Emily and I remained on antibiotics to ward off any as yet undiagnosed bacteria that might have caused the rupture of my amniotic sac. The oxygen level in her isolette was lowered by 10 percent, easing it closer to normal room level. She exhibited no incidents of apnea or bradycardia, two of the major banes of premature existence. Every three to six hours, her blood was drawn from her heels to test oxygen and carbon dioxide levels. With each test, the nurses continued to assure us that her blood gas levels were good.

Until then, Fox and I had never heard of blood gases, but we quickly became versed in how efficiently these gases—oxygen and carbon dioxide—were or were not operating in Emily's lungs and bloodstream, and how the balance between them was or was not being maintained. Her oxygen level had to be high enough to keep her tissues vital. But if it rose too high, the effect could be toxic. Without enough carbon dioxide, the portions of her brain that told her to breathe would not be properly stimulated. But if the carbon dioxide level became excessive, her blood could become acidic. I cringed each time the blood was drawn and joined Emily in protesting when her blood sugar level was tested eight times a day with a stab in her heel. When Emily recoiled as a chilly thermometer was slipped under her arm six to eight times a day, I pulled back, too.

During his periodic visits to the NICU, Dr. Friedman was always cordial. He gladly answered questions, never displayed annoyance, and never, ever lost his punctuation-mark smile. Leaning his elbow against Emily's isolette while I talked, he kept that cheery expression focused on me while I voiced concern about the discomfort that Emily and her fellow occupants of K9 routinely underwent. Humans are resilient, I am the first to agree, and can weather all manner of sadness and suffering. But often the scars remain. Even keeping Sigmund Freud out of the conversation, there are all kinds of studies to suggest that early childhood really is a formative period. The pain from youthful suffering can return to torment even the most balanced of adults. When I worried that if she did survive this experience, Emily would recall nothing but pain, Dr. Friedman had a smile and a ready rejoinder.

"She'll never remember it," he insisted. His response came so swiftly that I suspected this was another of those issues the parents of premature infants habitually introduce. Premature infants lack the neurological sophistication to process pain or to record the unpleasant sensation in some kind of psychological memory bank,

Dr. Friedman said. Their brains are not sufficiently developed to encode this data, he said. In fact, he added, until relatively recently, doctors believed that the risks of anesthesia greatly overshadowed the premature infant's capacity to feel pain. As a matter of course, surgery was performed on these small children with no anesthesia at all. Babies of Emily's size who did survive after massive medical intervention showed no greater tolerance or intolerance toward pain than other children, Dr. Friedman said. He reminded me once again that pain wasn't the issue here; getting her healthy was. In any case, he went on, these little kids seemed not to have the relationship toward pain that adults or larger children do.

"Then how come she flinches every time a needle gets stuck in her?" I asked.

"Reflex," said Dr. Friedman, and his smile blinked on with its own kind of reflex.

I looked down at Emily and hoped that her young response system would be powerful enough to kick the next person who jabbed her with a needle. Already, her heels were black and blue from so many needle pricks. Reflexively, Dr. Friedman smiled and moved on to the next isolette.

And so in short order we settled into an odd kind of routine. We moved into our new microcosm, the NICU, as if it were some Buck Rogers planned community, a retirement village in reverse. Although conveniences like chairs were not provided, parents were encouraged to spend as much time as they wanted in K9. The nurses chatted comfortably with us, often sharing personal details of their lives outside the hospital. Edna, for example, described how she had met her husband, an engineer who was also from the Philippines, at the christening of a mutual friend's child here in New York. She confided that at the moment, her major extracurricular project was to get her driver's license. She had been taking driving classes, she said, and in a few weeks she planned to take the road test.

The nurses reminded us that we could telephone the unit for information about Emily whenever we wanted. In fact, I soon discovered that an entry called "social" on Emily's daily progress chart made note of every visit or telephone call. "Mom visited, played with baby," it might say. Or, "No visits, no phone calls." Even if the latter notation occurred on the all-night shift, I felt chastised, and vowed to be a more attentive mother.

I found it easy to spend hours with Emily. In no time at all I ceased to see the monster machines that lurked above her. My brain seemed to enter K9 with its own giant economy size supply of mental Crisco. Anything it did not want to see, like the crudely named oxygen blender, it erased by greasing over. I fast became adjusted to the Mylar electrodes scattered about my daughter's small chest. I stopped compulsively watching the pulsemeter and oximeter next to her. I no longer regarded the endotracheal tube as some kind of hideous appurtenance. It was part of Emily; it almost seemed to belong in there with her, like her nose or her toes.

I genuinely enjoyed talking to Emily. While she slept, or while she was awake and seemed to be studying me with those piercing blue eyes, I prattled on. I suppose I half expected that she would join in the conversation. I talked to her while she clutched my finger. I talked to her while I stroked her back or stomach. I told her about her family, about this strange place that was temporarily her home, about the doctors and nurses and machines. I told her about the weather. If flowers or gifts had arrived for her, I told her about those, too. The poor child must have wondered if I would ever shut up. Rational thought was not my strong point in those first few days of her life. But at some level, I think I reasoned that what we were doing here was completing her gestation, but in an unnatural, out-of-the-womb environment. In utero, Emily could hear my voice and Fox's—or at least that's what all the how-to-have-a-perfect-pregnancy books had said. By talking to her, I felt I was offering her some kind of continuity with the world from which she had been so abruptly ejected. I persuaded myself that a familiar voice might offer some security against the cacophony of K9. Since I could not hold my child, I thought that talking to her might enhance whatever bonding process we could accomplish in this artificial habitat. I wanted her to know that mine was a voice she could trust.

Besides, it was fun to talk to Emily. It made me feel that maybe I really was a mother. Looking at her, talking to her, touching her, proved to me that she was real. I couldn't push her in a carriage down the street. I couldn't show her off to my friends. But I could relish every moment I had with her. As strange as the situation was, that was what we had to work with.

Growing up, I was showered with proverbs, maxims, and mottoes from my maternal grandmother. Sometimes they made me crazy, for these adages were often dour and laced with heavy moralism. "Waste not, want not," she would say. Or, "I used to complain because I had no shoes until I saw a man who had no feet." I loved my grandmother, but to protect myself against this steady stream of sermonettes, I took to thinking of her as the Homily Queen of North America. "Make the best of what you've got" was one of her favorites. This was what Emily, Fox, and I had, this brightly lit shrine to technology. I, for one, was determined to make the best of it.

Reality did not make it any easier to achieve that goal. When I finally was released from the hospital, nearly a week after I had checked in, it was hard to walk out empty-handed. It seemed that the lobby was exploding with couples taking their newborns home. Everywhere Fox and I looked we saw armloads of new life wrapped in pink, blue, and yellow blankets. We saw mothers walking awkwardly, but jealously clinging to their priceless packages, and fathers hovering nervously. We heard grandparents exclaiming rapturously. There were flashbulbs from many cameras. Carrying my purple tulips instead of my baby, I tried in vain to spread Crisco on this scene. This was another of those down-the-rabbit-hole inversions. When you leave a maternity ward, you are supposed to go home with a baby, not with vacant arms and a dangerously heavy heart.

Wordlessly, for we were both conspiring for composure, Fox and I drew close and walked out to a gray and rainy street to hail a cab. Looking down on the sidewalk, I spied a shiny coin. I decided this must be another omen. I picked it up. A lucky penny, just for Emily.

"All that time when we were trying to get pregnant," Fox said as the taxi took us home. "I thought you were just being jealous and resentful when you used to tell me about how much it hurt you to see people pushing babies in carriages. I didn't understand why you would cry when your good friends had babies. You tried to explain it to me, but I thought you were being selfish. I thought you were overreacting. I didn't get it."

He paused for a minute and his hand gripped mine. "I think I'm beginning to understand."

Back home, our message machine was crammed with calls. Friends and family from all over wanted to know every single detail about Emily. Everybody was demanding what is known in the news business as a complete fill: who, what, where, when, why —as if we could even come close to answering that last one.

Fox and I realized we were in a curious position. Of course we wanted our daughter home with us. But in the very best of circumstances—if all went well, as Dr. Friedman would say—that was not going to happen for several months. So as much as we hated the thought of parking our daughter in a clear plastic box across town, that was the best of our none-too-happy alternatives. We had to hope that she would remain in the hospital. If that was the case, we were going to have to work out some kind of system to help preserve what little of our sanity we had left. We wanted to talk to each person who called. We wanted every friend and relative to know exactly what was happening with Emily. But if we had to recite the day's progress report and prognosis twenty or thirty times a day, our tongues would turn to taffy.

It was not that we were not eager to talk about Emily. I was obsessed with her, and could think of nothing, or no one, I would rather discuss. But to ward off false optimism on the part of our friends and family, all of whom wanted to believe that everything would be fine, and that we would soon be bringing our big, healthy baby home with us, I felt compelled to recount the perilousness of her situation. Each time I ran through the long list of dangers, it reminded me anew of just how tenuous Emily's future really was. I would conclude the calls exhausted, having bored the caller with more details than anyone could ever want, and having depressed myself with the same scary possibilities.

So, right then and there, we devised the Emily hotline. We composed a short message and recorded it on our answering machine. Keep it positive, we told each other. Try and be upbeat and just tell people the short version of this huge, complicated story.

"Hi, it's Wednesday, we're so glad you called. Emily weighs 680 grams today. The doctors think things look good, for now. She's kicking and pounding. The nurses have nicknamed her The Fighter. We love her very much. We're grateful for your call and hope we'll be able to talk to you soon."

Each day, we would update the information. It seemed a sensible solution, but it also brought home to us how quickly and radically our lives had changed. Any whisper of stability, any trace of predictability, had completely vanished. One week earlier, we had been a two-career family, eagerly awaiting a later-in-life baby. We went to work, we saw friends, we had political opinions. We debated large issues and squabbled over small ones. We cared about the homeless and crusaded against illiteracy. We were upset about the spread of drugs and we despaired at the scourge of AIDS. Our dinner conversations might focus on the plight of political prisoners in distant lands, or of questions of justice right here in America. Now every ounce of our energy was directed at a small person in a surreal environment. It no longer seemed relevant who was president. The grand theater of world events seemed petty in light of the drama unfolding in our own lives. There was tragedy on every street corner. We hoped our own outcome would be less unhappy.

"Do you think we're becoming obsessed?" I asked Fox. "Have we lost all sense of reason and perspective?" I was standing in our living room for the first time since I had left for California. It seemed very lonely without Emily inside me.

He slipped his arms around my waist and held me close.

"I think we're two people who've just had their lives turned upside down," Fox said. "I think we're two people who have a very tiny baby whom we love very much. I think we're very scared about the future, about her future. And I think we have every reason to be."

We fast became steeped in the literature of prematurity. As reporters, Fox and I tended to consume data in an almost pathological fashion. When we wanted to know about a certain subject, we immersed ourselves in it. Emily's birth thrust us into a new arena of facts and statistics. By studying this material, we thought we might come to some better understanding of what had happened, and what was still happening. Insight and information, we reasoned, might give us some balance. We might feel a little less out of control.

We learned that though prematurity might be a random experience, it was certainly not rare. Every year in this country, about 250,000 babies are born with some degree of prematurity; that is, before they have completed the thirty-seventh week of gestation. Many are healthy enough to go home immediately. But between 150,000 and 200,000 infants—including some full-termers—spend time in an NICU. Moderately premature babies, those born four to nine weeks ahead of schedule, range in weight from 1,500 to 2,500 grams at birth. Stunning technological advances now give them a 90 to 98 percent survival rate. Very premature babies, like Emily, are those born in weeks twenty-five to thirty. They may weigh as little as 500 grams, or may topple the scale at a porky 1,750 grams. Each year in the United States, very premature babies number about 35,000 to 39,000—approximately 1 percent of all live births, or about 125 very low birth weight births per day. The chance for survival of these small babies is exactly what Dr. Friedman was forecasting for Emily—around 50 percent.

Some specialists use Acronymic to describe these babies, and refer to them as VLBWs, for very low birth weights. VLBW babies comprise just 1 percent of all live births each year, but account for half of all neonatal deaths in the first twenty-seven days of life. For these tiny babies, the relative risk of death in the first twenty-seven days of life is almost 200 times greater than for a baby of five pounds or more at birth. In short, very low birth weight remains the major determining factor of neonatal mortality.

Even after the first twenty-seven days, however, these very low birth weight babies continue to be at greater risk of dying. VLBW babies are five times more likely than normal birth weight infants to die later in the first year of life.

These numbers were sobering. I had always believed that information is power, and now I kept thinking that if I learned more about these statistics, I could somehow conquer them. But it was like trying to defeat a huge army that no one, least of all me, could see. The only weapon I had was my wits, and these days I wasn't too sure about them. But maybe by understanding what was going on, I could come up with a viable battle strategy. Maybe I could do something concrete to help Emily. And so in my hunger for information, I called a Harvard specialist to discuss why these babies had so much against them. I learned that the older preterm children, those born in the third trimester, were surviving in greater and greater numbers. But all this technology didn't seem to be making such a big difference for the very tiny babies. Was there a reason they had such a rough time of it?, I wondered. The doctor's answer was easy to understand, but not very encouraging. "They're simply too small," she said.

Fox and I marveled at how egalitarian prematurity was. Because low birth weight and preterm deliveries are often linked with poor maternal health, inadequate prenatal nutrition, and problems such as drug and alcohol abuse, the phenomenon is often associated in the public mind with a low-income population. In fact, prematurity ripples through all levels of society. Teenage mothers may have a very low birth weight baby as readily as a mother over forty. Prematurity honors no racial or ethnic distinctions. It sweeps through all classes, all ages, all races. In at least half the cases, there is no clear reason for the early birth.

The pervasiveness of this phenomenon that we learned about from our first forays into the annals of prematurity was soon reinforced by a barrage of well-intentioned anecdotal information. Like

blood gases, prematurity was not something we discussed with
most people on a day-to-day basis until Emily was born. Suddenly,
it seemed that everyone we knew or knew of had had some direct
or indirect experience with a premature infant. And everyone
wanted to tell us about it.

Amazingly, nearly all these stories had not merely happy endings, but joyous, extraordinary, fantastic endings. Not only did the
infants prosper, they all seemed to achieve incredible goals. These
champions from the Prematurity Hall of Fame never went on to
become drug addicts or ax murderers. They never settled for ca-
reers as truck drivers or convenience store clerks. They all became
star athletes; they were all brilliant scholars and they all excelled at
whatever highly specialized profession they chose. No one came
right out and told us that the entire Supreme Court was made up
of ex-preemies, but this was basically the message we were getting.

"My twin brothers weighed way less than two pounds each
when they were born," Joanna, my college roommate, informed
me. "They're thirty-seven now, they're both well over six feet, and
one's a doctor and one's a lawyer."

"My husband's great-aunt was born prematurely almost
ninety years ago," another friend ventured. "Weighed just a little
more than two pounds. Do you know she was one of the first
women in Oregon to practice law!"

"Albert Einstein was premature," a scientist friend told Fox.

"My sister weighed two pounds when she was born forty-five
years ago," a colleague in Washington told me. "We put her in a
shoe box and stuck her in the oven. She did just fine."

Sometimes, the enthusiasm of these callers was outmatched
only by their lack of tact.

"Oh, yes," said an acquaintance in Boston. "My husband has
a cousin who was born at just about Emily's stage. He's blind, deaf,
and a little bit retarded, but otherwise he's fine."

"Oh, well," said the mother of a childhood friend. "At least
you have your stepchildren."

My brother Peter reminded me that Mark Twain was born
prematurely. So were Voltaire, Rousseau, Charles Darwin, Victor

Hugo, Daniel Webster, and Anna Pavlova. Sir Isaac Newton was a premature infant, as were Pierre Renoir, Winston Churchill, and Napoleon Bonaparte. As Peter observed, Emily was definitely in interesting historical company.

Peter, an avid historian and sometime thespian, also noted that William Shakespeare had made reference to prematurity. He wouldn't have been stuck with his annoying and unattractive limp, Richard III announced in the play that is named for him, if he hadn't been born "unfinished" and "before my time."

We knew our friends and family meant well when they passed these stories and factoids on to us, and we greatly appreciated their supportive spirit. But soon we began to overdose on what we took to referring to as heroic preemie sagas. People who have been plunged into other life-changing situations—terrible illnesses, accidents, abandonment by a spouse, and so forth—have told me that they, too, grew swiftly tired of the "I have a friend who . . ." stories by which they were inundated. The heroic preemie sagas were not only highly embellished, but increasingly, they were filled with certain recurring themes. The shoe-box-in-the-oven component, for example, soon became a familiar feature.

"My husband had a great-aunt who lived well into her nineties," a friend of my mother's wrote in a note from California. "She weighed just a little over a pound at birth. But they put her in a shoe box and put it in the oven and everything turned out fine."

"In the nineteenth century, when babies were born early, they just kept them in the oven," a friend who taught history told me when she called late one night from California.

"Let me guess," I said. "In a shoe box, right?"

"Why, yes," my friend replied. "How did you know?"

Just in case we might have forgotten how much our lives had changed, or, for a moment, allowed ourselves to think we were living on the same planet as most of the people we had known before Emily was born, these conversations reminded us that we really were in some new galaxy. The matter of time seemed to be a major delineating factor. "Well, when do you get to bring her home?" was probably the most frequently asked question about Emily. As patiently as we could, we tried to explain the uncertainties and variables, the obvious risks and statistical probabilities. We tried to tell people, gently, that it was less a question of *when* we brought Emily home, but *if* we brought her home. We endeavored to convey the precariousness of her situation. We attempted to dispel false hopes—ours and anyone else's. But ours is a generation of heavy expectation. We don't do well with lack of predictability. Impatience is stamped on our collective chromosomes. We assume we will be able to schedule the important events of our lives, and we take for granted our sovereignty over the lesser occurrences.

This sense of false power and privilege sometimes leads to a serious inversion of priorities. Small disruptions take on the dimensions of minor catastrophes. If an article of clothing is not back from the dry cleaner on the appointed day, we fuss and fume. The Federal Express package that does not arrive on time is suddenly crucial, life will stop, perhaps the entire globe will explode, without it.

Over and over, we would take a deep breath and run through what was rapidly becoming a fixed speech once again. When we brought Emily home, we would say, was less important than whether she got through the next day, gained weight, stayed healthy, warded off infectious marauders. Emily was not a package from Saks, we wanted to say. We couldn't schedule her delivery time.

"I've bought her the cutest little playsuit. I'm not sure if it'll fit her, but it's absolutely adorable and I want to send it right over. I can have it sent by messenger—"

It was a good friend calling, a smart, interesting woman. She is very successful in her business, and oddly enough, her field is communications. She hadn't heard a word I'd said.

"Please," I said to her. "Please put it in a drawer and hold on to it." I tried to cushion my comments. I really didn't want to think about a wardrobe for Emily yet. If something awful were to happen, I was not sure I could stand to have frilly dresses and pastel playsuits around as a further reminder.

"It was really sweet of you to think of Emily," I told my friend. "But why don't you just hold off on sending anything over for her until we know if or when we'll be able to bring her home?"

"Well, when will that be?" my friend persisted. "I mean, when do you get to bring her home?"

Not everyone missed the point. From Los Angeles, my colleague Ed Chen sent a letter by Express Mail reminding us of the lessons he and his wife had learned when their son Matt had been born seven years earlier. Matt was eight weeks premature, and at birth weighed two pounds, three ounces. Compared to Emily, this sounded very old and very, very large. Ed churned the letter out on the newsroom computer a day and a half after Emily was born.

"God knows it won't be easy," Ed wrote. "But so many things in life are not."

Coming from a father who had been through the experience of a premature infant, those words really meant something. Ed, of all people, understood how brave these tiny babies are, and how helpless their parents feel. "I know, too, that you'll meet some of the world's most remarkable and dedicated and caring people at the neonatal ICU," Ed wrote. "And not just the medical staff, but some of the other parents. We found one another a great source of mutual support and sustenance throughout." I immediately pasted Ed's letter into the journal I had begun to keep for Emily. Someday, I hoped she would read these entries and marvel with me and Fox at the wonder of her birth and her fortitude. On a whim, I glued the lucky penny I had found outside the hospital onto another page. "A penny saved is a penny earned," my grandmother, the Homily Queen, used to say. Maybe this penny saved would earn Emily an ample share of good fortune. Maybe someday this shiny coin would be a family amulet.

But there were also mundane matters to attend to. I needed to rent a breast pump. In the hospital, a nurse had given me a five-minute lesson in how to express milk. In K9, the nurses and Dr. Friedman were encouraging me to pump regularly. Emily would

be ready for mother's milk any day, they predicted, so it was important to assure a steady flow of milk now. "The more you pump, the
more you'll get," they told me. Back at home, I discovered there
was no listing in the Yellow Pages for breast pumps. I began calling pharmacies and prenatal exercise facilities.

"You're lucky," said the proprietor of the sixth place I called.
"We just had one come in. They go out as quickly as they come in,
you know."

I said I didn't know, never having researched the availability
of breast pumps before, but promised to rush over and pick it up
immediately. I started to explain that I hadn't had a chance to
reserve a breast pump in advance of the birth because my child had
come so early, but the woman cut me off.

"Just make sure there's no dust on it when you return it," she
growled. "If there's any dust, even a speck, you lose your whole
deposit."

The machine made a creepy grinding noise, like an all-pur-
pose sound effect from a cheap horror movie. When it wasn't
grinding, it was whooshing. I watched as the milk filled the clear
plastic container, and then, with sadness, threw it out. Emily was
not ready for it. Each time I used the machine, it reminded me of
my loneliness. It was supposed to be Emily sucking at my breast,
not a plastic funnel. The milk was supposed to be nourishing her,
not ending up in the trash.

So for now I went empty-handed when I headed over to the
hospital. I was pulled there by a magnet called Emily. I needed to
be with her, even if it just meant standing alongside her and watching her.

For Fox the urge was less compelling. It was not that he did
not want to see Emily, but it was clear that the environment in the
NICU made him uncomfortable. Both of his parents had died in
hospitals, and now here was his tiny daughter, surrounded by machines that looked as if they would just as soon devour her as rescue
her. He hated the feeling of powerlessness. Fox is not a macho,
chest-beating guy who goes around swinging from vines or leaping

from tall buildings. But feeling that he could do nothing at all in this situation made him want to avoid the place.

"It's not at all unusual," said Leslie, Emily's primary nurse. "Take a look around here. Who do you suppose comes in here? The mothers. The men can't handle it. It's too hard for them."

Sure, Leslie said, usually the fathers showed up in the beginning. In rare cases, the father spent as much time in the NICU as the mother. Mostly they made sporadic visits. Once the babies "graduated" to the nurseries next door or across the hall, where there was much less equipment and the atmosphere was less intimidating, the fathers turned into Robert Young. In the well-baby nurseries, the fathers could handle their children and even hold them. Here in the NICU, it was parenthood-in-a-porthole. The fathers hated it.

"It's never easy for anybody," Leslie said. "But it's always less difficult for the mothers."

Leslie's regular days off had happened to fall in the first few days after Emily was born. In her absence, Emily had had a different nurse each day. They all seemed highly capable. They were patient, well-informed, and universally gracious. Nevertheless, I welcomed the prospect of continuity and consistency in the person of Leslie. Emily would remain her charge throughout her stay on K9, Leslie said. If and when we moved across the hall to the well-baby nursery, or next door, where the even weller babies were, Leslie would go, too. It was great news for many reasons. Leslie was just about my age. She was smart, with a master's degree and five years of teaching in the New York City public schools before turning to nursing. She'd spent eleven years at the hospital, all of it right here in the NICU. "Right from the beginning I knew this was where I belonged," she said. "I knew this was where I wanted to work."

Most of all, she radiated equal and enormous quantities of competence and confidence. Her shift started at 7 A.M., and by the time I arrived at eight, Leslie knew all about Emily and me. She had carefully read every notation on Emily's chart, and she had talked to some of the young pediatric residents who had been on duty these last few days. This impressed me, and made me feel less like a modular patient. Leslie was clearly a responsible professional who took her job seriously, but she also telegraphed a sense of warmth and concern. She cared about her job, and about doing it well, and she also cared about people.

"Forty years old, your first child," Leslie said. "This is really rough for you."

"Actually, it's a whole lot rougher for her," I said, and gestured to Emily. "But thank you."

Even in her baggy blue hospital pantsuit it was easy to see that Leslie was quite slender. Her hair was about shoulder length, dark brown with streaks of russet. She had an easy smile and a reassuring manner. In no time at all, Leslie and I found ourselves gabbing like long-lost girlfriends. I learned that she was single, and that she lived in an apartment owned by the hospital just a few blocks away. She had two cats, loved to read science fiction, and also enjoyed biography. Recently she had begun dating a somewhat younger man. We laughed, because even though she referred to him by the archaic description of "my sweetie," it sounded so risqué.

"Don't you love it?" Leslie said. "Men can date younger women and no one thinks anything of it. We go out with someone younger than we are, and it's this big deal." Like most New Yorkers, she could work and keep up a running dialogue at the same time, performing complicated maneuvers without losing her train of thought or speech.

It would be impossible to calculate how many babies Leslie had cared for in her eleven years here in the NICU at the hospital. Each year there had been several as small as Emily, or almost as small. Others were much larger, but much, much sicker. Some stayed for days; others for months. She said she had remained in touch with some of the parents—although, she had to admit, only those whose children had survived. When a baby died, she said— and she was careful, she did not say "passed away," or "expired," or some other euphemism—most parents just had to close the door. It was too painful to continue any kind of contact.

So obviously, in caring for these babies, Leslie and her nursing associates had to be equally adept at dealing with the parents. They had to juggle the egos of the doctors with the anxieties of the mothers and fathers. Working so closely with the parents, Leslie came to know them very well. She warned me early on about the stress that a long hospital stay with a small, sick child can put on a marriage. "It's a terrible strain," she said. "There really isn't any way around it."

Soon Leslie and I struck a pact. "You may not always like what I have to say, but I promise I'll be straight with you," she said. "If things look bad, I'll tell you." She vowed she would offer no false hopes. "When I get worried," she said, "I'll let you know." I knew instinctively that she could be trusted. In this crazy labyrinth of a hospital, she would be an ally for me and, most of all, for Emily.

Leslie had some advice for me. "If you're going to be here for a long time—a couple of months—you're going to have to learn to pace yourself," she said. "You can't be here all the time, you know."

Implicitly, what she was saying was that I was going to have to hand over my full trust to this operation. It was one thing to recognize intellectually that the doctors and nurses were running this show, and well they should. Their collective expertise and experience was immense. But now I was going to have to make the leap beyond the intellect. I had to let go.

"A lot of mothers find it helps to go back to their jobs, even part-time," Leslie said. Her voice was gentle. She was telling me it was not an act of disloyalty to Emily to carry on with my own life. I was not sure I was ready to accept this notion, but at least I was willing to entertain it.

I'd stolen the blue stool by then, and pushed it up close to Emily. Leslie leaned over the isolette and together we watched her sleep. Around us, the buzzers and beepers continued to blare and blast. Nurses and doctors called to one another. The in-house telephone rang, news, perhaps, of another small child about to be born seven floors below. But Leslie and I ignored all this. We were focused just on Emily.

"Fox thinks she's blonde; I think she's brunette," I said.

"It's a little of both," Leslie said. She bent her knees to study Emily more closely. "It's ginger. Her hair is the color of ginger."

Leslie was taking Emily's temperature now, slipping the thermometer under her armpit, and recording her vital signs on the sheet of paper that hung from her isolette. She moved deftly, and conducted herself with great efficiency. All the while, she kept up a running dialogue with her tiny charge in the big plastic box.

"You're okay," Leslie told Emily when she flinched at the cold thermometer. "There you go, all done."

"You're like her other mother," I told Leslie. She smiled. "Auntie Leslie," she said. She checked the respirator hose for condensation, then used a small vacuum tube to remove the excess mucus from Emily's mouth. Holding Emily's ankles in one hand, she lifted her fanny to change her diaper. In that position, the baby looked like a tiny fish being measured for length. Too small, the authorities would have to have said had they seen a fish of Emily's size.

Babies as small as Emily did not wear their diapers in the NICU; they laid on them. Preemie Pampers were the nappies of choice here, disposable squares of white cotton no bigger than purse-sized Kleenex. They fit under Emily like a fluffy white blanket.

I watched Leslie with admiration. She handled the baby so deftly. But the procedure made me feel my distance from Emily. Even this most basic element of baby care, diaper-changing, was performed in this hermetic setting.

"Leslie," I said, "do you think I'll ever be able to hold her?"

She closed the portholes and turned to look at me. "Absolutely," she said. "I promised I'd be straight with you, and I absolutely promise you'll be able to hold her." It was time for her morning break, and she was starting to walk out of the NICU. "I don't promise when."

I snapped open a porthole and slid my hand in. Emily was

lying on her side, facing me. Holding her was far off into the future. For now I would have to be content with just touching her. I stroked a finger along her back and hoped it felt as good to her as it did to me.

FIVE

Amazingly, the first week was winding down. Bolstered by a nutritional supplement known as "Hyperal" (for hyperalimentation), Emily was gaining weight, about twenty grams a day. Her head sonograms came back showing minimal cranial bleeding, less than one on a scale of one to four. "Looks great!" Dr. Friedman wrote in a brief note on Emily's progress chart.

Early one morning, before I arrived at the hospital, she had her first bradycardia. I burst into tears when Leslie told me. But Leslie was cavalier. "Look, it's going to happen," she said, adding that it was astounding that it had not occurred earlier. "See that kid over there?" Leslie said, and pointed to a baby in the corner. "He has about six of them a day." One little boy, who spent two months in the NICU before graduating to the well-baby nursery, used to have twelve to fourteen of them every day. "Every time you turned around, the kid was having a brady," Leslie said. Now that baby was scheduled to go home within the week. "He's fine," she said. "Just fine."

She confessed to me that Emily's bradycardial episode had triggered some of her more authoritarian tendencies, not to mention some salty language. As a former teacher of small children,

Leslie had learned never to take any guff from anybody under four feet tall. When Emily's heartbeat dipped below one hundred, the sure sign of a bradycardia, "I shook her, called her a little shit, and told her that if she ever did that to me again, I'd smack her," Leslie said.

I leaned over Emily's isolette and put my mouth next to the porthole. "You hear that, Emily?" I said. "She means it. You listen to Auntie Leslie."

Late in the week, Leslie warned me that Emily would proba- bly need a blood transfusion before long. I turned pale. But Leslie insisted that this was nothing to worry about. Blood transfusions were part of being as small as Emily, she said. In the NICU, transfusions were routine.

"You can't take that much blood out of these little kids with- out putting some back in," Leslie said. Blood was taken from the babies four to six times each day. For Emily, all the pricks to her heels and ankles had begun to take their toll. Her "crit"—another new term in our growing medical vocabulary, this one meaning the hematocrit level, or percentage of red blood cells in her blood— was dropping steadily.

But the word *transfusion* set off an alarm in my head. I had read and written too much about AIDS not to be terrified of it. Most blood banks, such as the one deep in the bowels of this hospital, could promise that their screening for the HIV virus that causes AIDS was at least 95 percent effective. But what about that other 5 percent?

"She's not getting any donor-anonymous blood. I won't have it," I told Leslie. "I'll start lining up donors immediately."

Leslie supported my position. "I think you're smart," she said. "Unless I absolutely had to, I wouldn't take blood from down there either."

Any encounter with serious illness is an abrupt initiation into the morass of hospital bureaucracy. Dealing with what Leslie called "down there," with the hospital's blood bank, I harkened back once again to Lewis Carroll and the Mad Hatter's tea party, where the guests kept telling Alice, no matter what her request, "Can't be done. Can't be done." Number one, the blood bank did not encourage donor-specified blood donations. In fact, the personnel "down there" went to great lengths to discourage donor-specification. It meant additional record-keeping for the staff. Second, each unit required several days for processing, so if you needed your donor-specified blood quickly, you were out of luck. Third, there was no such thing as a baby-sized transfusion unit. All blood was packaged in a single container size, roughly the hematological equivalent of extra large. Although a baby of Emily's size would require only a few tablespoons of blood per transfusion, an entire donation unit—seven or eight times what she would need—would have to be processed for each attempt. Leftover blood was, in the vernacular of the blood bank, "wasted." That meant it was thrown away.

"You're absolutely right," one of the hematologists agreed when I finally tracked down someone who seemed to have some authority. I still thought maybe I could convince them that packaging baby-sized blood units might in fact be a sensible endeavor. "It's ridiculous," she said. "But that's the way it's done." In a giant hospital with a merciless bureaucracy, this was not a battle this doctor was willing to take on.

I also learned that blood was stored for a maximum of twenty-seven days. So, in the case of a prolonged illness, it was best to stagger the blood donors, bringing them in every three or four days, or even once a week.

So that night when I got home, I put out the call to everyone I could think of who was relatively nearby: *Please Give Blood!!!* Fox watched and listened to this telephone campaign with a mixture of emotions. Just the day before, he had learned that he was ineligible to donate blood to his own daughter. He is a congenital overachiever who does not cotton well to anything he interprets as failure or rejection. In this case, the news that his blood showed traces of the hepatitis virus, presumably the result of living in Third World countries for fifteen years, was a major personal affront.

We talked about this over dinner. I had fallen into the habit of leaving the hospital around eight, or sometimes closer to nine. If Fox stopped by K9 at all, it was at about eleven in the morning—and then for about twenty minutes. I spent as much of the day with Emily as I could.

My total involvement with Emily and her hospital world left little time or energy for such mundane activities as grocery shopping. Fox kept our tiny New York-apartment-sized refrigerator stocked with the essentials: orange juice, a quart of milk, maybe some yogurt. Often he bought the kind of pasta and sauce that can be prepared in five or six minutes, which was two or three minutes more than either one of us was willing to spend in the kitchen these days.

More often than not, we went out to eat. Columbus Avenue is a restaurant rodeo, with something for almost everyone, although not too many of the places are really outstanding. For Fox and me, the main allure was proximity. We could walk out of our apartment, and in five to ten minutes find a passable place to eat. Tonight, we weren't sure we could handle even that five to ten minutes. Since all this had started with Emily, I had found it hard to be calm. Fox, reacting to my agitation, felt a sense of anxiety of his own. So after he pried me away from the telephone, he suggested that we go to the Chinese restaurant right up the block from us.

It was a dingy place with Formica tabletops, just the kind of no-frills atmosphere that suited my mood. We ate there often. Fox, who speaks flawless Mandarin, was instantly recognizable to the waiters. They exchanged greetings in Chinese, then seated us at a little table in the rear of the restaurant. Moments later, two ice-cold beers arrived in front of us.

"I didn't even hear you order these," I told Fox, then hastily took a sip. Jane, my doctor, was a follower of the old wives' tale that held that malt beverages promote lactation, and had granted her blessing to a beer every now and then.

Fox laughed, because of course he could have ordered goldfish soup and I wouldn't have understood him. Both of us were smiling, and for one wild moment we were relaxed and possibly even happy, almost the way we had been before I had gone to California only a little more than a week ago.

"Elizabeth, we're not going to make it if you don't ease up a little. This is going to be a long haul—if we're lucky—and you're going to have to start marshaling your energy a little bit." Fox had ordered chicken and was spooning some onto my plate. He preferred to eat his in the traditional Chinese fashion, with the food heaped on top of a bowl of rice, and the bowl held close to his chin.

"What I don't need right now is a lecture, Fox." my voice sounded snappish. I hated it. "We're both going about this in our own ways," I said. I hoped my tone sounded a little less brittle.

"That's true," Fox said. "But I'm concerned that your way is going to bring you down. You need all your energy for Emily. You can't do this if you're running on empty."

"Okay, all right, Fox. Enough." The sharp tone was back. I took a breath and tried to take the edge off. "More important, what are we going to do about the blood?"

"I don't know. I feel really terrible that she can't take any of mine. I guess I'm just morally inadequate."

"Cut it out, Fox," I said. "Blood has nothing to do with morality. You lived in primitive places for a long time. I think you're lucky it's only hepatitis.

"And anyway," I continued, realizing suddenly that I, too, was slipping into the lecture mode, "I can't give blood to Emily, either. Not this soon after the delivery."

This was a dead-end conversation. I wanted to change the subject. "So, has anything happened in the world today?" I asked.

"I got hit up by three homeless people, my editor yelled at me, and the subway got stuck for twenty minutes near Columbus Circle."

"Right. Anything else?"

Fox gave me a quick news summary. He called for the bill, and when it came, we opened our fortune cookies.

"You will receive good news," Fox's fortune read.

"Patience is wisdom," mine said.

It was just a quarter of a block to our apartment. We walked arm in arm.

In moments of reflection, when I sit back and ponder the good things, I am grateful to have a mother who manages to toe the line between loving involvement and cloying intrusion. Certainly she volunteers opinions with which I often disagree, but only rarely does she attempt to stuff her viewpoints down my throat. She is always interested in what goes on in the life of her youngest child, but still, she keeps a safe distance. We're lucky. Our relationship truly is based on love and mutual respect. In this case, to her enduring credit, my mother had decided to delay flying from San Francisco to New York until Emily's condition stabilized, and until Fox and I felt a little less frazzled. Sensitive enough to recognize that her presence so soon after Emily's birth might confuse an already frenetic situation, she realized, too, that Fox and I might feel obligated to take care of her. For now she felt we should be focusing our full energies on Emily. "As soon as you say it's okay," she told Fox in one of the first telephone calls when Emily's birth seemed so imminent, "I'll be there."

From the moment she first learned I was pregnant, my mother had awaited the birth with jubilation. She knew how badly Fox and I wanted this child, but she had her own reasons for celebrating the prospect of a new generation. The news from the prenatal testing that it would be a girl only increased her joy.

One of our favorite pictures together was taken not long before my grandmother, the Homily Queen, died at ninety-two. Grandma seldom smiled in real life, and almost never in pictures. She seemed to adhere to that ancient belief that some portion of her soul would be captured by the camera. If so, she didn't want to go on record as displaying some frivolity like mirth. But in this picture, Grandma was beaming. She was proud to be with her "girls," as she often called my mother and my aunt, and me and my cousin, Susan. My mother looked regal, with her strawberry-blond hair piled high atop her head. I looked businesslike, wearing one of those awful dress-for-success blazer outfits that made an entire generation of women in the early 1980s look like men in skirts. What the picture showed was the powerful continuity of spirit that had persevered in this line of women in spite of everything. As different as we were, the three of us looked connected. We shared a common seed, and if that seed had blossomed in distinct fashions in each of us, its roots were dug in deep. Widowed before she was twenty-five, Grandma had raised two daughters alone in the Depression by running a corner store in California's Central Valley. Her firstborn daughter, my mother, Jean, returned the favor by going to work to help support the family. To secure employment with the state of California, she lied and said she was eighteen, the minimum age. Actually, she was sixteen.

So they were strong, these genes that Emily had inherited. These women were tough and determined. They were self-sufficient. And often, they were very stubborn.

In many ways my mother and I were at once casualties and survivors of the women's movement. So many women leapt so far and so fast in the decade that began around 1970 that we often failed to pay due homage to the women who preceded us. We opted for different life-styles—jobs, mainly—in a social climate that permitted us to do so. At times we dismissed our mothers' generation by branding them with unkind phrases such as "just a housewife." But in recent years my mother and I had come much closer together. We honored each other's choices and forged new and stronger respect. One reason I was so happy to learn that I was carrying a girl was that I wanted to cultivate that same kind of caring, loving relationship with a daughter of my own. I heard myself telling a good friend that I did not want to die without the experience of that side of the mother-daughter bond. Now my mother was grappling with her side of this bizarre turn of events. Emily represented a statement of her own belief in the future as well.

On the phone from San Francisco the morning after Emily was born, my mother asked, "Is she bigger than a telephone handset?" I wondered where she had gotten that image. It turned out that the moment Fox called her to tell her Emily had been born, she raced to the public library to read everything she could find about premature infants. Still unsatisfied, she called a local medical center, then rushed over to pick up all the literature they had for families of very small babies. One brochure compared the size of kids Emily's age to telephone receivers. (Actually, as I told her with no small measure of indignation, the proud mother bragging about her behemoth babe, Emily was 13¾ inches long—half again as big as the average eight-inch telephone receiver.)

At the hospital, my mother and I went through the washing-up ritual in the parents' room. She was about to leave her purse in one of the lockers when a young black woman stopped her. She was wearing a satin baseball jacket and a Mets cap. "I wouldn't do that," she warned. "Things disappear around here. I lost sixty dollars last week. Somebody took it out of my coat, hanging right here."

We thanked her for the advice, and introduced ourselves. Her name was Monique. She was twenty-four, and had a baby in the well-baby nursery next to the NICU. Beverlee, her little girl, was the survivor of a set of twins born at twenty-eight weeks. Beverlee weighed almost two and a half pounds at birth, but Antonia, her sister, weighed just fifteen ounces. The doctors thought Antonia would die immediately, Monique told us, but somehow, she managed to hold on for three days. I was impressed by the maternal pride in Monique's voice when she talked about Antonia's accomplishment. She was, of course, sad that her child had died after just three days, but obviously very proud that this fifteen-ounce person had lived as long as she had.

"The doctors couldn't believe it," Monique said. "They kept saying there was no way she could still be alive."

I had only had a few days of experience there myself, but already I was learning that this was what happened in the NICU. Life and death were daily, compelling issues, events people in the outside world could ignore while they shopped at Bloomingdale's or caught the newest movie.

But my mother was still a newcomer; she hadn't been there

long enough to understand the enforced intimacy of this compact universe. An intensely private person, she is also a born diplomat. Since dead babies are not exactly dinner-party conversation—the topic does tend to make the guests uncomfortable—my mother adroitly switched the topic by complimenting Monique on the names she had chosen for her daughters. Monique explained that at birth, twins are identified by the hospital as "A" and "B," in the order they emerge. "Antonia and Beverlee," Monique decided.

"I think I know who's doing the stealing," she said. There was a teenage "drug mother" on the floor, Monique said, skinny and wired by who-knows-what combination of who-knows-which chemicals. Her baby, a boy, was being kept in the NICU for observation. Monique said she had noticed that the mother spent at least as much time in the family room smoking—and, she suspected, rifling peoples' possessions, as she did in the NICU with the baby. "Just keep anything you care about with you," Monique cautioned.

Clutching our handbags, my mother and I made our way down the hall to "Emily's room," as Jean was already calling it. I marveled at the graciousness with which she gave smiles and friendly hellos to each stranger we passed. My mother was near seventy. She was no doubt suffering jet lag from the three-thousand-mile flight the afternoon before, and in her own way from the anxiety and strain of Emily's untimely arrival. Now here she was, greeting people like some ambassador of good cheer in these unlikely surroundings. There were funny, unwritten rules of decorum here on K9. The place was too small and too crowded for any semblance of privacy. Every conversation was public, and every baby was subject to community scrutiny. Yet without some opening, some spoken or unspoken invitation, adults kept largely to themselves. In less than five minutes my mother had broken the ice. I was glad to have her there, for me and for Emily.

Her brochures had prepared her for the NICU shrine to technology. She seemed not to see any of it as she focused solely on her grandchild. "It's Grandma Jean," she told Emily as she stroked her back. We had never discussed what she would be called after the baby was born. "Grandma Jean" was what came out. It sounded fine.

Leslie watched the scene as if Jean were her own mother. She swiped the blue plastic stool and pushed it up so my mother could sit while she got to know her granddaughter. Years vanished from my mother's face as she filled up with love for this small person. We were very quiet, Leslie and I. The moment was too sacred to interrupt.

But silence and tranquillity were scarce commodities in the NICU. Dr. Friedman soon bounced in, all smiles as usual, and announced that Emily was ready for safflower oil.

"What is she?" I asked. "A salad?"

Humor was something else that did not abound on K9. I was dumb to think that Dr. Friedman might catch the allusion. He was very forthcoming about his medical knowledge and his own achievements, but he seemed too intense for jocularity without a purpose. In brief conversations throughout the week, he had told Fox and me he was a gourmet cook. He had also described himself as a voracious reader, particularly of fiction. Furthermore, he had said he was a dedicated runner. As a matter of fact, he made a point of ducking out of the hospital once a day, no matter what weather, to take in a lap or two around the reservoir in Central Park. And when Fox and I had inquired as to why he'd chosen the demanding and evolving field of neonatology, he'd smiled and said he just loved machines. In his view, neonatology was the best of medicine and high technology. "And," he added cheerily, "the patients don't talk back."

He explained that the safflower oil was to keep Emily's skin supple. He also believed that some of the nutrients from the oil could seep through her skin. Using a gauze pad, Leslie showed us how to apply the oil. I let my mother do the honors. After all, our motherly and grandmotherly privileges were limited. We had to relish what little "normal" interaction we could have with Emily.

Dr. Friedman had some more good news. Emily was making such terrific progress that she could now begin feeding on my milk. He told me to stock up on the small bottles used to transport and store moms' milk, and to begin bringing it in the following morning. I was elated. This seemed like a real step toward getting Emily healthy, and better yet, getting her home.

On the way out that evening, one of the nurses stopped me. Her name was Christine, and she carried the imposing title of night nursing supervisor. Christine was probably in her early thirties, but a little excess weight gave her a portly appearance and made her look older. Christine was big on enforcing orders and in making sure that on her shift at least, everything on K9 ran according to the rules. Through the nurses' grapevine, I had learned that Christine used to be in the Army. That explained her autocratic demeanor, but it did nothing to make me feel more comfortable with her. The truth was, she intimidated me.

"I hear that Emily gets to start feeding on your milk tomorrow," Christine said.

I told her yes, then waited for what I was certain would be some words of criticism or admonition. Instead, Christine softened and offered guidance.

"A lot of mothers up here find their milk supply is pretty limited," she said.

That was true: I had been pumping four times a day as directed, but my output was far from plentiful.

"It's the tension and the stress," she said. "You've got to drink a lot of fluids. We recommend water, lots of it, and also malt liquor."

Obviously Christine did not think that a beer now and then was going to turn Emily into an alcoholic.

"Oh, please," she said. "It's so diluted by the time it gets to her." Christine said the hops were the secret. "They help stimulate milk production." The friendly look she gave me now surprised me. "And it wouldn't hurt if it helped you relax a little bit, either."

Changing out of our gowns, my mother remarked on the plethora of young women in K9. She was right. It seemed like the majority of pediatric residents were female, and certainly all the nurses were. When Dr. Friedman made his rounds every morning, the covey of fledgling physicians surrounded him with something adulation. "Friedman's Flock," they were known elsewhere in the hospital, or "Freddie's Angels."

"How can you tell the doctors from the nurses?" my mother asked.

It was a good question. But usually the nurses wore light blue pantsuits, like Leslie's, or blue wraparound dresses, like those favored by Christine and Edna. The residents wore green hospital scrubs. A peculiarity of K9 was that whereas the residents rotated in on two-week shifts, the nurses tended to stay there for many years. Elsewhere in the hospital, it was common for nurses to move around. But the neonatological unit demanded special skills, as well as a particular kind of emotional constitution. Marjorie and Eleanor, two of the NICU nurses, had nearly fifty years of experience between them. Linda, a cool and quiet Filipino nurse on the evening shift, had begun working in the NICU fifteen years ago, and had never left. As a consequence, most of the nurses were at least in their thirties, and many were older.

"Anyway, the doctors look younger," I told my mother.

She sighed. Times had changed since she went to work for the state of California. Medical school was no more an option for her than a trip to the moon.

"They all look young to me," she said.

Over the weekend, Ethan and Sarah came down to New York. So while Fox played tour guide, escorting his children to the museums and major sights of New York, Mother and I held forth in K9. Today was Emily's introduction to mother's milk, an offering I foolishly thought she would receive with great enthusiasm. Instead, she reacted as if it were raw liver. One sense that premature babies do have is smell, and so to familiarize her with the scent of mother's milk, Leslie dabbed a drop on a gauze pad and let her take a whiff. She hated it! Her nose scrunched up in disgust, and if she hadn't been tied down with all her IV tubes and monitors, she would have taken off and run.

"Don't take it personally," Leslie said. She set up the Harvard pump that would send Emily's new foodstuff down a slender tube in her nose that passed through to her stomach. The pump fed her just one cc of milk per hour, an almost immeasurably tiny quantity.

At noon, Fox brought the kids by the hospital. Ethan and Sarah were eager to see their new half sister, who was still, after all, E.T. to them. But hospital regulations forbade children from entering K9. Ethan and Sarah could sit in the family room, and that was that.

"I don't see why I can't see her," Ethan said. "She's my sister. Anyway, I'm almost twelve. It's not like I'm a kid." He cast a superior glare at Sarah, who was eight. "It's not like I'm going to go around pulling out tubes or pushing buttons," Ethan said.

But rules were rules. On K9, the rules permitted only two adults to visit any one baby at any one time; no exceptions, and certainly no kids. "When she gets bigger and better, in a month or so, we might be able to bring her down here for you to see in the family room," Leslie told Ethan and Sarah. For now, we compromised by taking Polaroid pictures of Emily and letting Leslie explain all the various apparatuses she was hooked up to. Fox, Jean, and I watched with admiration as Leslie sat between Ethan and Sarah and told them the purpose of the endotracheal tube, pulsimeter, oxymeter, and all the other outer-space equipment crammed into Emily's tiny living space. She was patient, answering their questions in a clear, comprehensible fashion that we wished the doctors could emulate. We knew she must have been a very good teacher.

We noticed that some of the parents had done some interior decorating in their babies' isolettes. Many had little stuffed animals wedged in corners, between the tubes and pipes. Some parents had taped family photographs to the inside of the plastic walls. In this sterile, institutional environment, it gave a trace of home. So that night at dinner at our favorite Chinese restaurant, I hauled out the Polaroid and snapped a family portrait of Mother, Fox, Ethan, and Sarah. Emily's first "wall painting" showed her family. Sunday was Easter, so Mother contributed Emily's first toy, a miniature white bunny. Ethan and Sarah urged me to bring in another bunny, this one pink, that had come to the apartment with a flower arrangement. For good measure, they donated a little gray stuffed seal they'd brought from home. Suddenly, the decor in Emily's isolette went from hospital minimalist to F.A.O. Schwartz.

It puzzled me that there was no formal support group on K9 or in the NICU—no official network through which experience and encouragement could be shared. Having a premature infant was such an all-consuming event. Who better to relieve the strains and stresses than people who were going through it themselves?

But my friend Ed was right. Many parents and their children were in and out of K9 in a matter of days, even hours. Those parents tended to remain as strangers, barely exchanging nods or glances. Gradually the rest of us, we regulars who were, with luck, in this thing for the long haul, came to recognize one another. The rare nods and glances turned into frequent words of good cheer. For people in our outside worlds, the bizarre seesaw of prematurity was too foreign to comprehend. Unless, like Ed, they had been through it personally, they would ask polite questions, then completely glaze over when we parents lapsed into too-long, too-intricate answers or explanations. It was like trying to explain peanut butter to someone in China. They just didn't get it.

But here in the NICU, a bradycardia, for example, was a daily event. Soon after Emily had her first one, a mother from the well-baby nursery across the hall appeared to help ease my concern. Her name was Carol, and her little boy John was scheduled to be sent home soon, probably within a week. She was a few years younger than me, but otherwise, our stories were very similar: a much-wanted, long-delayed pregnancy; a ruptured amniotic sac; a middle-of-the-night delivery. One gestational week older at birth than Emily, John was significantly larger. That is, he weighed a full one pound, fifteen ounces at birth—four huge ounces more than Emily. I had seen Carol across the hall, holding John and rocking him in a big wooden rocking chair. We'd smiled at each other, and I'd hoped Carol hadn't seen the envy on my smile.

"Sometimes I'd be standing there, watching John just the way you're watching Emily now, and he'd have a brady, right in front of me," Carol said. "You just learn to shake them out of it. You can't be afraid of it. You have to give them a good shake and get that heartbeat back up."

Carol had come over to talk to me quite on her own. From across the hall, she'd seen me crumble when Leslie had told me about Emily's first bradycardia. Later, without my knowing it, she had conferred with Leslie about the event and my reaction. In the outside world I might have cursed her as a busybody. Here in the NICU, I blessed her for her marching over to see me, and for her sensitivity in helping me through this small crisis.

My mother's presence made it easier for me to socialize. I could chat with Carol or Monique without feeling that I was abandoning Emily. When the nurses or doctors were doing their rounds in the NICU and the parents had to vacate the place, we huddled in the hallway and traded our own version of real-life heroic preemie stories. We could brag about our children, just like normal moms. It was as if for a moment we were real mothers of real babies in a real day-care setting, not frightened women whose fragile infants might or might not make it to the day-care stage. Thrown together by the force of circumstance, we were instant best friends. We had no history to bind us, as most friends do. Rather, we had the present, and a very compelling sense of what each of us was going through, right then, at that very moment. In some ways that bound us closer than the people we called friends outside K9, people who could never know the anguish of watching a baby cry mutely because his breathing tube was blocking all sound.

My newest best friend was LaTanya Cooke, mother of the alarm-happy baby in the far corner of the NICU. I'd heard the nurses express their frustration over Cooke, as they called this little boy, as he habitually set off his beepers. The nurses had their own nicknames for the babies, reflecting personality traits that seemed apparent from the moment these kids arrived on earth. One little girl was known as the Kvetch. She was the smaller of twin girls, and she always looked dissatisfied. "If she didn't have the tube, you know she'd be whining," one nurse, Georgeanne, muttered. Emily was dubbed "the Fighter" almost from day one. Baby Cooke's penchant for activating his alarms at all hours of the day and night earned him the dubious moniker of "the Fussbudget."

"You just know this kid's not going to be a happy person," said Marjorie, a nurse who had put in more than twenty years in the NICU.

One day I crept over to take a peek at Cooke, a small bundle of dark flesh with his back turned to me. He had masses of curly hair, and though the nurses called him "Cooke," his mother's name, I noticed that the name tag on his isolette listed him as Jacques Louis Jackson. Jacques Louis had been born three weeks earlier than Emily, but at precisely the same gestational stage. His birth weight had been 760 grams, the same as Emily's.

His mother and I met in the family room after LaTanya slammed down the pay phone on the wall and turned to face my own mother and me with a furious expression. "I'd like to kill him," she said, and we all knew we would be fast friends. It was her boyfriend, Jacques Louis's father. He kept telling LaTanya that he loved the baby, but she just couldn't get him to come in and visit. "He's always busy. He says he's working all the time," she fumed. "Well, I'm busy, too. I work, too."

LaTanya was confident and poised. From a quick glance she looked to be in her early thirties. It turned out she was not yet twenty. She lived at home with her parents, far from the hospital, in the distant reaches of Brooklyn. Her subway ride to the hospital was nearly an hour long. She worked part-time in a city agency. After we'd all scrubbed up and donned our gowns, we walked down the hall to the NICU together. Emily's isolette was the closest to the door, so LaTanya stopped to visit with us.

"I've been talking to Emily when you're not here," she said, and I confessed I had done the same with her son. "She keeps her eyes so wide open, like she knows just what's going on."

"Like she knows what's going on and she wishes she were somewhere else," I said.

Then LaTanya told me that another baby Emily, Emily Smith, had been in residence in the NICU when she and Andre first arrived. Emily Smith had gone home, big and fat and healthy, LaTanya said. "So you see, the name's good luck. Your Emily will do just fine, too."

LaTanya was particularly afraid of what she called "the AIDS." Just a week or so earlier, an adult female cousin of hers had died from it. LaTanya had gone to the funeral. In the NICU, the normal proscriptions of polite social interchange did not apply. Here I barely knew this young woman, and I heard myself commiserating in my best Emily Post tones, "What a shame. Was it drugs or sex?"

The tactlessness of this question did not bother LaTanya. "Could have been either," she said, and we kept on walking.

Like LaTanya, I remained terrified that contaminated blood would somehow end up in my baby's veins. My worst fear was that Emily would never go home from the NICU. In my second worst fantasy, she would flourish and go home for two or three happy years, only to be diagnosed as suffering from AIDS because of a faulty transfusion. "I have no intention of bringing you through the perils of prematurity," I wrote in Emily's journal, "only to subject you to the risk of bad blood." Probably I had read too many tragic accounts in *People* magazine. But the worry was real, enough so that the mere mention of the words *blood* and *transfusion* could make my own blood stop cold.

So I stiffened when Dr. Klein told me it couldn't be put off any longer—Emily was definitely going to need a transfusion. Dr. Deirdre Klein was a young pediatric resident, and because she had been on duty the morning Emily was born, I fooled myself into thinking she had some special stake in my baby's future. She had a casual manner, and a way of softening her unhappy news with a smile. The big red Annie Hall–eyeglasses she sometimes wore gave her a schoolgirl quality. She joked freely with the nurses, and in turn they called her Didi, her nickname. I doubted that she could be stuffy or standoffish, like some of the other doctors, even if she tried.

I rushed to the pay phone and called my brother Peter in

Toronto. But Peter had a terrible case of the flu. His wife Kay, a veterinarian, said he was infectious and that even though he could be in New York in a matter of hours, his blood would not be suitable.

Once again I gave thanks for my mother's support and her crafty native ability to circumvent the authorities. Technically, my mother was over the age limit, sixty-five, for blood donors. But age limits had never stood in her way before, and she wasn't about to let them now. We conspired to subtract a few years—why not? My mother is tall and thin. Her hair is its own natural strawberry color, with not even a trace of gray. Suffice it to say she looks far younger than her years anyway. "Just come with me in case I forget how old I'm supposed to be," she said. The next morning, we met for a big hearty breakfast and I accompanied her to the blood bank. She did not mind bending the hospital's rules to donate her blood, but she was uncomfortable with the prospect of lying outright when asked her age. Desperate for good clean blood for my baby, I had no such scruples. "Nineteen twenty-three!" I chirped when they asked for Jean's birth year. That would make her sixty-five on her next birthday.

No one even blinked. They raced through the questions about medications, medical history, height, weight, and so forth, and then escorted her into the room where the blood was extracted. We knew that if we made prolonged eye contact, we would both burst out laughing.

Thirty-two hours later we watched as Mother's blood inched slowly into Emily's veins. From across the hall, John's mother, Carol, came over to share in the excitement. As her hematocrit level had dropped, Emily had grown very pale. Little by little she was turning pink again.

"Our little rosebud," my mother said. She looked at her granddaughter with joy in her eyes. "I'm so happy that that's my blood in her. I'm so glad that part of me is in her."

I slipped my arm around Jean's shoulder. "That's not just your blood," I told her. "That's your spirit."

•   •   •

Very early the next morning I was sitting on the blue stool I had now done my best to claim as my own. Emily was clutching my finger, my favorite mother-daughter position. This was what passed for contact between us, and I relished every microsecond of it. As long as we could trade even this tiny touch, I reasoned, we had something.

I looked up and, standing over the isolette across from Emily's was a young woman I hadn't seen before. She was wearing a hospital nightgown under her NICU gown and was juggling an IV pole in her arm. Her hair was disheveled; I recognized the disoriented look of a mother who had very recently given birth.

"Is it sterile?" she said, and pointed to the isolette. The two nurses on duty were occupied with other babies, so there was no one else around to give her instruction in the customs of the NICU. She walked to the wall sink and washed her hands, then gingerly opened the porthole and studied her baby. In a few sentences I learned that her name was Carla Field, that she was a dentist, and that her husband was an investment banker. They lived in the suburbs, in New Jersey. Molly, their daughter, had been born early that morning, at twenty-eight weeks. By now it was a familiar tale: ruptured membranes interrupting an until-then normal pregnancy, no real reason for the premature labor, and suddenly, a very tiny baby.

At this moment, as she cast her first real, uncensored gazes on her daughter, it was hard—and probably irrelevant—to tell her that she was lucky that her child, well over two pounds, was so big and, relatively speaking, so far along in her gestation. Neonatology was a new field, filled with statistical and technological marvels. Nowhere was the extent of the power of intervention more evident than in the critical twenty-fourth to twenty-seventh week period. Starved for information about my own child, I had learned that even now, a baby born at twenty-four weeks could expect only about a 10 percent chance of survival. At twenty-seven weeks, the figure soared to 90 percent. If Emily was in the middle, at twenty-five weeks and about 50 percent, Molly, at twenty-eight weeks, was virtually in the home stretch.

But Carla was troubled because in the birth process, Molly's umbilical cord had wrapped around her neck. From the neck down Molly was pink and I thought rather plump, weighing a hefty 1,120 grams. But her face and neck were the color of coal, the result of the twisting of the umbilical cord. The effect was curious, a two-tone baby.

"The doctor said this will pass, that it won't be permanent," Carla said. "I hope he's right."

Carla's work as a dentist helped her feel at ease in this living laboratory environment. She seemed to be maintaining a cool, almost clinical detachment as she examined her newborn child. When she hauled her IV pole around and came to look at Emily, she peered at her with a kind of detachment, as if she were a mouthful of teeth.

"Twenty-five weeks," she said. "Molly was twenty-eight."

This was something new: competitive prematurity, or, my preemie is bigger than your preemie. Carla was full of questions, all the same ones I had asked myself when Emily and I had first arrived. How long would Molly have to stay in the NICU? How long would she have to stay on K9? How long before she could begin feeding her mother's milk? How long before she could hold her baby and play with her? I told her these were questions she would have to ask Dr. Friedman, and tried to explain to her that the very nature of this place was unpredictability. But I could see that Carla was not the kind of woman who was accustomed to unpredictability. I judged her to be about thirty-two, give or take a year. Aside from the fact that she had been born twelve weeks too early, Molly was obviously a scheduled child. Dental school had been scheduled; marriage had been scheduled; setting up her own practice and buying their house in the suburbs had clearly been scheduled.

"How long before you can start wearing normal clothes?" Carla asked. "How long did it take you to lose all your weight?"

Emily was just ten days old at that point. I hadn't even thought about stepping on a scale since her birth; I hadn't had the time or inclination. I had no idea how much I weighed, nor did I particularly care.

"My friend who had a premature baby at Columbia–Presbyterian said it was great," Carla mused. "She lost all her weight in a week." Then she changed the subject, wondering, "How often do they let you visit the babies?"

Finally, there was a question I could answer. "As often as you want," I said. "They keep the place open twenty-four hours a day."

Carla returned at midmorning, this time accompanied by a family entourage. She'd shed the hospital-issued nightgown for one of her own, with pink roses and matching slippers and duster. Even the pink NICU gown seemed to be part of the outfit. She'd done her hair and put on makeup. She looked great—not a bit like a woman who'd had a baby a few hours earlier, and I told her so.

Carla's family was warm and friendly. Her husband was on hand, and so were both sets of grandparents. They trooped in en masse to admire Molly, oblivious to NICU rules that limited visitors to two per infant. Their confidence gave them a certain authority. But in the family room after their visit, it was clear that all their self-assurance hadn't completely paid off. I'd stopped by to wash up after a quick coffee break, and found myself sharing the sink with Carla's mother. She was steaming.

"Carla's sister drove all the way in from Long Island," linking the *g* and the *i* in an inadvertent parody of the New York accent, "and they won't even let her in to see the baby. I think that's just ridiculous." Until then I hadn't noticed the other member of Carla's party, a large woman in blue jeans sitting on the couch with her arms folded and an unhappy expression on her face. I agreed, and told her we'd been upset when Emily's half brother and half sister from Boston were not permitted to meet her. Carla's mother was unimpressed by anyone else's tale of woe. "But she drove all the way in from Long Island!" she repeated. "In traffic!"

Back in the NICU with Emily, I was struck once again by how diverse we were, we parents of premature infants, and how differently we all coped with the experience. Some parents obviously couldn't deal with it at all: There were several babies in the

unit who hadn't had a single visitor the whole time Emily and I
had been there, and others, like the infamous Kvetch baby, whose
parents had popped in once for a perfunctory look at this smaller,
sicker twin, then lingered across the hall in the well-baby room
with the larger, healthier child. I'd seen several very young mothers
whose own mothers made me feel geriatric. Often their stays in the
NICU were brief, for babies who were admitted only for observation frequently were fortunate enough to go home quickly. Sometimes the explanation for a short sojourn in the NICU was not so
positive, babies with very serious problems often died quickly.

One night, a young mother flounced in wearing a red chiffon
peignoir under her serviceable pink NICU gown. It was trimmed
with white fur, as were her clip-clop high-heeled slippers. Her dark
hair was styled in ringlets piled high on her head, and she wore
dangling gold earrings. It turned out she was not yet seventeen.
She breezed in, peered at her child in his isolette, and vanished,
clip-clopping down the hall at a racehorse pace. When she left,
LaTanya and I exchanged an incredulous glance with Georgeanne,
a nurse with nearly ten years of experience in the NICU.

"Welcome to the honeymoon suite," Georgeanne said dryly.
Then she laughed and told us about the couple who'd shown up
around midnight several years earlier in full wedding regalia—
everything except the cathedral-length veil. Evidently marriage was
a detail they hadn't quite gotten around to before their child's early
arrival.

"You stay up here long enough, you see it all," Georgeanne
said.

Another night, about a week after Emily was born, I noticed
an attractive black couple hovering over an isolette in one of the far
corners of the NICU. The parents smiled at me in an inviting
fashion, so I walked over to say hello and to join them in admiring
their baby boy. By my standards, he was huge, about three pounds.
His name was Clifford John, and his parents told me they planned
to call him CJ. His mother, a designer of hats, was tall and slender,
dressed all in mulberry under her hospital gown. The father, Clifford, was a full head shorter than his wife, stocky and balding. A

church organist on the weekends, he taught music in the Newark public schools during the week. CJ was his first son, and if ever there was a proud daddy, it was Clifford.

From the nurses I had learned that premature infants sometimes look out of kilter when they are born. Parts can seem very much out of proportion. They may have huge feet or heads. Their noses may seem fit for a giant. Sometimes, it is their sexual organs that look as if they were borrowed from an adult.

CJ's father was crowing about his son's hands and feet. "Look at those hands!" he exclaimed. "I can tell he'll be a basketball player."

"Or a pianist," the baby's mother chimed in.

"Look at those feet," his father went on. "You just know he's going to be a tall boy, don't you?"

I didn't want to be rude, but what I was really looking at was the kid's penis. It was immense. Robin, the nurse on duty, was standing alongside us, watching and listening politely as I agreed that CJ had the hugest hands and feet of any kid his size I had ever seen. He would make a wonderful basketball player or a brilliant pianist, and he would certainly be very tall, I agreed. When his parents left, Robin and I cracked up.

"Get that kid a diaper!" Robin said in the same urgent tone she might have used for a real emergency. "He's distracting the women on the floor."

The rare note of levity was welcome. Far too often, the mood in the NICU was heavy and somber. I had noticed early on, for example, that the parents of the baby next to Emily spoke to almost no one, not even their baby's nurse in their daily visits. It soon became apparent that as they were from Ecuador, and spoke only Spanish, there was what the hospital would call a language barrier. I tried to imagine how awful it must be for them. The place was overwhelming enough to me, and I spoke English. Imagine trying to understand all the medical terminology in translation. The two young NICU receptionists, both from Puerto Rico, were equally conversant in Spanish and English. But often they were not on duty, or in some cases they could not leave their station. There was no hospital interpreter, so these parents were often reduced to communicating in sign language, pointing at the baby's stomach, for example, or gesturing to one piece of equipment or another.

Their family name was Diaz, and their little boy's name was Charles. He was born at twenty-nine weeks. His stomach was distended like a balloon, and on the rare occasions when he did open his eyes, he looked wan and exhausted, as if the mere effort of raising his lids had done him in for the day. When I asked Robin about Charles, she just shook her head, reminding me that officially, the nurses were not allowed to talk about the babies with anyone other than the parents. "He's a mess," was all she would say. "That kid is really sick."

Both his parents were short and solidly built. They never missed a day of visiting him. Mrs. Diaz, probably about ten years younger than I was, had long, dark hair, parted down the middle, and wore large, light brown framed glasses. I noticed that where the rest of us had taped pictures of our babies' families in the isolettes, Mrs. Diaz had hung a small religious icon. After a few days of exchanging polite but wordless smiles, I finally got the courage to try my high school Spanish. It seemed to me that there were dinosaurs roaming the earth the last time I actually studied the language, and in the back of my brain I dimly remembered being grilled in useful conversational phrases on such things as how to change a tire, something I could barely do in English. But I had the odd feeling here in the NICU that we were all in this thing together. I wanted to at least attempt to say something to Mrs. Diaz.

"Es su primer niño?" I asked gingerly. Is that your first son? I was amazed when a full sentence came out, for in fact my last formal instruction in Spanish had taken place in my junior year at Berkeley High School.

Mrs. Diaz—and that is the only way I ever knew her—brightened. She seemed pleased that someone would make the effort to communicate with her in her own language. She responded with a torrent of Spanish. I thought she was telling me that she and her husband already had a little boy at home, but I wasn't positive.

"Despacio, por favor," I said: slowly, please.

And so we began a tentative daily exchange that centered on the health of our children.

"Muy malo," she said of Charles. He was very sick. To help feed him, the doctors had implanted a tube in his chest that went straight to his belly. Whereas Emily wriggled and kicked, Charles lay there listlessly. The pain he was feeling was reflected in his mother's countenance. Her face was a mask of anguish.

But Mrs. Diaz was too polite not to have something nice to say about Emily. *"Mas grande!"* she would exclaim, even when the scale showed that Emily had lost weight, not gained.

Our discussions were rudimentary. I stumbled around and no doubt made a grammatical fool of myself. But we could smile at each other, and we could share the overpowering confusion and fear we both felt. In any language, a parent in this setting feels completely unhinged. We agreed, in our best present-tense Spanish, that there were two things we must never lose sight of. It became the way we bade farewell to each other every day as one or the other of us left. Sometimes we squeezed each other's hands; sometimes an arm slipped gently over a shoulder; sometimes it was just a wave.

"Esperanza y patienza," we would say.

Hope and patience. Without either, we agreed, we might as well give up.

SIX

The crisis struck around midnight on April 5, Emily's tenth day of life. At noon the next day, Dr. Friedman made a terse notation on her chart:

"Emily has developed probable NEC."

NEC stands for necrotizing enterocolitis, one of the worst hazards of prematurity. "Literally," said Marjorie, the nurse who had worked in the NICU longer than anyone else, "it means a death to the bowel wall." It was late at night, twelve hours after the diagnosis had been made. All day I had been waiting for a short, simple description of the disease my child had contracted. It took Marjorie to put it in such clear terms.

Its causes are unknown, but NEC manifests itself when the usually friendly bacteria in the intestine turn unfriendly and attack the tissue in the intestinal wall. The bacteria produce bubbles of gas that swell up and interrupt intestinal functioning. If the intestinal wall perforates, the infection may spread through the entire abdominal cavity. In such cases it is almost invariably fatal. In less severe bouts of NEC, the intestine may repair itself on its own. Often, surgery is required to extract damaged tissue and to rejoin living sections. NEC hits full-term newborns and premature infants alike, but is most devastating in very small babies like Emily.

One theory, Dr. Friedman said, is that NEC is somehow conveyed to the baby through the feedings. "My milk?" I asked him. My knees faltered. Had I poisoned my own child? "Well, we're not saying that, exactly," Dr. Friedman said. As always, he delivered this information in calm, rational tones interspersed with the now familiar smile. He spoke with the same dispassion he might use to report the weather: "Cloudy on Sunday, your kid has NEC." But the impact was not lost. I felt that at any moment Fox, Emily, and I would drop through some unseen chasm. We had been warned by my friend Ed and others that when the setbacks come for premature infants, they are seldom minor. This was definitely a big one. Many babies die of NEC. A colostomy is frequently necessary. For babies as small as Emily, the prospect of surgery holds its own litany of serious risks. She weighed well under seven hundred grams. The trauma of the trip to the operating room alone could kill her.

"NEC is definitely a fascinating subject," Dr. Friedman said, and now his voice picked up, reflecting his interest. He said he had written several papers on NEC that had been published in important medical journals. As a matter of fact, he continued, among neonatologists, "I'm considered something of an expert on NEC." He smiled.

The setting of this conversation made it all the more unsettling. K9 was like a child that had gone through a growth spurt while no one was looking, and suddenly, everything was too small and ill-fitting. The halls, narrow to begin with, were lined with unused equipment. Sechrist ventilators and unused isolettes were parked there like shopping carts outside a grocery store. The nurseries overflowed, reminiscent of overcrowded housing developments. To pump milk at midday, nursing mothers huddled behind a half curtain in a cluttered storage room. An old pink hospital gown had been draped across the window separating that room from the adjacent nursery, but still, if a mother stood up too quickly, she could easily put on an inadvertent topless performance. There was nothing resembling a conference room, no place where one could conduct a conversation with anything close to privacy, and not even a bathroom for the parents. Outside in the hallway, around the corner from the elevator, there was a unisex stall toilet. Occasionally, the lock even worked.

So here we were once again, Dr. Friedman and I, leaning against Emily's isolette like a lamppost. Actually, he was doing the leaning. The whole time he was talking to me, I could barely take my eyes off my daughter. From time to time, to be polite, I made eye contact with Dr. Friedman while he discoursed on NEC or answered my questions. But Emily remained my primary focus. She was lying on her back with her fists clenched tight. Occasionally she would open those clear blue eyes and look in my direction. Even without the illness, she was withstanding daily assaults to her system that no adult would tolerate. I couldn't bear to think that this brave, strong child was being asked to face yet another Sisyphean obstacle.

Around us life went on in the NICU. Nurses bustled over their babies. Bells and alarms raged. Dressed in ritual black, a family of Hasidic Jews—grandparents, a young and nervous-looking father, and others who must have been uncles and aunts—davened and prayed in Hebrew near the warming table where their small infant, the latest arrival here in the NICU, lay splayed out. At the isolette next to us, Mrs. Diaz stolidly maintained her quiet vigil. Carla breezed in, perfectly coiffed with a chic new haircut and nails freshly manicured with rosy pink nail polish. Dangling a little white bag, she called out to Dr. Friedman, unconcerned by the fact that he was in conference with someone else. "I've got the milk, Dr. Friedman," she said. "Where should I put it?"

Each day the NICU seemed more and more to be a microcosm of the world outside, where personalities paraded, egos cavorted, and suffering went on in silence. Each day was a reminder of just how relentless mundane events can be. At this very moment that my daughter's life lay in jeopardy, two young residents were chuckling over some private moment of mirth in the corner.

Carla had stopped to inspect her daughter. Molly was one tone by now, a source of great relief to her parents. Like most of us who had settled into K9 for the long haul—we hoped—Carla had begun decorating her daughter's isolette. But where most of us had hung photographs of our families, and where Mrs. Diaz had put a religious picture, Carla had taped a picture of their house.

Emily had already been placed on antibiotics, Dr. Friedman said, returning me to earth and the calamity at hand. There would be frequent X-rays to explore the extent of possible damage to her intestine. Until her condition stabilized, feedings would be stopped.

"But you should continue to express your milk," Dr. Friedman advised. He was not about to offer any kind of odds on how Emily's illness would progress. But his congenital optimism, his "sixth sense," as he called it, inclined him to think that Emily would pull through this disaster. NEC was a major peril for premature infants, he repeated, but many babies did recover from it completely.

"When she can tolerate it, when she gets better, we'll want to start her up again on your milk," he said.

At that moment I was feeling pretty glum. "If she gets better," I said.

"I'm always optimistic," Dr. Friedman reminded me. "Let's say 'when,' not 'if.'"

Standing there with Emily, I remembered that she had seemed lethargic the day before, not her own true self at all. But I was new to this world of prematurity, so I hadn't known to sound an alarm. I thought maybe she was just tired. "Baby needs sleep, baby needs sleep," Miss Lee, the Korean nurse, kept telling me. Besides, I already had a reputation in the NICU as a neurotic troublemaker, the kind of mom who actually wanted to be informed about what was going on with her child. Leslie, among others, thought this was perfectly reasonable, but many of the young residents considered it an annoyance to have to interact with parents they might only know for two weeks, the duration of their rotations in the NICU. Just that morning I had introduced myself to the resident, Daniel Ho, who would be assigned to Emily for the next two weeks. Dr. Ho was remote; his manner was efficient, crisp, and no-nonsense, as if he were dealing with the repair of cars or computers, not babies. I watched Dr. Ho and his fellow residents as they conducted their daily rounds. They displayed no emotion, moving in a herd from isolette to isolette, and referring to each baby as "he," regardless of gender. "They're really smart, the cream of the crop," Leslie agreed. "But when it comes to social skills, forget it." Unlike the nurses, who were required to take psychology courses, the resident physicians had no formal education to prepare them for personal interaction. All their training and superspecialization turned them into brilliant technicians. Often the cost was any vestige of humanity.

"I'll be drawing more blood from him and having it sent down to the lab," Dr. Ho told me.

"Her," I said.

Through his thick, wire-rimmed glasses, Dr. Ho gave me a blank look.

"Her," I said. "You'll be drawing more blood from her. Emily is a girl, not a boy. Have you noticed?"

Now Dr. Ho tossed me an expression of disgust. "We call all the babies 'he,'" he said. "It's less complicated."

Once I was alone with Emily, I picked up the binder that held her progress reports and leafed back to previous days. Just two days before, noting the introduction of fats into Emily's diet, Dr. Friedman had written that Emily "continues to do quite well." If Emily received an "A" on that grading, I felt like calling home to report my own top mark when I read Dr. Klein's notation from the same day: "Mother visiting often, with good bonding displayed." But yesterday's entry was less favorable. "Appears less active today," Georgeanne had noted in an entry that confirmed my own observation. In an entry marked midnight, Dr. Stein, another resident, had noted that Emily's abdomen appeared tense. "Baby pulls up legs when abdomen is touched," Dr. Stein wrote, confirming that Emily was probably in a great deal of discomfort. Under the "neuro" heading, Dr. Stein observed that Emily was "less active, but responds to pain." Through reading the chart, I learned that Dr. Stein had suspected NEC the night before and had ordered Emily to be placed on antibiotics. It seemed like a major development, and I wondered why, since she knew we wanted to be informed of what was happening to Emily, Dr. Stein had not bothered to call Fox and me at home.

"Well, what could you have done?" Dr. Stein replied when I asked her about this later in the afternoon. She was young, certainly under thirty. She was tall and attractive, and wore her hair schoolboy short and slicked back with gel. She presented an image of uncontestable self-assurance.

I tried to explain to Dr. Stein that what I could have done was not the issue. Emily was the only baby Fox and I had, and under the circumstances, it sometimes felt presumptuous to say we had her at all. The hospital had her. A plastic box held her. We had never so much as embraced our own child. Information was our connection, I told Dr. Stein. To deny us that was to deny us part of Emily.

She was unmoved by my small soliloquy. "Well, it was midnight," she said, and turned to walk away.

That night, I sat at the round teakwood table I had been carting around for fifteen years worth of houses and apartments. In spite of myself, I felt tears slipping down my cheeks as I wrote in Emily's journal. All I knew about NEC was that it was potentially among the most serious pitfalls of premature existence. I was frightened.

But I also knew that in Emily, I was dealing with a very determined individual. She squeezed too hard and stared too hard for there to be any doubt about that. She was tiny, but she was also tough. When she looked up at me, there was a determined expression on her face. "Calm down, Mom," she seemed to be saying. "We're going to beat this thing." It was clear that Emily was no quitter.

"I get scared," I wrote in her diary, covered with pink and blue flowered fabric. "But then I look at you. You're brave, you're strong. You're not giving up."

Emily was giving me courage lessons. I was happy to accept them.

• • •

One calamity begot another. Her illness meant that Emily's blood was weaker, and it also meant more blood tests, more frequently. Emily was starting to resemble a pincushion. Every time I turned around, there was another nurse or doctor, plunging another needle into another area of her small body. Even in her enfeebled condition, Emily managed to cringe and kick in protest. Between the illness and the injections, her hematocrit level, the ratio of red cells in her blood, was dropping steadily.

"We're going to need to transfuse him again," Dr. Ho pronounced.

"Her," I said. "You're going to need to transfuse her."

I accepted this news with some nonchalance, since by my calculations, there should still have been plenty of my mother's blood left. But Dr. Ho informed me that the blood bank had no further donor-specified blood on reserve for Emily. This was when I learned about what I came to refer to as the "zap-it-all, zap-it-now" policy of the blood bank. Irradiating small quantities of blood was too problematic, so each time a transfusion was required, an entire adult unit of blood was, as they called it, "wasted." Donated blood required a minimum of twenty-four to thirty-six hours for screening and preparation. Dr. Ho was certain Emily would need a transfusion before then.

"We'll have to give him donor-anonymous blood," he said.

I was too chilled to correct the pronoun. Dr. Ho's glasses had a habit of slipping down his nose, and he pushed them back idly before departing.

For once, the fishbowl quality of K9 had an unexpected benefit. Moments after Dr. Ho took off, Carol, the mother of baby John, was standing beside me at Emily's isolette.

"You're just going to have to trust in the screening process," Carol said. John had had dozens of blood transfusions, Carol told me, all of them from donor-anonymous blood. She and her husband were unable to donate, and they hadn't found friends or family members they could trust who shared their baby's blood type. Besides, Carol said, given the past and present sexual activity level of many of her friends, she actually felt safer with blood screened by the hospital.

"They're really careful," she said. I told her she was probably right. Friends had begun coming to the hospital to give blood, and Dr. Klein had slipped and told me that two of Emily's donors had been rejected, one for hepatitis and the other for herpes. "Anyway," Carol said, "you don't have any choice. The baby needs the blood. You've just got to do it, and have faith that it's the right thing."

At that moment, Carol's presence was so reassuring that I did not stop to wonder how she could have known of this predicament in such detail, and so quickly. But I looked up and in the other room, there was Robin, the nurse, smiling at us. After overhearing the discussion between me and Dr. Ho, she had approached Carol and urged her to talk to me.

Robin's gesture was yet another example of how the nurses seemed to hold this whole place together. The doctors gave the orders, the administrators took care of business, but the nurses kept things human. They were the buffers and the barometers, riding the balance between the parents' panic and the doctors' detachment. In the process, they managed to keep the kids as their primary objects of attention—and often their affection, as well.

One morning, early on, I was in the NICU at about seven o'clock when Eleanor, another nurse who had put in twenty-plus years there, was making her report on the night's activities to the nurse who would succeed her on the day shift.

"All my babies are doing fine," I heard her say in conclusion. I thought the possessive pronoun was interesting.

Ten or so minutes later, I happened to be riding the elevator to the basement cafeteria. During pregnancy I had been scrupulous about my diet. But the long hours here at the hospital and the stress that seemed to come with the turf had returned me to my worst pre-pregnancy eating habits. My appetite had died and once again I was back to drinking coffee. In the elevator that morning, Eleanor was the only other passenger. She was a large woman with meaty legs and a solid, sturdy body. She wore her graying hair in the kind of parted-to-the-side permanent wave style I remembered from my elementary school teachers in the 1950s, sort of like Betty Crocker before her 1968 makeover. Eleanor's big arms looked as if they could encircle the world. So did her smile.

"I noticed that you refer to the kids as your babies," I said to her. "I think that's really nice."

Eleanor threw me a huge, beatific grin.

"They're all my babies while they're up there," she said. "My babies and God's."

From Robin the message was less reverential, but equally compassionate. Robin, in her late twenties, was the unit's resident swinging single. Her concern for children had sent her from elementary school teaching to neonatological nursing. But along with her love of babies, she confessed that one reason she liked working on K9 was that she could work three twelve and a half hour days, then party, play, and relax for the next four days. When her shift started at 7:30 A.M., Robin looked like she had rolled out of bed fifteen seconds earlier. Her hair was pulled back with a rubber band, and she wore not one touch of makeup. After her midmorning break, around 10 o'clock, she would return looking like a cosmopolitan cover girl—in a nursing uniform. Her lashes were brushed thick with fresh mascara, and her lids glistened with shiny shadow. Her hair was now moussed and gelled to bouffant perfection, and sometimes it was pulled back with a velvet bow. I teased her that she went from looking like something the cat would rather not have brought in, to looking like the cat, all sultry and sleek. On everyone else, the blue hospital scrubs looked baggy and dull. On Robin, they looked like a high-fashion jumpsuit.

"You can have one, too," she said. "All you've got to do is go to nursing school and get a job up here. No problem."

Robin ran on high voltage energy. She had a quick, easy laugh that could de-stress tension in a moment. Without trivializing the very real pressures on K9, she managed to make light of them. When Emily's sunglasses and bilirubin lights went on, Robin bade Emily welcome to the K9 tanning parlor and offered to loan her some sun block. When they were removed, she squealed "Beach Blanket Babylon comes off!" Robin had a knack for reading people quickly, and for sensing sudden shifts in mood. She traced this skill to growing up in a large, loving family. Robin was one of five sisters from Long Island, all born close together. They were all the very best of friends, she told me.

To keep her trim figure in shape, Robin had recently taken up running. There was a pool in her apartment building, she told me, and whenever she could find time, she tried to do forty-five minutes of laps. Before I was pregnant, I was always compulsive about my body, too. But now I worried that an hour of aerobics or jogging was an hour away from Emily. When Fox went for a run each evening, I resented it, and took it as a sign that he was more interested in himself than in his daughter. Who knew what would happen to Emily while he was running around the reservoir? I demanded. I refused to acknowledge at that point that there might be something other than a selfish motive to his exercising; that maybe running helped ease the stress for him.

Robin heard me out while I vented these feelings; like Leslie, a stint in the NICU had made her into an amateur marriage counselor. To my amazement, she not only took Fox's position, but encouraged me to start doing something for my own body as well. "Whatever's going to happen is going to happen, whether you're here or not," Robin reminded me. "You've got to take care of yourself, too."

Robin's concern was another reflection of just how tight the K9 universe really was. We stepped into each other's lives without a moment's pause. Robin was the one who had sent Carol over to talk to me about blood transfusions. In another setting, I probably would have bristled at that kind of intrusiveness. Here on K9, it felt like a favor from a friend.

In Emily's journal late that night, I noted that I had "reluctantly" authorized the use of donor-anonymous blood for her transfusion. "In any event, there was no choice. You needed the blood," I wrote in the book I was intending for her to read when she grew up. In the same day's entry, I wrote about the frustrations of dealing with the blood bank bureaucrats. I described them as behaving like border guards in a Third World country.

But they were who I had to deal with. There was no alternative but to put out the word to everyone I knew: Emily needs blood.

I added a plea to the message on our answering machine. I called everyone I could think of who might have suitable blood. A colleague in Los Angeles contacted her friends at *Newsday,* our sister newspaper, where she had worked before. In twenty-four hours she had rounded up four potential donors, all strangers to me, but people who had heard of Emily's plight. Many were parents of young children themselves, and they were eager to offer their help.

Meanwhile, my college roommate Joanna was on her way to New York. Joanna is tall and assertive. Nobody messes with her and lives to talk about it. Joanna once was a model and has remarkable eyes. She works with a youth service organization in the San Francisco Bay area, and probably did not need to make the business trip to Washington that she abruptly scheduled. But that way she could get her coast-to-coast air fare paid for. From Washington she grabbed the air shuttle, and at ten o'clock in the morning, one day after Emily was diagnosed as having NEC, I met her in the hospital lobby.

We felt like spelunkers, working our way through the subterranean caves of the hospital on our way to the department of hematology. "Did you sprinkle little crumbs behind us so we can find our way back?" Joanna asked. When we finally reached the blood bank, there was another of Emily's donors. Rolling up his sleeve was the husband of a woman I knew through work. I had never met Ralph, but when Debbie, his wife, learned that Emily needed blood and that Ralph had the same type, she dispatched him immediately. I worried a little because Ralph and Debbie had been trying for almost four years to have a child of their own. I thought the process of giving blood to someone else's newborn might exacerbate the pain of their own empty arms. But Ralph dispelled my concerns. Even if they couldn't have a baby them-selves, he said, "At least my blood may help your baby live."

So this was the mark of real caring, two adults volunteering their veins for a very small baby. Friendship means sharing, it means giving of yourself, the Homily Queen always said. Could there be a more basic act of giving than this, the act of sharing blood?

On the other hand, while it is true that my mother groomed me always to make my guests feel at ease, the donor room was the strangest place that my perfect-hostess genes have ever kicked into action. There, reclined on Roman orgy-style couches of mocha-colored plastic were two friends, one old, one new, each clutching a giant orange Styrofoam ball and each with a needle fixed firmly in the arm. As we traded patter, I looked around and spied the cans of fruit juice used to reward donors after they had given blood.

"May I get you some pineapple juice?" I asked them. In my mind I sounded demure, but in reality I sounded ridiculous. Joanna nearly fell off the couch, she laughed so hard.

"Pineapple juice?" she said. "Pineapple juice? What is this, Aloha Airlines? Honey, you can do better than that."

Ralph, an architect, had to hurry off to work, but Joanna could stay for a few hours. I wanted badly for her to be able to see Emily, my tiny pride and joy. Joanna wanted to see her, too. For almost twenty years we had fantasized about what it would be like when we had children. We had both been through unsuccessful first marriages, and together we had watched our years for poten-tial child-bearing narrow. Now Joanna had a little boy, Nicholas, and I had Emily. We were old friends who had stumbled through jobs, marriages, and dead-end love affairs on our way to what we wanted most, children and a family. We wanted to be able to exult together. It was as simple as that.

But even Carla, who seemed to make pretzels out of hospital regulations, hadn't managed to smuggle her sister in to see her baby. As with Ethan and Sarah, I had to be content with sitting in K9's so-called family room and showing Polaroid pictures of Emily to Joanna. Whereas some people who had seen pictures of our bionic baby had recoiled at how small she was and how she lived with such a myriad of machines, Joanna looked at the pictures of this tiny baby with her serpentine tubes and said exactly what I wanted to hear: "Oh, sweet baby! Look at how beautiful she is." Joanna's eyes were filled with tears, too. "She's going to be fine, Lizzie," she said, using her old love name for me. "I just know she is."

Outside the hospital, we linked arms in a gray rain. Joanna insisted on stopping to buy some opthalmologically approved stuffed animals for Emily. They were black and white, stripes and polka dots. "It helps them learn to focus," Joanna said. So now, along with her seal, her bunnies, and her assortment of family photographs, Emily also had an elephant and a zebra in her isolette. It was turning into quite a friendly little crowd in there.

The medication and the transfusions quickly took effect. Within two days Emily was rosy and alert. She was back to performing the Butterfield Stretch, the name we had given to her feat of extending one arm far over her head and stretching all the way to her toes. It was an exact replica of a gesture I've seen both Fox and Sarah carry out on many occasions. It may not sound like such an amazing exploit, but Emily's arms were weighed down with IV boards, needles, and tubes, so the movement required herculean effort.

Daily X-rays failed to reveal further deterioration in Emily's intestines. Gas bubbles were present, consistent with a diagnosis of NEC. But the photographs indicated no major rupture or blockage, which was cause for optimism in the view of the doctors. But her belly was still swollen, and terribly tender to the touch. Because Emily was so scrawny, her distended stomach looked even more grotesque and distorted, as if it had been inflated, like a balloon.

That was the first thing Fox commented on when he visited Emily three days after the disease was first detected. "My God, she's so skinny," he said. I found myself pouncing to her defense. "But at least she's alert and moving around. You should have seen her two days ago."

The implication, of course, was that I had been there, and he had not. It was a reflection of the huge and growing gap between us, and that was how we interpreted what we were going through with Emily. Charges and imprecations flew. I felt that Fox was insufficiently responsive. He felt that I was obsessed. I blasted him for going back to work immediately after her birth—although at the time I had encouraged him to do just that—and suggested that he cared more for his job than for his family. He retaliated that having a baby was the only thing in the world that mattered to me and that marrying him had merely been a vehicle for me to attain that end. And if he didn't work, he growled, how would he support his other kids? I wondered why he couldn't get across town and have a look at his daughter more often. I was there every day. Why couldn't he be there, too? He replied that I was turning Emily into a competition—the how-much-time-have-*you*-spent-with-her-lately? syndrome. And he chastised me for forgetting about our marriage in my concern for our child.

It was then, right when Emily got so sick, that the fighting began in earnest. Somewhere in the depths of our brains we knew how damaging prolonged stress and crisis could be to a marriage. We knew that even when children survived serious illnesses and long periods in the hospital, their parents' marriages often did not. Anxiety translated far too easily into animosity. Fear eroded existing weak points, like unseen, underground pressures on an earthquake fault. Rather than pulling them closer together, many couples found that the strain split them apart. I had written about such couples over the years, husbands and wives who had seen a child through a long and devastating illness, then found that their anger toward each other was too great to permit their marriage to continue. "We do see a lot of divorces up here," Leslie confirmed.

For us, it was like trying first to balance on the edge of a greasy cliff, and then attempting to waltz across it. I was spending virtually all my waking hours at the hospital. At night, if the phone rang at home, I levitated, convinced it was K9 calling to say that Emily was dead. Only while using the breast pump or grabbing a bite to eat at the hospital did I so much as look at the newspaper, once my lifeblood. It was the spring of 1988 and the presidential campaigns were heating up. Once a White House reporter, I barely knew or cared who the candidates were. What difference did it make who the President was when my child was struggling for life? For his part, Fox had escaped by burrowing into his work. He was part of a team of reporters at the *New York Times* who were investigating an important racial incident in New York state—the Tawana Brawley case. At the same time, he was following the primary elections with growing interest. For a number of years Fox had covered Massachusetts politics. Recently he had written a profile of Governor Michael Dukakis that was scheduled to run in the *New York Times Magazine.* One day, Fox reported to me with great enthusiasm that Dukakis was closing in tight in several key Midwestern states. I couldn't believe he expected me to care about politics. "You'll have to forgive me," I replied, "if I don't give a shit."

That was how different this process was for us. I was trying to manage the unmanageable; he was trying to retreat from it.

It was a classic example of gender role adaptation, Kate Patterson, the fertility shrink, explained when I called her in desperation. "Completely different coping mechanisms," she said calmly. "You're interpreting the same problem in vastly divergent fashions." As I began to look around and listen to other mothers in the NICU, I felt less of a need for professional analysis. It was quite clear that Fox and I were not alone in responding to this situation so differently.

John's mother Carol was making plans to take him home. Only now, as it became clear that the child would survive, did she feel that her husband had risked bonding with the baby. Like Fox, he seldom visited when his child was in the NICU, Carol said. Now that I thought about it, I could only remember having seen him in K9 once, even with John seeming to be thriving in the nursery that housed the healthiest kids.

"We fought," Carol said. "We fought a lot through all of this."

In a setback of her own, Monique's daughter Beverlee had

been moved back into the NICU from the well-baby nursery. It seemed that Beverlee, too, showed signs of NEC. Monique looked absolutely drained. She scared up a chair somehow and sat by Beverlee's isolette. Her back was to the rest of us, and her body language made it clear that she was not interested in interacting. I noticed that she was alone too. She wore a wedding ring and talked about her husband, a former policeman who now owned his own security business, but I had yet to lay eyes on him.

To LaTanya, the increasing tension between Fox and me was apparent and understandable. The two of us were almost always alone at our babies' isolettes. When Fox did come to the hospital, I was often snappish and sarcastic. "Glad you could make it," I would say, not caring who was listening. LaTanya could not help but hear digs like that, and one day, in the family room, she happened to walk in on the tail end of an especially nasty conversation between Fox and me.

"So what!" I steamed into the receiver. Fox was telling me that before Emily, there had been love and a marriage. He was saying I was obsessed with what was happening at the NICU. Then my face went purple when I heard Fox slam the receiver down.

I was furious. "He hung up!" I said. I was glad that LaTanya was there. It gave me a human to vent to.

"Your husband, right?" she asked.

The notion of privacy on K9 was such a joke that LaTanya and I were better off acknowledging right up front what was going on. She told me that she and Jacques Louis's father were having a rough time, too.

"We fight a lot," LaTanya said. "He keeps telling me that he loves Jacques Louis. But if he loves him so much, how come he never comes to see him?"

We had already settled into little rituals. As was our habit, we tied each other into our hospital gowns, the way big sisters do for little sisters who can't yet reach behind them to tie the bow. LaTanya was so strong and feisty that it was easy to forget how young she was. She had not endeared herself to the K9 nursing staff because she sparred with so many of them. But I kind of admired that quality in her. In the best sense of the word, she was tough. In any situation, she would fight to get what was coming to her. Here on K9, she would get what was coming to her son.

LaTanya and I were washing our hands together now, still babbling.

"Well, at least you got him in here," LaTanya said. "I can't even get Jacques Louis's father into this place."

"Oh, right. He comes in here and all he says is that Emily looks so much skinnier than the last time he came. I don't need that, LaTanya. I don't need him to come in here and tell me she looks like a fragile little bird. I know that."

"It's like you get used to seeing these babies when you're in here so much," LaTanya said. "They look normal to us. But when somebody comes in who hasn't seen them, they think they look scrawny and strange."

"He's jealous." I had just blurted out what I considered to be one of the big issues between Fox and me. He said it was an evil and angry accusation. But it was how I felt. "He says I spend too much time here. He wants me to pay as much attention to him as I pay to Emily."

By now LaTanya and I were walking down the hall toward the NICU. We were just passing the supply cabinet when LaTanya asked me, "What do you think of my hair? I changed it."

I took a step away to study her face. She still had pimply teenage skin, one of the few indications of how young she was. Usually she wore her hair short and curled around her face. But today she had combed it into a more upswept style. It went straight up off her face, then burst into little curls.

"It makes you look older," I told her. I thought that was what she would want to hear. "Much more sophisticated."

LaTanya stopped before we could turn the corner into the NICU. She said she wanted to move to her own apartment after Jacques Louis got out of the hospital.

"Which borough do you think is better?" she asked. "The Bronx or Queens?"

I didn't want to tell LaTanya that I had been to The Bronx exactly twice, both times for stories. My Upper East Side bureau chief was horrified when he learned I had taken the subway. My experience with Queens was confined primarily to LaGuardia Airport. Sometimes, I realized, our common experiences as mothers of tiny babies born too soon made it easy to overlook the very real differences between LaTanya and me. For a moment I reflected that if I had started as young as she did, I could have had a child her age. That was an odd image, because LaTanya did not seem a bit like a daughter. She felt like a friend. Outside, in the portion of the planet that masqueraded as reality, my friendships were based on history, on shared pasts and experiences. Here there was no past, only a very urgent present. I told LaTanya that I had heard good things about both the Bronx and Queens, and that wherever she found a good apartment, that would be the right place to live.

"Hi, Emily," LaTanya said as we entered the NICU. She tapped gently on Emily's isolette. "It's me, honey. It's LaTanya. I'm Jacques Louis's mother. You two are going to have a long lifetime to play together."

News traveled faster in the NICU than on the AP wire. We soon learned that baby Molly was being moved across the hall to the healthier babies' nursery. Or, as her mother enthused, "She's graduating! So soon!" Carla would probably use the same boastful tone if Molly, age fifteen, had just earned a degree from Harvard.

LaTanya and I shot each other a can-you-believe-it expression. It was great that Molly was doing so well. But what about our kids? When would they get to graduate?

Later that day, Carla burst in on me while I was using the breast pump. "Oh," she said when she saw me sitting there. "I really need to use it. Will you be much longer?" When I told her I needed to pump for at least five more minutes, she looked disappointed. "In five minutes I can get all the milk I need," Carla said. Then she surprised me. Instead of leaving, she sat down to chat. This was another of those bizarre, only-in-K9 conversations. There I was, nude from the waist up, talking to a woman who had been a stranger just a week before. Even now, I would hardly have numbered Carla among my most intimate acquaintances. She was a little too pushy for my taste, and a little too fueled by some innate sense of privilege. Outside K9, she was not the kind of person I would be likely to pick out for a pal. But here again, the common nature of our experience gave us some basis of understanding.

Carla said she had already gone back to work. Because she had her own dental practice in New Jersey, she could block out time during the day to shoot across the bridge to spend time with Molly.

"At first, I was writing 'HOSPITAL' in my book for the hours that I was here," Carla said. "But I thought it looked too grim, so I just started writing 'MOLLY.' " Carla smiled. "I made a sign to hang on my office door when I'm using the breast pump there," she said. "It says 'PUMPING STATION.' "

One thing that had kept me from rushing back to my office was that I thought I would be unable to concentrate on my work. Every time the phone rang, I would fear that it would be the hospital, calling to say that something awful had happened. I couldn't imagine conducting an interview. How could I ask questions? Wouldn't my concern about Emily overpower my ability to think about anything else?

"Don't you have trouble looking into people's mouths and thinking about their cavities?" I asked Carla. "I'd be afraid I'd drill a hole in the wrong tooth."

But Carla was much cooler about all this than I was. Maybe it was because things seemed to be going so well for her child. Maybe she was just more confident that Molly would prosper, no matter what. Carla always looked terrific, stylishly dressed and well made up. She said she never had trouble finding a parking place when she came to visit Molly. Life seemed almost charmed for her. She said she had no trouble focusing on her work.

"Just the opposite," she said. "It's a distraction." Her work consumed her completely, Carla said. When she was at her dental office, she couldn't think about anything other than what she was doing, including Molly. Besides, Carla said she enjoyed talking about Molly with her patients. A premature infant was sort of exotic, Carla said. "People are really curious. They want to know all about her." She let out a big laugh. "And that's the best part," she said. "I'm happy to tell them."

I buttoned my blouse and set about disengaging the plastic container filled with my milk. It attached to a long plastic tube that in turn was hooked up to a cone-shaped device that fit over the breast. These little nursing kits were standard issue on K9, and Carla was all ready with hers. She had her back to me, unbuttoning her gray silk dress. Her baby was doing so much better than my own; Molly was Dr. Friedman's star patient. That had to be why Carla found it so easy to trust the system.

"I guess I just worry too much about leaving Emily alone," I said. "If something happens, I want to be here."

Carla sat down in the rocker, uncoiled the plastic tube, and started to pump. This was the first time she and I had had anything resembling a real conversation.

"You just have to figure that this is the best place for them right now," she said. "You have to believe that they can do a whole lot more for your baby here than you can." Carla was rocking back and forth in the chair, with the cone clamped to her breast. She actually looked comfortable in this strange little corner.

"They really know what they're doing," Carla said. "You just have to let them do it."

My conversation with Carla lingered with me. Maybe she's right, I thought. Maybe I could regain some of my rapidly vanishing sanity if I went back to work. Maybe it would help me order my days a little more rationally. Maybe I would be less testy, less frantic about Emily. Carla and her husband always looked cheerful and affectionate when they came to visit Molly. It didn't look like they went home and fought about their sick child. They even held hands when they walked down the hallway. Before all this started, Fox and I used to do that, I remembered.

So later that day I mentioned to Leslie that I might go back to work, at least part-time. Leslie took a step back and gave me a big grin.

"That's great!" she exclaimed. "I've been waiting for you to say that."

Emily looked good today. She was rosy and responsive, and she seemed almost comfortable. Leslie said her saturation levels and bowel sounds were good. The latter was an especially optimistic sign. "Listen, you can't make this place your whole life," Leslie said. "I keep telling you that. You're going to go nuts if you do—or maybe I should say, even more nuts."

The way Leslie saw it, we still had to operate on the assumption that we were in this thing for the long haul. "If all went well," as Dr. Friedman liked to say, it would still be several months before I could take Emily home.

"You need to start normalizing your life," Leslie said. "It probably wouldn't hurt for you and Fox to think about taking a weekend away somewhere."

"Oh, God, Leslie, I couldn't do that," I said. "I'd think about Emily the whole time. I'd be on the phone to you constantly. I'd be a basket case." I caught Leslie's glance. "Okay, *more* of a basket case."

But work was different. I could plan it so I wouldn't have to go anywhere. My office was on the same subway line as the hospital. I could be in easy contact by telephone. I could be at the hospital if anything happened.

My sanity—what was left of it—wasn't the only reason to go back to work. Right after Emily was born, one of my editors asked if I wanted my maternity leave to start immediately. I didn't. I didn't want to use up that precious time while Emily was still in the hospital. I wanted to be able to spend my leave with her after she came home, the way I had planned when I first found out I was pregnant—the way every other mother and daughter did.

I slipped down to the family room early that evening and called my office in Los Angeles. My colleagues were elated. If I was talking about going back to work, then things must be going well, right? My editor and I arranged for me to do an interview that had been postponed when Emily arrived. I have always operated on the theory that once you make up your mind to do something, it's better to do it right now, right this minute, than to postpone it. The longer you put it off, the longer it is not to do it, whatever it is, or at least that's the way it's always worked for me. I took a breath and told my editor I would do the interview the very next day.

At home that night, Fox was ecstatic. Working would take my mind off the hospital, he figured. Maybe he would get his old wife back, the one who was a companion, not the one who left before he awoke and stumbled home tired and cranky.

"Maybe you'll finally talk about something other than hematocrit levels," Fox said. He was boiling the water for pasta with store-bought sauce. It was the world's easiest dinner, and it was all that we had the energy to prepare.

More than once since Emily's birth, Fox had said he feared he was losing me. He felt that I was forgetting everything in my life except Emily. It was a theme he repeated tonight.

"You're obsessed," he said. "You're not the same person. You're totally wrapped up in Emily, in her surroundings. That's all you think about, all you talk about."

This is where we would start to scream and shout, and then would cry. To me it made perfect sense that I would be wrapped up in the life of my daughter—our daughter. What else was there besides this tiny child, fighting so hard for the life she was entitled to? What else compared to her courage? And what else mattered?

"Me," Fox would say. "What about me? Where do I fit into this picture? I'm your husband. I'm not the enemy. You're turning away from me. You're cutting me out. You're excluding me from your life. I matter, too. I'm Emily's father. Come back, Elizabeth. Don't do this to me. Don't do this to us."

While Fox was cooking the pasta, I had set the table, the one with the lace cloth I inherited from my grandmother. I poured us each a glass of wine.

"To Emily," I said, as if there were anyone else I would think of toasting.

• • •

The next day I went to the Carlyle to meet the young man I was supposed to interview. It was Ethan Canin, the author of the book I had been reading on the fateful plane ride. Ethan arrived without a tie, so as graciously as possible, the maitre d' threw us out of the fancy restaurant. We headed for the café, where both of us felt more comfortable. Ethan was a medical student in addition to being an author. His publisher had told him of my situation when I cancelled the first interview and immediately he asked about Emily. Ethan looked concerned; he knew how precarious the lives of very premature babies could be.

But then we talked about his book, and about his life. Things were going smoothly, I thought. I was wearing a grown-up dress, and might even pass as a normal person. We were eating lunch, just like normal people do, and talking about plots and structures and literary theory, and about love and family and the things we wanted most in life.

Just then I heard a series of electronic beeps. The sounds seemed to scream out of nowhere. I dropped my pen. I felt the blood drain out of my face. It sounded exactly like one of the isolette alarms in the NICU.

Ethan watched my reaction. "Relax," he said. He pointed to a man at an adjacent table. "It's only someone's wristwatch."

I felt as if I had just failed Normalcy 1A. It was pretty clear that I wasn't as ready to go back to the real world as I had thought. My original plan had been to go back to my office and write up the interview. Instead I fled the hotel and nearly ran the twenty blocks to the hospital. As scary as that place was, it had come to feel, in an odd way, safe. It was Emily's home. More and more I guessed it was mine, too.

Back in the NICU, I found a note taped to Emily's isolette. Now the plastic box not only held my baby, it was a mailbox, as well. I had been told that two social workers were assigned to K9, but I had yet to meet either of them. One was a short young woman with a mass of brown hair, Brenda Stone. I knew this only because she wore a name tag, not because she ever stopped to introduce herself. Chugging up and down the hall of K9, always carrying a clipboard and a thick stack of papers, Brenda forever looked too harried to talk. She had a look of remote intensity, the kind of expression that pierced through humans, wood, and walls alike in its determination to reach its final destination. Brenda had an office at the end of the hall, right next to the NICU. But she darted in and out without so much as a smile or a hello to anyone. Brenda must have been very, very busy.

The other social worker, Iris Brick, had been on vacation since we arrived in K9. Now she was back. The note taped to Emily's isolette was from her. She made it a practice to meet with all new parents of preterm children, the note said. She would be available to meet with us any time this week.

I dialed her hospital extension with eagerness. At last, I thought, Fox and I will have some kind of an emotional sounding board. In my fantasy, the social worker would be someone who could advise us on how to cope with the growing strains between us; how to redirect our anxiety about Emily into some channel that did not destroy us. I imagined a woman who was loving and wise. I figured that this woman would have had years of experience working with the parents of premature infants. Our problems would seem minor to her, and easily solved. She must have heard every story in the book.

But Iris was another casualty of an understaffed, overpopulated big city hospital. She came panting in to the NICU, fifteen minutes late for our meeting. She looked like she had just run two back-to-back marathons. Iris was a mountain of a woman, tall and quite overweight. She wore a kind of muu-muu, a jersey print dress that made her seem larger still. Still sunburned from her vacation in Mexico, she gave the impression of a giant Damson plum.

Iris barely stopped for introductions. She wanted to get right to work. "Great!" she said when we sat down in the family room for our little get-to-know-one-another chat. "You have excellent insurance coverage. That means you can afford outside counseling."

Now she actually looked at me. She had a sincere, this-is-the-way-it-is expression. Most couples whose children spent long stays in K9 experienced varying degrees of anxiety, Iris said. It was only normal. However, there was no way she could minister to all of them. People who could afford to see therapists or counselors outside the hospital were strongly urged to do so. "I really have my hands full with the public assistance cases," she pleaded. She shuffled a mound of papers like a big stack of cards. "There just isn't time for all the private patients." She looked hastily up at the clock. In fact, she said, she was running out of time now. She got up to leave for her next appointment.

Wait a minute, I thought. I wasn't through. Iris and I must have had all of four minutes together. There were a lot of questions I wanted to ask. But she was practically out the door.

"Wait, Iris," I called out to her. "Have you thought about having some kind of parents' support group up here?" Hands on her hips, Iris turned around. She wasn't glowering exactly, but neither was she looking overjoyed about what I had to say.

"Some kind of organized activity where people could meet regularly and let off steam? Something where you could trade information, and help each other during tough times?" My voice sounded shrill, almost whiny. It sounded like I was begging. I was.

"How about this?" I asked. Iris was looking impatient. She was shifting her ample weight back and forth. I noticed she was wearing backless high-heeled sandals. It was a major feat of engineering that they could support her as well as they did. "How about some kind of orientation program for when you first get here. You know, like 'Welcome to K9! Here's What To Expect!' "

Iris said her department had considered something along those lines, but nothing had gotten off the ground. The hospital population was just too diverse and too disparate. "You can't get everybody in one place at one time," she said. "It's impossible. People say they're going to come, then they never do."

Then Iris brightened. She had an idea. "That would be an excellent project for you to organize," she said. She sounded like she was talking to a mentally retarded nine-year-old. Next she was

going to suggest I make braided key rings. "It probably would help
you manage your anxiety."

I cringed. "Manage my anxiety?" What kind of talk was that?
What book of social work-ese had that phrase escaped from? Then
Iris gave me what was probably intended as a compliment. "It
looks like you're holding up all right," she said. "You'll probably
make it. You'll probably do okay."

Iris was moving toward the elevator. She promised we would
talk again soon.

The meeting with Iris had been a washout. No doubt I was
expecting too much. I heard the words *social worker* and thought it
would be someone who would make everything better. Even a little
bit better. Instead I found an overworked hospital employee.

But walking back down the hall toward the NICU, I suddenly felt my disappointment replaced with a sense of excitement.
Carol had arrived with her husband Frank. They were carrying a
ton of baby things. Carol was stuffing a diaper bag with Preemie
Pampers. Frank had a huge smile.

"This is it! This is the day!" he said. "We finally get to take
our boy home."

Carol looked up. Her grin was bigger than Frank's. "I can't
believe it," she said. "Finally. I just never thought this moment
would come."

Carol's baby John weighed just over four pounds, the cutoff
weight for sending babies home from K9. He seemed like a monster to me. Carol had dressed him in little blue overalls. He looked
like what Fox would call a real baby. The clothes were made for
Cabbage Patch dolls, Carol said. This was one of the morsels of
wisdom culled from the grapevine of moms of premature infants:
Buy doll clothes. They fit.

But the joy that Carol and Frank were feeling was tempered
with trepidation. John was still experiencing bradycardias. So along
with his supply of disposable Preemie Pampers, Carol was packing
his monitor. She said she had hired a nurse who was trained in
infant CPR.

"You're going to do fine," Carol said as we gave each other a farewell hug. "You just wait. Emily's going to be out of here before you know it. We'll be walking our kids in the park together as if none of this had ever happened." She handed me a slip of paper, a scrap she had torn off a daily chart tablet. "That's my home phone number," Carol said. "Please call any time, even if you just want to talk.

"Promise to call, please," she added in a tone of mock sternness. I nodded and bent down to smile at John one last time.

I wished that Iris, the social worker, could have witnessed this farewell scene. Carol had shown the warmth and encouragement that I was longing for. But it took a mother, not a social worker, to truly understand.

Outside the hospital, the flowering fruit trees were exploding into bloom. Clouds of white blossoms softened the city's unyielding concrete. With the profusion of sweet smells and color, Central Park had lost its menacing qualities of midwinter. Now it felt inviting, a giant garden that promised solace. Some mornings, following Robin's advice, I jogged across the park to be with Emily, and other days I took a leisurely stroll in midafternoon. In a perverse way it helped to be around all those screaming kids who were out with their moms or nannies. With very little imagination at all, I could pretend that one of the little babies in the ruffled hats was Emily and that the mother pushing the navy blue pram was me.

Her condition remained unchanged, which was to say, it wasn't great. I'd stopped asking how much she weighed. One look told me that the answer was "not enough." Emily's veins were so tiny that there was a limit to how much nutrition could be administered intravenously. The nutritionists and doctors were juggling their formulas, trying to add fats that would translate into much-needed calories for Emily. But now Dr. Friedman was advising the surgical insertion of a tube in her chest.

"Just like Charles," Leslie explained when I asked how such a device would function. It was called a Broviac tube, and it was slipped in through the baby's jugular vein. The tube allowed increased quantities of nutritional supplement to be pumped in. "She'll gain weight much faster," Leslie promised. "It's the best thing to do."

Charles had a small incision in his neck where the tube was introduced. The opening in his skin meant that all contact with Charles had to be conducted under sterile conditions. Each time the baby was handled for any reason, the nurses put plastic gloves on. Some of them wore face masks to keep from breathing germs on the baby. The first time LaTanya saw this done on a baby, she decided the child must have AIDS, and that the nurses were trying to protect themselves. "Oh, no, not him," she said when she saw Charles being treated in this fashion. Leslie explained that it was the baby they were trying to safeguard, not the nursing staff.

Leslie also saw that I was standing near Charles's isolette, staring at the wound in his neck. I was trying to figure out how the tube worked. I was also worrying about the incision.

"I can't believe you're thinking about vanity at this point," Leslie said, reading my mind. "The scar is so small it's almost imperceptible. When she grows up, it won't even show."

Without that scar, without the Broviac tube, she might not live to grow up at all. Walking in the park, I wondered how soon Dr. Friedman could schedule the surgery. There was really no option. She was wasting away, and if the NEC didn't get her, starvation probably would.

Inspired by Monique, whose baby Beverlee was making steady improvement, I'd bought a small music box in the hospital gift store. It was shaped like a little pillow, trimmed with lace and embroidered with flowers. Like Beverlee, Emily perked up and looked around, trying to locate the source of the sound when she heard its music. The song it played was "You Are My Sunshine."

So now in the park I took a giant leap into the future. I tried to put all this sickness, all this hospital stuff, far behind us. I pictured Emily at her wedding. I saw all of us—Ethan, Sarah, Fox, my mother, Leslie,—sharing in the celebration. I saw Fox beaming with pride as he took his beautiful daughter on his arm and escorted her to the floor for a dance. Emily had on a wonderful, full-skirted white gown. The song they were dancing to was "You Are My Sunshine."

"Promise me you'll come to her wedding," I said to Leslie when I went back to K9. "Promise me you'll dance and you'll throw rice. Promise me you'll be there."

Leslie did not hesitate for even one second. "I promise," she said. She gave me a big hug that seemed to last a long, loving time.

SEVEN

"You must never slam her doors," Dr. Robert Wolf chastised when I closed Emily's porthole with a little too much enthusiasm. The hospital's pediatric surgeon was a tall man in his late forties whose brown hair had obviously begun to grow thin many years earlier. The way he carried his body, lumbering a bit, it looked as if he had recently grown five or six inches and had not yet adjusted to his new stature. He had a habit of folding his arms on his chest and scrunching his eyes and his mouth simultaneously between significant phrases. It was clearly a gesture of many years' standing, and along with his galumphing walk and his mild admonishments, it gave him an avuncular quality. I wrote in Emily's journal that night that he reminded me of an overgrown Bob Newhart.

Dr. Wolf was a man given to intellectual small talk. He confessed, for example, that he was a hard-core history buff. At present, he was deeply engrossed in a recently published history of the Civil War, *Battle Cry of the Republic*. The book had received excellent reviews and was already climbing the best-seller list. The book was prompting Dr. Wolf to reconsider the presidency of Abraham Lincoln. Standing there at Emily's isolette, he conducted a small colloquy on the war between the states. In the middle of the NICU, he began quoting from the Gettysburg Address. Under the heading of "curiouser and curiouser," this small, insufferably hot room filled with miniature humans was now taking on the qualities of a university extension class. Emily's education was progressing daily.

There was also a stuffy side to Dr. Wolf. He took himself, and his medical abilities, quite seriously. On the other hand, this quality was probably an asset for a regular-sized man with large hands who performed delicate surgery on two-pound people. Still, Dr. Wolf blanched when I playfully referred to my daughter as "Mighty Mouse."

Of all the doctors I had met so far, Dr. Wolf handled Emily with the most tender touch. He lifted her legs as if they were precious porcelain that might shatter at any moment. When he probed her stomach, he stroked it softly afterward, as if that might take the sting out of it. Still, Emily winced. So did Dr. Wolf, and so did I.

His verdict was that without some dramatic and unforeseen development, Emily would certainly need surgery. At the very minimum, Dr. Wolf wanted to explore to see what damage might have occurred. If there was a blockage, he would need to clear it. It was possible, he warned, that Emily would emerge with a colostomy. But for most of these NEC babies—a generic term by which Emily was now known around the NICU—that was a procedure that could be reversed by the time the child was two years old.

I hoped Dr. Wolf was right about this, for I remembered how cruel kids could be in the locker room in junior high school, poking vicious fun at anyone remotely different from everyone else. The girl with the large breasts was always the subject of wicked ridicule, and the girl with no breasts yet was no better off. Would my child, with a plastic bag hanging out of her stomach, be viewed as a freak? Dr. Wolf seemed to share my unspoken confidence that this would even be a matter for consideration. At this time, the colostomy appeared to be the most extreme of possibilities. He seemed to be ribbing me gently as he assured me that very few of these colostomy kids went off to college with trunks full of Baggies.

He seemed sanguine, too, that once Emily was big enough, she would be able to withstand the actual operation. There were pediatric anesthesiologists who were trained to customize the anesthesia for especially small babies, Dr. Wolf told me. Once again I marveled at the medical specialties that remain obscure until one really needs them. I had met a lot of people with a lot of interesting jobs over the years, but I had never met a pediatric anesthesiologist. I wondered at what point in the process of medical school a fledgling doctor underwent a kind of epiphany and decided "That's it! That's my field!" And I thought about what brand of personality would want to spend his life putting children to sleep.

Dr. Wolf reminded me that he routinely performed surgery on preterm infants like Emily. In fact, right there on K9 there were several on whom he had operated. NEC was a very scary diagnosis, he conceded. But generally, the condition did respond to surgery. And if Emily gained enough weight and was sufficiently strong, he saw no barrier to her pulling through an operation.

His words were reassuring, and so was his manner of quiet confidence. Still, I dreaded the thought of anyone, even a man so obviously competent as Dr. Wolf, cutting into my daughter and sewing her up.

Dr. Wolf was much more sober about the scheduling of surgery. Emily was far too small to withstand it, he said. He echoed Dr. Friedman's pronouncement that it was unlikely at this small size that she could even survive the trip to the operating arena in an adjacent building. Before he could even think of operating on Emily's abdomen, Dr. Wolf said, she needed to gain weight. "The bigger she is, the better," he said. Although he had in the past performed successful surgery on babies below a thousand grams, Dr. Wolf preferred for Emily to be as large, and therefore as strong, as possible. The longer we could postpone the operation, in other words, the greater were her chances of surviving it.

"I'd like her to weigh at least one kilo," Dr. Wolf answered when I asked about his minimum weight requirement. "But bigger is even better."

A kilogram is 2.2 pounds. But Emily was so small that the method of measurement was almost irrelevant. She was not a whole lot over one pound at that point, just a little over half a kilo. Dr. Wolf wanted her weight to double.

Step one in the fattening-up process was the insertion of the Broviac tube. Nutritional supplements could thus be passed directly into her arteries. This would not only remove the strain from her tiny veins, but enable the dietitians to increase the amount of calories she was receiving.

"Can't they just give her cheesecake?" I asked. Dr. Wolf smiled, scrunching his eyes as he did so.

He presented me with a new form to sign. It was an authorization to permit surgery to insert the Broviac tube. At the bottom of the page, I saw a line marked "mother," and scribbled my name. This was the first time I was formally exercising my official capacity as mom, and I wished it were for something other than consent for surgery. A permission slip for my child to go on a field trip, for example, might have been nice, or maybe an indication to her teacher that I had reviewed her report card. As I signed the document, I was left feeling uncomfortable that the procedure was necessary at all, scared that anything would be slipped through an artery as narrow as a piece of vermicelli. At the same time I was upset when Dr. Wolf told me his schedule would not allow him to perform the surgery for at least another two days. On one hand, I didn't want Emily to have the operation at all. On the other, I wanted her to have it immediately.

As they prepared to leave, Dr. Wolf introduced me to his assistant, a surgical resident named Dr. Wayne Weissman. He was tall and trim, slightly suntanned, and wearing a fashionable haircut. I thought he looked like a tennis teacher, and could easily imagine him courtside in Miami or Beverly Hills. Until then, he had spoken not one word, but now Dr. Weissman lingered to chat for a moment. Dr. Weissman—I wanted to call him Wayne, but it was clear he took his title too seriously to permit that kind of familiarity —volunteered that in working alongside Dr. Wolf, he felt he was learning from the master. It was like an aspiring painter apprenticing with Rembrandt, Dr. Weissman was saying; "They just don't get any better than Bob Wolf." But when I questioned him, he told me he had no real interest in going into pediatric surgery at all. That was a special calling, one that demanded highly refined skills and talents, Dr. Weissman said. His own inclination, he went on, was to go into cosmetic surgery.

"Great," I told him. "Emily's scar will look terrific, and if Emily and I get through all this, you can do the face-lift I'm going to need afterward."

Sitting with Emily for all those hours, Leslie and I coined a new love name for her. We called her Emil-lee-lee, an affectionate permutation that only the two of us used. It was an indication of the deep tenderness we both felt toward this sweet pea of a child, and it was a sign of the growing closeness between Leslie and me. Because we were together for hours and days on end, we knew funny little details about each other's lives: what kind of pasta we each preferred, where we liked to vacation, the names of pets we had as children. I knew what kind of carpet Leslie was shopping for; she knew what books I was reading. She disclosed that after such long, intense days at the hospital, she hated to go home and cook for herself. Often she ate at a Greek-run coffee shop just around the corner from the hospital. On her recommendation, I tried their meat loaf one night, and the next day reported to her with gusto. Anyone who had overheard us would have thought we were discussing the chef's special at Lutece.

No matter the subject, Leslie and I talked openly, and with a growing bond of trust. We took risks, probing into each other's lives and venturing opinions with no fear of reprisal.

It certainly did not strain Leslie's powers of perception to detect the friction between me and Fox. She saw the tense politeness, and heard me snipe at him for little or no reason. She listened patiently to my complaints when he was not there. More than once, Leslie offered advice that friends who had known me for years might not have dared to dispense. In many ways, Leslie's take on the situation was even more accurate than that of the fertility shrink, who theoretically knew more about our particular psychological dynamics. Leslie, however, had watched the interaction of countless parents in her eleven years in the NICU.

She had cared for one child whose well-known parents were divorcing at the time of his premature birth. Neither parent would speak to the other, Leslie recalled. She became a kind of traffic cop in that case, she said, making sure that the two parents were never in the NICU at the same time.

"We'd get these phone calls, 'Is *she* there?' or 'Is *he* there?' " If by chance both parents did appear at the hospital at the same time, Leslie would send someone down to the family room to talk to one parent so the other could leave.

"There are parents who blame each other. I mean, publicly," Leslie said. "Can you imagine? They come in here, they stand beside their little kid, and they start accusing each other—loudly—of causing this predicament."

Leslie remembered one father who permitted his wife just one visit with their infant daughter, born with severely stunted limbs. But after that the father told everyone they knew that the baby had died soon after birth, and forced the mother to go along with his story. Nurses who called the house with information about the child were required to identify themselves by their Social Security numbers; the father kept a list by the phone. Leslie remembered the pain on that mother's face and in her voice if by chance she answered the telephone. Eventually, Leslie told me later, the father had the baby transferred to another hospital. No one knew if the child had lived or died.

Leslie told me stories like these to remind me that Fox and I were not the first to go through marital hell in the course of having a very premature infant. Like LaTanya, Leslie watched me return near tears after talking to Fox on the telephone. She was careful never to pry, but she was always willing to listen when I needed to blow off steam. That happened, unfortunately, a great deal.

We were careful, Fox and I, to try never to lay guilt or blame upon each other around the issue of Emily. But of course at some level we both had to wonder, had we done something to bring on this terrible situation? We had had a huge fight the night before I went to California. Had the screaming and yelling triggered some kind of hormonal imbalance that brought on labor? But these questions were just too painful to confront at this point, not with baby Emily holding on so valiantly.

Instead we delicately skirted the real issue, Emily, and our unutterable fears that we might lose her, and jousted over peripheral topics. Fox complained a lot about the cramped, overheated conditions of our New York apartment. It was no smaller or hotter than it had ever been, but suddenly, in Fox's view, it was unlivable. I laid into him about his sleeping habits. For his entire adult life, Fox had worked until the middle of the night, then slept until midmorning. The habit dated to his days as a correspondent in Asia, where a 5 P.M. deadline in New York meant filing a story at 5 A.M. Now I told him he was slothful and selfish. Fox had decided it was no longer workable to bring Ethan and Sarah down to New York to visit; after their last trip, the weekend after Emily's birth, they had told their mother and him that I seemed preoccupied and tense. I countered, in my most rapacious shark mode, that it was perfectly reasonable for him to fly up to Boston to see those two children, but perhaps from time to time he could take a cab across the park to see his other child. I knew it got to him to pit his children against one another. I knew it was dirty pool and that I shouldn't do it. But I was angry at the world about this lousy hand that had been dealt to Emily. I did it anyway.

"This is a terrible, terrible time for both of you—for all three of you, really," Leslie would reassure me. She said it with patience and caring. From her, it didn't sound like a lecture, or like some outsider awkwardly trying to identify with a situation he could not possibly identify with.

"Just don't do anything now," Leslie would counsel. "Don't make any decisions and don't do anything. Wait until all this is over." What she was saying, really, was: Don't leave him—not now, anyway—and don't throw him out. However this comes out, you're going to need each other when it's over.

My big grievance continued to be that Fox seemed more worried about his job than he did about Emily. I was too angry and upset to recognize, as Leslie urged me to do, that what he was doing was displacing his own anxiety. Leslie kept to her counsel. "This is the wrong time to make any decisions or draw any conclusions. Just wait."

In turn, Leslie shared intimate details of her life with me. I learned that she had struggled for years with anorexia nervosa. The picture on her hospital identification card portrayed a gaunt, cadaverous creature. In real life Leslie's brown eyes were lively, but on that laminated card they looked hollow and sunken. She weighed ninety pounds when it was taken, Leslie told me. That was when she hit rock bottom, when despair and depression made her view food as an unnecessary appurtenance. Her family worried; her friends told her she looked awful; everyone tried to get her to eat. "When you're that depressed, when you feel that bad about yourself, you just don't care," Leslie said. "It doesn't matter what you look like." Therapy and hard work had helped her to defeat that demon, and now she was twenty pounds heavier than when her identification picture had been taken. Leslie's hospital uniform— baggy pale blue pants and a loose blue-checked top—was particularly sexless, but from time to time I would see her as she was leaving the hospital in what I called normal clothes. I was always struck by how pretty she looked. Her figure looked slender and petite, not skin-and-bones skinny.

While she was working to gain weight, Leslie said the other NICU nurses cheered her on with friendly teasing. When she crossed the hundred-pound Rubicon, one nurse, Wanda, began calling her "Fats." The mood was intense here in K9. It was crowded, and the working conditions were far from luxurious. The nurses, too, went through their highs and lows, as each of "their" babies improved or faltered. A foul humor here could poison the air in an instant. Instead these women coped with the inherent adversities of their situation by pulling together. Never mind the respect with

which they treated each other—and that was enormous. The cama-
raderie they had developed was truly remarkable.

"So much for the theory that women can't work together," I
told Leslie one day.

"Yeah," she said, "but that theory was only invented by men."

Leslie and I felt like we knew each other's families. She had
met my mother, my husband, my stepkids and, of course, my
daughter. But we talked about my father and brother, too. Leslie
told me about her sister, married with kids and living in the suburbs. We talked about her mother, retired from teaching in the
New York City school system. In large part it was her mother who
had inspired Leslie to follow her path into teaching. Leslie came
from a background—increasingly rare in this day and age, it
seemed to me—where service to others mattered. Her mother had
made an investment in the future by working with children, and
now Leslie was doing the same.

We grew sad, both of us, when Leslie talked about her father.
He had died several years earlier on the seventh floor of this very
hospital. When her mother and sister folded under the strain of her
father's long illness, it was Leslie who was forced to be the strong
one in her family, Leslie who was pressed to decide that life support systems would no longer do her father any good. Leslie missed
her father horribly. "For a long time, when the elevator doors
would open on the seventh floor, I couldn't even look," she said.

But often we talked about less somber subjects. In time I
learned that the threads of russet woven through Leslie's hair came
from a bottle. Trained in the beauty academy of Los Angeles,
where natural hair color ends in the sixth grade, I prided myself on
being able to pick out a color job ten miles away. But Leslie's had
fooled me. "Henna," she said, and although the rest of her hair
wasn't red at all, the shiny strands absorbed all the color. "That's
because they're really gray," Leslie said. "And they're gray because
we're so old."

A key part of her route to recovery from anorexia had involved regaining her self-esteem, and then learning to really take
care of herself, Leslie said. In part this meant learning how to

reward herself, how to acknowledge that she was a worthwhile person who genuinely deserved a little healthy self-indulgence. Nurses' salaries are notoriously poor. It was one of the few times I heard Leslie sound remotely bitter or angry. But she had learned that spending some money on herself did make her feel better. Her hair color came from a fancy salon on Madison Avenue. Once a month, she scheduled a facial or a massage, again at an elegant establishment that made her feel pampered.

"You could use that right now," she said. Sleeplessness and anxiety were carving deep lines in my face. But in the context of a child who was struggling for life, self-enhancement felt self-centered and frivolous. I had no patience for the small luxuries that had once pleased me. What was I supposed to do, nibble on cucumber sandwiches and select nail polish colors while my child wrestled with the future of her existence?

"You're wrong, you know," Leslie said. "This is when you really need it. You're not going to do Emily any good by letting yourself fall apart."

It was advice that might equally have been offered to or extended by the broken hearts club. I knew, because I had extended the same counsel myself many times. My friends claimed that according to my medical philosophy, a nice hot bubble bath could cure anything from cancer to unrequited love. My mother had always taught me that before contemplating suicide, take the proverbial hot bath, put on a ton of makeup and a wonderful dress, and head out in the world. Now I regularly issued the same exhortation.

To a friend whose husband brought home a social disease, I railed, sounding like a street corner evangelist, "Put down those tranquilizers! We'll go and get a facial instead." When another friend found herself left high and dry by the boy of her dreams, I trundled her off for a fattening lunch at a too-expensive restaurant. A college classmate survived the alcoholic breakdown of her husband, but did not know if she would make it when his girlfriend showed up at the front door to nurse him through it. We spent the next day having Japanese massages, the kind that make your bones feel like they are cracking—the perfect antidote. In each such instance, our primary topic of conversation was exactly what Leslie and I seemed to spend much of our time talking about: men.

Leslie wanted to get married. What woman in her late thirties did I know who didn't? Certainly I had aspired to that same goal long before I met Fox. But men who were smart, interesting, and also available were rare. The paucity of decent males seemed to give the ones who were around a license to be arrogant.

"You put yourself out there, you hope, and then nothing," Leslie said. It was a familiar refrain.

Leslie's sweetie was finally back in town. It was a bad sign, we both agreed, when he didn't call her immediately. While Emily slept, clutching my finger, we discussed potential strategy, all the while keeping our eyes on Emily's monitors. It soon became clear that if Leslie wanted to see this man, she was going to have to call him. We rehearsed various possible conversations. But neither of us was prepared for the harsh response when she finally did reach him.

"He said he didn't feel 'right' about the relationship," Leslie said. I shuddered. How many times had I heard a variation of that refrain? Men who waffled, and said something stupid when what they meant to say was "I liked you enough to sleep with you, but not enough to do anything more than sleep with you." Even if Leslie was not deeply in love with this man, even if things had not progressed that far, I knew how much this must have hurt. I knew her pride and ego must be aching, and that her hopes must feel like they had been run over by a tank.

But I underestimated Leslie's guts. All those times that men dumped Drano on me, I skulked away and cried quietly for a while. Leslie handed it back in kind. I applauded her temerity.

"So after he said that to me," Leslie said, "I told him, 'Well, in that case, you must really have felt terrible about that night you spent in my apartment. I really feel sorry for you, you jerk,' then hung up the phone."

To me these lessons were at least as important as the Civil

War. If Emily was listening, we knew she was getting an earful of the eternal female verities.

In the family room on the day Emily's Broviac tube was scheduled to be inserted, Dr. Ho had been delegated to explain to me why the procedure had been postponed. If I hadn't been so mad, I might have felt sorry for this poor young man, totally lacking in anything resembling social skills, feebly attempting to make some kind of faint emotional connection. He might as well have been trying to explain quarks. It just wasn't working.

Dr. Wolf divided his time between two hospitals, Dr. Ho said. If things backed up—if one operation took a lot longer than he had anticipated, or if a genuine emergency arose—there wasn't a lot of room to maneuver in the schedule.

"This is a genuine emergency," I said. "My child is slowly starving to death."

"Right," Dr. Ho said, and before he could continue, I interrupted him.

"Wrong," I said. I felt my teeth clench, and I fought the urge to scream at this man in green hospital scrubs. "It is absolutely not right that my child is starving to death. It is completely wrong, absolutely wrong. There's nothing right about it."

"But it's not really an emergency," Dr. Ho said, ignoring my outburst. Nervously he pushed his glasses back on his nose, even though they had not fallen down. "I mean, the timing is not absolutely crucial."

"You mean if she's dying slowly it's different from if she's dying fast?"

"If it had been absolutely critical to put the tube in at a certain time, Dr. Wolf would have done it right then and there," Dr. Ho said. He was speaking in slow, patient tones. "A couple of days obviously wasn't going to make that much difference or he would have done it immediately."

Dr. Ho, a man with the personality of a tabletop, was trying to sound very calm and rational. He might, in fact, have been discussing carburetors. Medical school had prepared him for all the mechanical aspects of this job, but he was clearly out of his element when it came to the interpersonal requirements. Apparently no one had ever told him that when a child is sick, a mother becomes irrational in direct proportion to the degree of illness. Emily was pretty sick, and I was definitely distraught. I took a deep breath and tried to approach the situation on Dr. Ho's terms.

"Okay, so when can we do this?"

Dr. Wolf would not be back for at least another two days, Dr. Ho said.

Now I really hit the ceiling. "Two days?" I exploded. "Come on, two days and my daughter may be dead."

Other parents who had arrived to visit their children were donning gowns and washing up. They pretended they were not listening, but of course they could hear every single word.

Dr. Ho assured me that I was overreacting. If Emily's life were at stake at this moment, Dr. Ho was certain the surgery would be done instantly. But I had to understand, the scheduling was very complicated. Unexpected interruptions often came up.

At this point I realized I was wrong. It wasn't carburetors he was thinking about, it was airplanes.

"It's a lot like trying to schedule landings at LaGuardia," Dr. Ho said. I was not sure I was hearing him right. Was he actually likening the timing of my daughter's surgery to finding a time slot for the Pan Am shuttle? "If the weather's bad, the traffic backs up," Dr. Ho said. "Or sometimes things just get really crowded, and so the planes are late."

I decided it was time to remind Dr. Ho that we weren't just talking about inconveniences in air travel here.

"Are you aware of the insensitivity of your analogy?" I asked him. He pushed his glasses back on his nose and looked at me incredulously. He must have skipped the class in medical school about What To Do When a Parent Challenges You. "Has it occurred to you," I asked, trying to keep from shouting, "that we're talking about a child, not a metal mode of transportation with wings and exhaust pipes?"

Dr. Ho was not yet thirty, and already he had fallen into the physicians' pit of assuming that a patient would accept whatever he said with complete faith and reverence. I assumed he had gone to medical school, not veterinary school, yet here he was, treating me like a cow. I was supposed to digest his information like fine-quality feed. He glowered at me, but said nothing.

"You'd look pretty stupid if I wrote this up as a story and quoted you," I told him. I was hoping he would receive what I intended to be a gentle rebuke as an instructional message. Maybe it would help him in communicating with the next set of parents. But Dr. Ho flared. "You wouldn't dare do that," he said. "You would have no right to quote me." He got up to leave.

I still didn't know when Dr. Wolf would insert Emily's Broviac tube. I asked Felipe, the receptionist, if I could use the in-hospital telephone, then requested that the operator locate Dr. Wolf. Several minutes later, I recognized Dr. Wolf's voice at the other end of the line. It was possible, he said, that he might be able to perform the procedure late this evening, when he was finished with everything else. I panicked. This doctor was highly compe-tent, I was sure of that, but did I want him sawing into Emily's jugular vein after a long day in the operating room? Wasn't this a particularly delicate incision? "It's routine," Dr. Wolf replied. I hadn't intended to insult him, but in my concern for Emily, I had worded my question clumsily. "I'll be the judge of whether I'm too tired to work," Dr. Wolf snapped.

I hadn't realized I was speaking to him in the surgical arena. Our conversation was on a speakerphone, and everyone in the oper-ating room was listening. Now I better understood his impatience.

"I don't have time for your ambivalence," he told me. "I'll see you the day after tomorrow. We'll do the procedure then."

Leslie was not on duty when I arrived at the hospital very early the next morning. It was Georgeanne who was taking care of Emily. She told me there had been a fire at Dr. Wolf's other hospital, in Queens, and that as a result he would be able to insert Emily's tube at ten-thirty that morning. Though I felt bad for the parents of the children at the other hospital, I rejoiced that Dr. Wolf would be able to take care of Emily today. I assured Georgeanne, just in case she had had any doubts, that I had been nowhere near Queens in the last twenty-four hours.

Our usual drill was that I would wake up very early, call K9 for a report, then take the bus to the hospital. When he was in town, Fox often tried to stop by on the way to work, at midmorning, or maybe in the evening when he finally escaped from West Forty-third Street. But this morning, Fox didn't come. Calling from the telephone on the wall, I begged him to, once I learned that Dr. Wolf would perform the procedure. With a feverish mixture of terror and optimism, I urged him to hurry over.

"I can't," he said. "I'm writing inserts on my magazine piece."

After a series of postponements, the profile Fox had been working on for the Sunday magazine was finally scheduled to run. Fox was impatient with his editors, who kept ordering what seemed to be petty changes. He was anxious to have the whole project behind him.

The inserts were due by eleven that morning. By that time, with luck, Emily's surgery would be complete.

"Tell your editors the inserts are going to be late," I pleaded. He replied that I ought to know enough about newspaper deadlines to know that was impossible. If they needed the inserts, they needed the inserts, and they needed them now.

"They have kids, Fox," I argued. "What are they going to say, 'No, you can't be there for your daughter's surgery?' "

"Elizabeth—" Fox was getting impatient. He hated it when my neediness turned to pushiness.

"Anyway," he said. "The surgeon is there. There's really nothing I can do for Emily at this point."

"But Fox," I wailed, "you can do something for me. You can be here."

Dr. Wolf nodded pleasantly at me as he strode into the NICU. Fifteen minutes later he was washing his hands in the family room and depositing his pink gown in the used laundry basket.

"Everything went smoothly," he said. "She's fine."

I couldn't stop my tears. I really believed this simple operation would be Emily's salvation. My instinct was to throw my arms around Dr. Wolf and hug him in gratitude. Fortunately, my brain sensors were functioning sufficiently to convince me that this would be inappropriate.

"Thank you," I said, pumping his hand over and over. "Thank you, thank you, thank you, thank you."

Dr. Wolf gave me his scrunched-up smile.

"You're welcome," he said.

The miracle came true. Emily did begin to gain weight almost as soon as the tube was put in. My optimism returned in mammoth quantities.

"Things are looking up," I said on the message that day on the Emily hotline, as we now referred to our answering machine. "She's starting to gain weight, quickly and steadily. The doctors are encouraged, and so are we."

The Broviac tube meant that Emily, like her neighbor Charles Diaz, was now subject to sterile procedures. The nurses donned rubber gloves and face masks when they adjusted her bandages or changed her diaper. Emily's limited experience with human touch now had a rubber barrier to it.

Her latest blood donor was a colleague of mine, Richard Eder. The father of seven children, Richard leapt at the chance to help save the life of our small baby.

"That's Pulitzer-prize-winning blood," I told Emily when the packet containing Richard's blood came up from the lab for transfusion.

"For God's sake, Elizabeth, stop pushing her," Fox upbraided me. He worried that while I hailed Emily's strength and courage, I was coming to demand too much of her. More than once he had expressed concern that if we did get to take Emily home, I would have overly high expectations for her; I might say, in essence, Look kid, you made it through this awful and amazing ordeal, don't give me any of this "I can't" garbage.

To some extent his fears were grounded. My favorite people have always been those who work hard to achieve excellence. I admire people who set goals and strive for them, even if it means struggling. The funny thing was, Fox shared this view. Both of us shuddered at what we saw as a decline in standards among members of our own generation and, more fearfully, among those a generation behind us. There was a festering do-enough-to-get-by-but-nothing-more mentality that really troubled us. Coupled with the doctrine of entitlement, the result was a growing sense of complacency: Why bother to work hard for something when it's owed to you anyway? Why knock yourself out to earn something when you can just put it on your credit card? Whether it was a healthy baby, a high-paying job, or a useless bijou from electronics-land, it was your birthright, wasn't it?

So probably Fox was right. Probably I would be one of those pushy, demanding mothers who shove their children toward over-achievement and early neurosis. As Joanna's blood had dripped into Emily's body, I had reminded her that Joanna was an expert skier, tennis player, and swimmer. Ralph the architect had prompted me to lecture Emily about artistry. Now, long before she could dream of reading, I was urging her to appreciate a precision wordsmith.

"Don't worry," Leslie told Fox. "She can work it out in therapy, just like the rest of us."

Still more experts had joined Emily's team. One was a specialist in infectious diseases, Dr. Abington. His title made me think he must deal with things that came out of the Amazon. He was a taciturn fellow, all business. His expression was impossible to read, neither grim nor encouraging. His manner was somewhere between diffident and imposing. In either case, he seemed unapproachable. I started to ask a question about the possible origin of Emily's NEC, but stopped. Dr. Abington did not invite inquiry.

The mysterious stranger with the round, steel-rimmed glasses turned out to be a Ph.D. in chemistry or nutrition, Leslie said, or maybe it was nutritional chemistry. He, too, was the silent type, measuring the various tubes of lipids and other substances being pumped into Emily, then peering into the isolette to study Emily, herself. He never talked to me or any of the other parents, but once I did catch him with a half smile. Leslie said his name was Ed.

In response to Leslie's observation that Emily seemed to be favoring her right arm, and that her left wrist seemed sometimes to be flexing oddly, a pediatric orthopedist inspected Emily. He commended Leslie for her notation, then assured me that her wrists looked terrific, and for that matter, so did her arms and legs. "A natural athlete," he predicted. "Great potential muscle tone." Leslie and I looked at Emily and had to laugh. She probably weighed all of a pound and a half, and here we were, extolling her physique.

Every other day or so a physical therapist stopped by to check Emily's reflexes, and from time to time an infant kinesiologist made an appearance. The cluster of physicians attending Emily looked like an odd football team in a perpetual huddle. They traveled in a pack, with battalions of eager young clipboard-clutching interns and residents adding to their mass.

Just about the time Drs. Wolf and Weissman arrived on the scene, Dr. Alan Rosenblatt, the hospital's other staff neonatologist, returned from his vacation. From the dates that he attended medical school, I calculated that Dr. Rosenblatt was no more than forty. He was a tall man with a barrel chest and a hearty girth. Under his hospital gown he wore pastel, button-down shirts and madras-plaid bow ties. He had roundish horn-rimmed glasses and wore a yarmulke atop a haircut that made him look like Buster Brown. He came from Tennessee, and had a soft, gentle cadence that seemed like a lullaby in contrast to the rifle-fire New York voices around him.

In contrast to Dr. Friedman's peppy optimism, Dr. Rosenblatt was a perennial worrier. They made a strange team, Mutt and Jeff, Pollyanna and Cassandra. Slowly, I was learning that to get a true reading of Emily's condition I had to take an average of their various attitudes and opinions. "Doing fine!" Dr. Friedman would chirp. "Not so good," Dr. Rosenblatt would mutter. Trailed by his own marching band of residents, Dr. Abington merely cleared his throat. Dr. Wolf offered his scrunched-up smile. There was no risk of any kind of emotional involvement with them. Clearly the safe sense of detachment came with their turf. Like Gerber, babies were their business.

The charts showed that Emily was gaining weight, and my eyes confirmed this each morning when I joined her. But I also watched her writhe, I assumed in pain. Her tiny face contorted into horrible grimaces. Sometimes her hand gripped my finger in spasms, as if she were reacting to severe discomfort. "The infection persists," I wrote in her journal.

A week after the Broviac tube was inserted, Emily returned to her full birth weight. *"Mucho mas grande,"* Mrs. Diaz agreed, sharing my elation. *"Mas pequeño,"* I replied, pointing to Charles's stomach. It had shrunk dramatically. Charles's color looked better, too. At his worst he had seemed almost chartreuse. Now he was a toasty brown. He seemed more alert, too, looking up and responding to the sound of voices.

The Diaz family had conducted a remarkable vigil for this small baby. Mrs. Diaz stayed beside Charles for several hours each day. Her husband came to the hospital at least once a day, too, sometimes late at night. Very often, an elderly couple whom I took to be Charles's grandparents joined the watch as well. They were short, weathered, and gray, and displayed the same stolid forbearance as Mr. and Mrs. Diaz. If Charles survived, as it looked now that he would, he would surely be enveloped in a close and loving family.

No doubt because of her difficulty with English, Mrs. Diaz seldom spoke. Her silence seemed to give her strength, as if she had tapped in to some ancient reserve of quiet endurance. "That's one brave lady," Leslie said.

But Leslie was not on duty the day Mrs. Diaz's emotional defenses tumbled. It was Belinda, a Filipino nurse with a voice like a hummingbird, who told Mrs. Diaz that if she would like to, she could hold Charles. Mrs. Diaz was so disbelieving that Belinda sent for Felipe, the receptionist, to translate.

Mrs. Diaz watched impassively while Belinda dressed Charles in a tiny white T-shirt and wrapped him in a blanket festooned with small teddy bears. I envied her tranquility, for I knew that if it were me about to hold Emily, I would be bouncing off the walls. For just the briefest second, Belinda would have to disconnect Charles from his ventilator so she could reattach it outside the isolette. A hand pump stood nearby in case his breathing faltered. Someone pushed the blue stool over so Mrs. Diaz could sit with her baby.

In the next moment, every portrait of the Madonna and Child that I had ever seen came to life. Or rather, those works of art paled, because no painter or sculptor could hope to capture the love and joy that overtook that woman. Her face softened. All the worry and anxiety that had strained her features until now disappeared. She became ageless. Tentatively at first, she cradled the baby in her arms and looked at him in wonderment. Soon she was gently rocking him. *"Es mama,"* she whispered, so quietly that only those standing within inches could hear.

I hadn't realized how hard I was crying until I felt Belinda's arm on my back.

Are you all right?" she asked me.

I didn't want to spoil the moment with words.

"I'm just so happy for her," I said. "For them, I mean."

"It must be hard for you," Belinda said. "It makes you want to hold Emily, too."

I shook my head. Of course I wanted to hold Emily. But right now, this wasn't about me, or my remorse about not being able to caress my child. I will not pretend to be an unjealous person, but at that moment there was not one shred of envy. I was only happy for Mrs. Diaz.

Even as she handed Charles back to Belinda to return him to the isolette, Mrs. Diaz displayed a new serenity. With Charles safely sealed into his compartment, she turned and ventured a small and tentative smile. Only then did I notice that her eyes were moist as well. Instinctively, we folded into each other's arms and shared a deep embrace. On her way out of the NICU that day, Mrs. Diaz reminded me of our watchwords.

"Recuerde," she said softly: remember. She gave me a small squeeze. *"Esperanza y patienza."*

For now, I still had to content myself with fantasizing about what it would be like to have Emily in my arms, or in the arms of our family. Often I found myself visualizing her at home. The scenes were so real that I almost convinced myself they would happen. I could see Emily at various stages of development: crying, laughing, throwing food, walking. I could see her at the Glades, our summer house, chasing bunnies and running into the sea. Sometimes I saw her as a teenager, driving us all crazy by spending hours on the phone. I imagined her playing different sports—baseball, tennis, skating. Whenever I pictured Emily, she was smiling. Often she was laughing as well.

Out of nowhere while walking in the park one day, I saw all of us on a ski trip. Fox, Ethan, Sarah, and I made an annual pilgrimage to Utah to ski each winter, and on winter weekends we often tried to sneak in ski weekends in New Hampshire or Vermont. My college roommate Joanna and I had skied together in California, and also in Canada. One of our fantasies twenty years earlier when we dreamed about having children was to have kids who would learn to ski together. As usual, there were children around me laughing and shouting in the park when I suddenly had a vision of Joanna and her family and Fox and me and all of the Butterfield kids—Sarah, Ethan, and Emily—skiing in Italy. Joanna had told me about hitting the slopes there during European modeling assignments, but neither Fox nor I had skied there, or even talked about skiing there. But in my little reverie all the people around us were speaking Italian, and the signs on the slopes were printed in Italian. This whole pretend picture brought me a brief smile, for I have always figured that if you are going to fantasize, fantasize big. This one pictured Emily alive, happy, healthy—and

on skis. At the moment, that was the biggest fantasy I could manage.

I mentioned this imaginary expedition to Georgeanne, the
nurse who was caring for Emily that afternoon. Georgeanne had
an especially wry sense of humor that helped her deflect the ten-
sions of her job. She wasted no time in razzing me.

"Well, obviously, if you're going to take her skiing, you'll
have to take her nurse with you," Georgeanne declared. She assumed a sultry pose that looked particularly ridiculous in her oversized hospital uniform. "I've always had a weakness for Italian
men," she quipped.

From then on, it became a standing joke between Georgeanne, Emily, and me. From time to time, even when she was
working in different nurseries on K9, Georgeanne would glide by
Emily's isolette. "Italy," she would say in her most beguiling voice.
"Italy, Emily. Hurry and get better, because Mommy's going to
take us to Italy."

One day Fox was present when Georgeanne reminded Emily
of my bribe. He looked completely befuddled.

"Italy?" he asked. "Italy?"

Georgeanne and I replied almost in unison: "Never mind.
You had to be there."

Across the room, baby Beverlee was improving daily. It
turned out she had not had NEC, just some unexplained intestinal
disorder. Often the nurses positioned Beverlee so she could sleep on
her tummy, an option that was not available to Emily with all her
tubes and swollen belly. Beverlee seemed downright coquettish at
times, thrusting her fanny into the air and batting long, dark eye-
lashes at anyone who lingered to admire her.

"The vamp," said Georgeanne, and thus Beverlee's NICU
nickname was born.

Monique, Beverlee's mother, was looking better, too. For the
first arduous days of Beverlee's illness, she had shown up wearing
blue jeans and her Mets cap. Her hair was limp and unwashed. But
now Monique had been to the beauty parlor. In a lacy spring dress,

she was almost unrecognizable. Her whole spirit had lifted as Beverlee had pulled through.

Monique was twenty-five. In ten years she had had three kidney transplants, and still underwent regular dialysis. Her health was so precarious that doctors had told her repeatedly that she would never be able to have children. If she did conceive, they warned her, a pregnancy would seriously jeopardize her health. But Monique fooled them. She had had not one baby, but two. Antonia was born first, weighing three quarters of a pound. Beverlee came next, at two and a half pounds. The doctors thought Antonia would die at birth. To Monique's unending pride, she had lived a day and a half.

"I had Antonia cremated," she said one day. "I'm keeping her in a little urn in the living room, on the coffee table." Even with Beverlee making such a strong recovery, she did not want to be separated from the smaller of her twins.

When we were together, LaTanya, Monique, and I would complain about whichever doctor or nurse was driving us crazy that particular day. LaTanya had a special gripe about one of the night nurses. "She doesn't ever tell me anything," she grumbled. "I call, but she won't say anything. Just 'He's fine, I have to go.' "

Sometimes we gossiped about other parents. We were all somewhat steamed, for example, about Maria, who had come to be known as the Drug Mother. Monique said Maria had been caught in the act, stealing money from someone's coat in the family room. It validated Monique's suspicion that Maria had stolen her money and keys. "The hospital knew what was going on," Monique said. "They just didn't do anything." LaTanya was more concerned about Maria's baby. "She's just going to take that baby back to a house full of drugs," LaTanya said. "What kind of life is that?"

We could also marvel at our small miracles, our babies. When full-term babies were sent to the NICU, we would look at them with a curious kind of horror. Babies of six or seven pounds—never mind eight pounds or more—looked grotesque to us, almost deformed. Our eyes and senses had adjusted to thinking that babies came in two-pound packages. "Who would *want* one that big?"

LaTanya said one day when an eight-pounder with a suspected heart problem was sent to the NICU. All three of us—LaTanya, Monique, and I—had had vaginal deliveries. We shuddered to imagine what it must be like to give birth to one so huge. "How do they get them out when they're that big?" I asked.

We made plans for a K9 reunion. We took pictures of each other with our babies so that many years from now, the children would know what all this looked like. We speculated playfully about which of his K9 girlfriends Jacques Louis would choose, Emily or Beverlee.

We tried not to sound foolishly optimistic. But among each other, we could drop our guard and pretend that the future was not an illusion.

"I think he'll choose Emily," LaTanya said one day after Monique had left. "I kind of hope he does."

I walked over with her to admire her little boy. Jacques Louis was gaining weight steadily. LaTanya and I were shoulder to shoulder, peering in at her baby. In every possible sense, we felt very close.

"Me, too," I said.

 EIGHT

Swirling out of her throat, Emily's Broviac was taped to her chest in a little serpentine heap. Atop her isolette, a clunky looking Harvard pump steadily pushed liquid diet through the tube. Very premature infants like Emily are so small that they must be fed almost constantly, and in very small quantities. In Emily's case, the nutritionists had devised a regimen high in lipids, or fats. Robin and I watched the thick white fluid creep through the tube. "Every woman's fantasy," said Robin. "A nonstop diet of milk shakes and whipped cream."

Whatever the magic formula they had arrived on, it seemed to be working, for Emily appeared alert and was steadily gaining weight. The antibiotics seemed to be taking effect. "Today I felt we were getting our old Emily back," I wrote in her journal.

Daily X-rays continued to indicate that the initial damage caused by the NEC did not seem to have worsened. Bowel sounds, albeit dim, bolstered the heartening suggestion that Emily's intestinal activity had not come to a halt, a constant threat with NEC. The intestinal disease experts adhered to their theory that Emily had incurred an intraabdominal abscess that could be removed once surgery was feasible. Even Dr. Rosenblatt, the perpetual pessimist, ventured the occasional note of his version of cheer.

"Uh-huh," Dr. Rosenblatt would say. But his face, when he said this, looked less granitelike, and his fingers were crossed.

Outside the NICU, meanwhile, Fox and I were endeavoring to conduct at least some semblance of a normal life. We still went to the dry cleaner, we still bought muffins at the bakery across the street each morning, we still read the newspaper and watched the eleven o'clock news, and we still pretended to care about the events of the world. Fox went to work each day, making his way through the panhandlers and the hard luck cases on his way to the Seventy-second Street subway. At Times Square, he often saw the same heart-ripping scene of a young woman begging while her baby crawled on the filthy steps of the subway. The child's face was smeared with dirt, her hair was unwashed and stringy, and she sucked on a bottle that sometimes rolled down the steps along with her. As a correspondent in Asia all those years, Fox had witnessed and reported on equally sad sights, over and over. But now this daily reminder of the extremes of childhood tragedy took on a new perspective: Emily in her clear plastic box, fighting for each moment of an uncertain future, and this small, nameless child on the steps of the subway, breathing without appurtenance, but with no firmer prospect of hope or opportunity. Childhood is supposed to be a joy, not a battle, Fox would think as he dropped coins in the baby's mother's outstretched cup.

His work on the Tawana Brawley story, in which a black teenage girl claimed to have been abducted and raped by white police officers, meant he was spending time in the Hudson Valley, where the incident was alleged to have occurred. He hated the drive up the windy Taconic Parkway in what seemed to be a never-ending cold spring rain. He despaired of dead-end reporting on this story that frequently really did take on the dimensions of the proverbial wild goose chase. And in unhappy, late-night phone calls from Poughkeepsie, he often complained that I was failing to show sufficient interest in his work. Fox liked to remind me that he had made major compromises in his career for me. He never did like New York, he kept telling me, but he had moved there for me.

He would rather have had a foreign assignment, but here he was, toiling away in the United States—and he was doing it for me. I could have moved to Washington to be with him, he would charge. And if he hadn't moved to New York, we wouldn't have had Emily.

These charges never failed to get a rise out of me, for it was still my view that Fox was more involved in his job than he was in the baby. Kate, the fertility shrink, persisted in her position that Fox and I were a textbook illustration of the way men and women bring differing interpretations to the same problem. Fox's anxieties showed up in his relationship to his work, and his feeling that I was obsessing about Emily at the cost of everything—and everyone else—in our life. Our mutual assaults functioned in much the same way as Emily's Broviac tube: in through the jugular, and dumped directly into the belly. Only what we were depositing was not nutritional supplements, but pure bile. We not only yelled at each other, we also left angry, accusatory notes. I took to dreading the sight of yellow-lined paper on the table.

"Fox identifies with his job," Kate would tell me in calls I placed through the hospital phone system. She was always very calm and dispassionate, and I always felt, and sounded, completely frantic. Fox had his share of telephone sessions with Kate, as well. It was as if we were tattling, as if we both knew our behavior was reprehensible, but we wanted Kate to say that the other guy's words and actions were even more reprehensible.

"Everything else is topsy-turvy," Kate would reassure me. "He needs to feel that there is some stability, some predictability, in at least that one area of his life, his work." Besides, as Kate bloodlessly pointed out, Fox and the *New York Times* had been together a lot longer than Fox and I.

Though I resented his absences from the hospital, part of me had to admire Fox for his continuing ability to function professionally. On that front, I was a mess. Leslie, Pat, and others kept encouraging me to try to integrate my job back into my life. Emily was doing well, they said, and her progress would continue whether or not I was there at the hospital, hovering over her isolette day and night.

But I hated going into my office. I hated fielding what I took to be insincere inquiries about Emily from people whose actual motive was to ask me to do something. I hated going over the story, time and again. I hated the way people who knew nothing about prematurity seemed to attach magical significance to the exclusive topic of her weight: "Oh, you mean she doesn't weigh two pounds yet?" These were the same people who never really got it about the incredible highs and lows of premature existence. They wanted things to be steady and predictable. They wanted her to weigh five pounds so that she could then be delivered to us, on schedule. If they seemed genuinely interested, I would run through the medical game plan: We're trying to fatten her up so she can have the surgery, then we'll see what happens. But even this was too conditional for most people to accept. They wanted concrete answers. They wanted predictability. "Great!" they would say. "So she'll have the surgery and then you'll bring her home!"

It was hard enough to fend off these people, whose failure to understand the precariousness of Emily's tiny life depressed and confounded me. But what I hated even more were the people sitting around me who could not even bring themselves to say, "How's she doing?"

So I took to sneaking in after hours. I was spending at least twelve hours a day at the hospital, anyway. If I left there at eight o'clock at night, my office was sure to be empty. My concentration level was limited, making it impossible for me to think about working a full eight-hour day, in any case. This way I could put in a good four hours, going through my mail, sorting through telephone messages, and even communicating by computer with Washington and California. I could file stories, or I could electronically edit those that had been filed earlier. It was a depersonalized way to do business—no unnecessary human contact, no petty and meaningless exchanges, no risk that I might use my AK-47 tongue to tear some hapless victim to shreds. I loved it.

"You're cutting people off," Fox warned. "You're closing

them out so they couldn't help you even if they wanted to, even if they tried."

I protested. But of course he was right.

It took almost a month for Emily to regain, and finally surpass, her birth weight. Despite my ongoing remonstrations that "weight isn't the only criterion here, you know," I felt jubilant the morning Emily weighed in at 780 grams—twenty grams more than the day she was born. We all made jokes about how her new nickname should be Miss Piggy.

"The next landmark is a thousand grams," Dr. Friedman said. He was obviously pleased with her progress, but the goal seemed unimaginably distant. He might as well have said a thousand pounds.

The NEC was in a "holding pattern," Dr. Friedman explained. There was no evidence that it was getting any worse, but also no indication that it had improved. We just had to keep hoping that Emily would get big enough for surgery. Once the damaged areas were snipped out, Dr. Friedman believed, Emily could proceed with a speedy recovery and eventual discharge from the hospital. He still held to his original projection that Emily might well be able to go home in early July, right around the time that she was supposed to be born.

Since it seemed as if things were going well, Fox and I felt bolder about enlarging the scope of our own life. We decided it would not be disloyal to Emily to accept a few invitations, maybe even see some old friends. At some level we knew this was essential, because we were in serious danger of hacking away at each other like a pair of starved hermit vultures. On the other hand, even vultures would probably stop at fatally attacking their own mates.

I had painfully mixed feelings about expanding my world beyond the confines of our apartment and K9. One day, while taking a walk near the hospital, I had been gripped by guilt when I found myself lingering in front of a store window filled with colorful spring dresses. Window shopping! I shuddered (although it had

always been one of my favorite mindless activities). What kind of a
mother was I? How could I even think about about shopping or
personal adornment at a time like this?

So it was a godsend to disguise some of those gingerly at-
tempts at a social life in the cloth of professional obligations.
That way, I could assure myself that these encounters were really
necessary, part of our jobs, not just some decadent expression of
self-involvement. It still felt strange to be thinking about even
pretending to enjoy ourselves when our daughter was working and
fighting so hard.

By another happy coincidence, I was assigned to interview
Frank Ching, the author of a new book about his thousand-year-
old Chinese family. Frank and Fox had been pals in Hong Kong
and Beijing, but had been out of touch in recent years.

Frank's book was immense. He seemed to have decided to
devote a page to each year of Ching family history. In the past I
had always tended to recoil at Big Books, as in Yikes! No pictures!
But now, sitting at the breast pump four times a day, I had come to
love books that were big, chunky, and as escapist as possible. My
powers of retention were limited, but for the short term, I could
devour these big meaty tomes while the milk machine gnawed
away.

Ancestors, Frank Ching's book, transported me to an ancient
culture in another part of the world. By the time we were to meet
with Frank and his wife Anna, I felt prepared to conduct an intelligent conversation.

But as we sat down to dinner, my confidence deserted me. We
had picked a glittery restaurant near Rockefeller Center that served
something that might be called nouvelle Chinoise cuisine. The
place had gotten glowing reviews. It was filled with trendy, glamorous people wearing the kind of clothes and jewelry I could never
understand, much less carry off; even the hostess was wearing Gior-
gio Armani. The conversation had the urgent hum of a huge jet
about to take off, and the waiters seemed to have perfected the
science of bored impatience. There were a lot of people wearing
strange hairstyles and ugly eyeglass frames that years ago would

have been considered hopelessly nerdy. Now they were Haute Nerde.

It was not so much that I felt dowdy and out of place, which I did. It was that all of this felt terribly extraneous. After weeks of discussing Preemie Pampers and blood gases, I wasn't sure I could manage anything else—and I wasn't sure that I wanted to. About China, all I could remember was what Noël Coward once said: "China. Big." My own world these days was just the opposite: Baby. Small.

Fox saved me that evening. Numbly I took notes and asked the occasional idiotic question. Fox kept up a conversational pace that allowed Frank to be interviewed without even knowing it.

It was not a success, this tentative foray into the world outside Prematurityville, but for some reason, we decided to try it again several days later. It was as if we were still operating on some unspoken assumption that if we could act normal, our life might become normal. Fox kept comparing Emily to what he called "regular" babies, or sometimes "real" babies. I hated both terms. Even so, at some level, we both seemed to think that if we could regularize our life, then maybe Emily would become regular, too.

Once again, we used a professional commitment as our ruse. "Do it," Leslie urged me when I told her about the black-tie dinner that PEN, the international writers' organization, held annually. "It'll do you good to get dressed up," Leslie said.

But walking into the ballroom at the Hotel Pierre, I felt the same sense of being a complete alien that I had experienced at dinner with the Chings. If extraterrestrial creatures really were living among us, I had to admire them for having conquered this feeling of complete weirdness. I felt no more comfortable than if I had just landed on Asteroid X.

The room was filled with famous authors and high-powered publishing types. In this crowd, the conversation really was about compelling social issues. While they reached for canapés and juggled slender goblets of champagne, guests in formal attire were discussing censorship, imprisonment, and other hideous violations of human rights around the world. But they were also talking about big advances and outrageous agents' fees. Literary atrocity seemed to know no limits.

The room was ostentatiously decorated, with four-foot-tall flower arrangements on every table. The color theme was a smoky blue with glittering gold. After the sparseness of K9, it all seemed so unnecessary, so excessive. Was one of these famous writers going to jump up and shout, "Après moi, la deluge?"

From across the room I spotted a woman I knew from publishing. She was tall, blonde, and beautiful. Just a week before Emily was born, she had had a baby girl of her own, at the same hospital. Oh, God, I thought, please don't let her come over here right now and talk about babies. I don't think I can listen while she describes her baby's most recent accomplishments. I just don't think I can smile politely if her husband pulls out pictures.

I was lucky. We exchanged a smile and a wave, but neither of us made any effort to approach the other. Weeks later I learned that that very day, her little girl had undergone tests for cystic fibrosis. Blessedly, the tests were negative. The child was fine. But I will always regret that we did not stop to comfort each other that evening, that we did not take time to share the sheer terror of being the mother of a small, sick child.

After dinner, I told Fox I wanted to go to the hospital. It was almost midnight, and we were dressed to what they used to call the nines. "Are you sure?" he asked. I glowered at him, and without further question, he gave the cab driver the address. The night guards there were a fairly strange group anyway, but then so were we parents of NICU infants.

"K9," Fox said to the startled guard as we clipped past him in full evening regalia. Upstairs, we washed to the elbow, as always, and slipped on our pastel smocks. This late-night crew barely knew us, but if they were surprised to see us at this hour or in this attire, they never showed it. As Georgeanne liked to remind us, they had already seen it all.

"She's sleeping," Emily's night nurse, Claire, said. "And she looks very comfortable."

I just needed to see her, not even to touch her. Why disrupt what looked to be a moment of perfect rest? The tape holding her breathing tube in place looked tight; it was pulling slightly at her chin. My instinct was to reach in and loosen it, but that surely would have awakened her. I decided it could wait until morning.

"Good night, sweet Emily," said Fox. "Daddy says good night." His voice was very tight, the way it gets when he is trying not to cry.

Back at our apartment, the Emily hotline remained very much in operation. The calls from friends and family were a constant source of encouragement and support. The briefest messages— "We're thinking of you," "We're praying for you," "We're pulling for you"—offered enormous comfort. With the time difference working in my favor, I could call friends on the West Coast late at night, New York time. But often I was just too tired.

Most days, I left the apartment too early to return the calls to California. Sometimes I called from the pay phone in K9's infamous family room, but it was Fox who fielded most of the phone calls. "It just keeps ringing!" he would complain. "I can barely get out of the house."

His old friend David, his roommate from college, called regularly. So did a handful of mutual acquaintances. But mostly it was my network of women friends, my "committee," as we called these soul mates of many years' standing. Scattered throughout the country, they sent cheerful cards and little gifts and bombarded our phone lines. Some had never even met Fox until our wedding. Some had yet to meet him. In the dim and distant days before Emily's birth, Fox had sometimes expressed what sounded to me like jealousy about my relationships with many of these women. He feared that I shared more with them than I did with him. Curiously, they became a kind of life net for him, as well.

"So what's really going on?" Joanna—or Ruth, or Sharon, or

Ellen, or Diane, or Patricia—would ask after she had been briefed on Emily's health.

"How are *you* holding up?" Elizabeth, a friend in Los Angeles, always remembered to ask.

"This must be really hard on you two," Mary, Cecilia, Lucinda, or Carol would remark.

And soon, in long, heartfelt conversations, Fox began to truly understand the rich nature of women's friendships. From far away, these friends listened with no hint of judgment. Their love and support came free—and freely.

Still, for all their compassion and concern, these friends could not be expected to begin to understand the bizarre world that Fox, Emily, and I were inhabiting.

One evening while Emily was sleeping, this gap between what I used to think of as real life and what went on in the NICU became especially clear. I was sitting quietly with Emily, perched on the blue stool as I often did, when I looked up to see a young woman gazing at my child. Her expression was one of complete understanding. She, too, was blind to all the tubes and monitors. What she saw was simply a tiny child.

"She's so beautiful," the woman said. She was about thirty, with light brown hair and soft brown eyes. She was completely at ease in the NICU—a veteran, I figured out at once.

"This was Timothy's spot," she said. "What's your child's name?" She read the name tag. "Emily? Emily is in Timothy's spot."

She explained that Timothy was the smaller of her twins. He had spent weeks and weeks in the NICU, right here, in the very spot where Emily's isolette was planted. Paul, Timothy's identical brother, had already been sent home. Timothy was in the well-baby nursery. The doctors expected that he would be released any day.

"Emily's really sick," I said. "NEC."

"Listen, we nearly lost Timothy a couple of times," she said. "Not to NEC, he never had that, but to other problems, big problems, with his lungs, mostly. It was awful. I don't have to tell you how scared you get."

"But you know what? I think this is a lucky spot. We saw a lot of babies die while we were up here. But Timothy made it, even though there were a lot of times when the doctors didn't think he would. I think Emily's going to make it, too."

The next morning, there was a note taped to Emily's isolette. We had never bothered to introduce ourselves, but now I learned that Timothy's mother's name was Megan. She lived just fifteen blocks away from us. She had confessed the night before that she was more than a little scared about having both her boys at home. In her note, she was offering me moral support, and inviting me to stop by and give her some. It was another gray, drizzly day. "Hang in there," Megan wrote, "and remember that April showers really do bring May flowers."

Several days later, another pair of K9 alumnae returned for a visit. There was a great commotion in the family room, where a small crowd had assembled. Several of the nurses were there, as was Felipe, the K9 receptionist. Monique and LaTanya were both sitting on the plastic couch, too. There we all were in our pastel smocks, looking very much like overgrown nursery school students who were about to start a finger-painting project.

"They used to throw me out of here," an immense black woman was saying.

"Like you, Mehren," Georgeanne said when she spotted me. "We had to make her go home at night."

The mother must have weighed close to three hundred pounds. In a big, multicolored sweater, she looked even larger, and was holding court like some visiting celebrity. But the real star attraction was her little girl. I judged her to be about two. She was wandering from person to person, studying each face carefully with a kind of childlike omniscience. Don't try to put anything over on me, this kid was saying with her steady gaze. I've already seen more than most adults can hope to experience in a lifetime. In one hand this sage little moppet clutched a doll with long, silky, lavender hair.

"Valerie Patricia Leticia Margaret Antonia," the mother said when I asked the little girl's name. "I named her for all my sisters, plus Valerie, just because I liked it. I had a lot of trouble getting pregnant, and if she was going to be my one and only, I had to take care of everybody with one name."

She was recalling how for months, she had done everything short of camping out in K9.

"A real pain in the ass," Georgeanne said. But she said it with fondness, and the mother took it accordingly. Just like me, I thought, and Georgeanne and I laughed as our eyes met briefly.

Valerie had been born at just a little over twenty-five weeks. She was another child who had come early for no apparent reason, a story that was getting to be very familiar around K9. The doctors did not think she would survive her first two days. According to her mother, Valerie had encountered every possible pitfall of prematurity.

"You name it, she had it," the mother said.

"NEC?" I asked. For the baby's sake, I hoped she had avoided this particular peril. But looking at this inquisitive, happy little girl, it would have provided a perverse kind of consolation if the answer was yes. If Valerie had beaten NEC, I could definitely have hope for Emily. That's what they should do, I thought. They should bring in survivors of these awful preemie scourges and show us neurotic mothers that some kids do make it.

"No, I think that's the only thing she missed," the mother said. She gave me a soft look, the expression of someone who has also stumbled through this particular form of trench warfare. "Is that what your baby has?" she asked. I shook my head yes. "Mmm," she said. "That's rough."

"Cerebral palsy?" asked LaTanya.

"Honey, they all have cerebral palsy." It wasn't an especially funny response, but we all laughed anyway.

"Yes, she has a little bit of it," the mother continued. "She gets physical therapy. She'll be fine."

Valerie had crawled up on my lap. With one hand she was stroking her doll's hair, and with the other, mine. I found myself squeezing this little bundle, living proof that you really could walk out of this place in one piece. Suddenly Valerie tugged hard at my hair.

"No, Valerie, it does not come out," I explained. The child laughed, and so did the rest of us. I hugged her tightly.

"What if I want to keep her?" I asked Valerie's mother.

"No way. Don't even think about it," she said, smiling. "I worked too hard for this baby to ever let her go."

Her good cheer and her energy were contagious. I went back to be with Emily feeling buoyant. I laughed to myself when I realized that this odd sensation was called confidence. I had almost forgotten what it was like.

Sometimes, sitting with Emily, I leafed through the big blue binder atop her isolette that contained her daily medical evaluations. A lot of it was hard to understand, in part because the doctors tended to have such awful handwriting, but in larger part because it was written in medicalese. I could figure out that "meds" meant medications, but after that, with a series of numbers and pharmaceutical abbreviations, I was lost. The notations from the nurses recorded things such as Emily's still inflated abdominal girth, the status of her lungs, her excretory functions, and her response to various daily procedures. Reading any of it helped increase my sense of involvement with this small, plastic-encased person who was my daughter. I was still engaged in mothering-at-a-distance, and any small crumb of information made me feel less excluded.

Since I was in a particularly upbeat frame of mind following the encounter in the family room, I was surprised when Leslie chastised me for an action that by now was something of a daily habit.

"I'm afraid I'm going to have to ask you not to read Emily's record book," Leslie said. Her voice was more formal than I had ever heard it, as if she were speaking to a stranger. Her face looked cold, too.

"What?" I said.

"It's against hospital policy," Leslie said. "I've been asked to tell you that you are not permitted to read a patient's records so long as the patient is in the hospital."

This edict puzzled me. Leslie and who knows how many other nurses had watched without comment for weeks while I paged through Emily's records. It was a moment before I realized Leslie was looking over my shoulder, behind me, and into the hall while she spoke. I waited just a moment, then turned around to see Carolyn Foreman, the head nurse of the NICU, standing in the hallway. Whether or not she was listening to every word, she was certainly watching as Leslie gave me this new set of instructions.

I turned back to Leslie and lowered my voice. "Is this some new mandate?" I asked her. "Is this some new rule they dreamed up this afternoon? You know perfectly well that I've been reading this book every day since Emily and I got here. No one has ever said a word. Why now?"

Leslie directed her eyes toward Emily. "Look, Elizabeth, personally I don't care whether you read her records or not. I can also see why you would want to, although it's certainly not the world's most stimulating reading material. But I have to tell you that you're not permitted to do it, and that if you continue to do so you may be asked to leave the NICU. And now I think we'd better drop the subject."

The head nurse had walked into the NICU.

Since Leslie's shift was almost over, I waited until she had left for the day before I asked to see Ms. Foreman. Ms. Foreman was a tall woman who wore horn-rimmed glasses and favored tweedy, conservative attire. Often, when she was in K9, her silk bow ties would bounce out over her pastel smock. She did little hands-on nursing since it seemed to occupy most of her time just to oversee the functioning of nursing services here on K9. Ms. Foreman was crisp and efficient, a woman who was clearly covetous of whatever power she could carve out.

I asked her about Leslie's pronouncement.

"Those records are hospital property," Ms. Foreman said. "They do not belong to the patient or to the patient's family."

"But am I not entitled to information about my child?"

"I'm going to tell you again. The records are hospital property. You are not permitted to read them or even look at them. If you do, we will make arrangements to bar you from the intensive care area."

With that she turned and walked away. I wondered if this little exchange would be included in Emily's records. Somehow, I doubted it would.

One of the wonderful things about working with Leslie was that no tension or bad feelings ever stayed in the air between us. The next morning we were old buddies again, Emily's mom and Emily's Aunt Leslie. We both knew she had been put up to what had taken place the day before. There was no reason to talk about it. Instead we talked about the latest good news, which was that baby Beverlee had been moved to the well-baby nursery next door. Whatever intestinal problems she had had turned out not to be NEC. She had responded well to treatment and seemed to be on a healthy path toward leaving K9.

To celebrate the event, Monique had gone to Macy's and picked up some preemie clothes for Beverlee. "I wish they hadn't had to shave her head like this," Monique said when I visited her that afternoon. Beverlee had had an IV line running into her head, and to accommodate it, the NICU nurses had had to clear the area of hair.

Since Emily had been born, I hadn't had a chance—or the nerve—to think about clothes. Early on, a good friend in California, a fashion writer named Mary, had said on the telephone that she wanted to be able to picture Emily in her isolette. "What is she wearing?" Mary asked. I burst out laughing, because of course the answer was nothing. Now, as I shared Monique's excitement about her daughter's new wardrobe, I did feel a little pang. Would Emily ever wear anything other than a breathing tube and a Preemie Pamper?

Beverlee's new outfits looked like they had been made for fashion-conscious mice. They were pink, and remarkably tiny, a little top and matching bloomer-style shorts. Holding up this miniature outfit, I was carried back to childhood. "They look like doll clothes," I told Monique. My own favorite plaything, after all, had been a baby doll considerably larger than Emily.

Compared to the tightly regimented NICU, the well-baby nursery seemed like a playroom. Whereas virtually all contact between babies and parents in the NICU occurred through portholes, in the well-baby nursery, Monique could lift the plastic hood off Beverlee's isolette, seemingly at will. She was allowed to sit with the child, actually holding her. It was a pose I had often seen Carla assume with Molly, across the hall in another of the nurseries. In spite of myself, I often felt envious. I knew that this experience of having a premature child was an ordeal for every mother up here. But now Monique was clutching her child close to her, unsaddled with tubes, and actually changing her clothes. I had yet to so much as hold Emily. The closest I came to holding her was when I would lift her little fanny to slip a fresh Preemie Pamper, no bigger than a purse-sized tissue, under her. In bleak moments I wondered if the day when I would get to hold Emily would ever come.

The move out of the NICU had had its effect on Monique, too. She was looking better and better. She smiled more readily and seemed less oppressed by the hospital atmosphere. Soon LaTanya joined us, too, and watched admiringly while Monique deftly dressed Beverlee in her new clothes. How, I wondered, had Monique become so adept at this process so quickly? If this were Emily, I thought, I'd be afraid I might break her. LaTanya and I were both a bit in awe, for not only was Monique touching her child at will and changing her clothes, but the whole time, she was conducting a running dialogue about the stroller she was about to buy for Beverlee. Now that Beverlee was definitely coming home, Monique continued, friends were planning to throw a shower for her. She knew they would buy her lots of wonderful gifts, maybe even a crib. "But a stroller's something you use so much," Monique said. "You want to be able to pick it out yourself." She had her eye on a lavender one. Though Emily weighed significantly less than Jacques Louis, LaTanya and I still shared the dubious distinction of being the mothers of the smallest babies in the NICU. For us, buying a stroller seemed too far into the future to contemplate.

Monique had brought a Polaroid camera with her, so we snapped some pictures of her with Beverlee. The prints reminded us, just in case we had forgotten, that even though Beverlee seemed immense, she still barely filled up Monique's forearm. This huge strapping behemoth of a child weighed all of about three and a half pounds.

"These pictures are awful!" Monique said with what I hoped was mock displeasure. "Beverlee's got her eyes shut in every one of them."

She slipped Beverlee out of her new party clothes and returned her to her isolette. When Beverlee was promoted to these new quarters, she also moved on to a real diaper—one that actually closed around her with little tape grips. The effect was to make her look not just bigger, but also healthier and more mature. More like the "real babies" that Fox kept talking about.

I noticed that Beverlee's little music box, the lacy little pillow-shaped toy that had inspired me to buy one for Emily, had made the trip from the NICU with her. It was sitting in a corner of Beverlee's isolette, not far from the wedding picture of Monique and her husband that was taped at Beverlee's eye level. LaTanya and I wandered back to the NICU to assume our places next to our own babies.

Without thinking, I wound up Emily's music box and it began playing for her. Instantly, she awoke and looked around to place the source of the sound. Her responsiveness made me ashamed for having lapsed into a moment's self-pity. Emily was tough, that was for sure, and above all, she was brave. So many adults I knew knew nothing of the kind of pluck and fearlessness that Emily showed us daily. To people who led comfortable, unchallenged lives, courage was a mere abstraction. It meant nothing until it was tested. Emily's courage was tested with every breath she took.

She grabbed my finger and squeezed tight.

• • •

Two days later, on Leslie's day off, one of the Filipino nurses, Belinda, approached me as I was sitting with Emily. Belinda had an almost musical lilt to her voice, and I loved to hear her talk. She and her husband, a male nurse who worked in another hospital, had come to the United States for the higher salaries offered to health care workers. Six months ago, they had had a little girl of their own.

Early on, Belinda had given me a little spiral-bound baby book that was designed especially for newborns who required intensive care. It was called *Footsteps,* and Belinda told me it was the last copy in the hospital. One of the administrative types, she said, had decided they were frivolous giveaways whose cost could no longer be justified.

Belinda had enormous brown eyes that always looked cheerful, as if someone had just told a good joke. She seemed dauntless, always full of energy when she started an afternoon shift that would see her working until late at night. Despite my entreaties to the contrary, she persisted in calling me "Mrs. Mehren." I would tease her, and tell her that Mrs. Mehren was my mother. But that was my name to her, so that was what she called me.

"Mrs. Mehren," she said this afternoon. "Would you like to hold Emily?"

I was not certain I had heard her correctly.

"Excuse me?" I said.

Belinda understood why her words would be impossible for me to comprehend. So often, Belinda had been there to shore me up when bouts of negativism came. Don't worry, she would tell me. It's going to be all right. It really is.

"I said that if you would like to, you can hold Emily today," Belinda said. "I'll just need to get a T-shirt, a hat, and some blankets for her to get her ready to be moved out of the isolette."

"Why are you even asking me, Belinda?" I said. Suddenly I felt I had been basked in hope. In Renaissance paintings there was always a great band of light from heaven, and right now I felt like I was standing in it. "I mean, is there a question? Of course I want to hold her."

Belinda disappeared for a moment, then returned with a front-wrapping T-shirt that would have been too small for the baby doll I grew up with. Lifting the lid of the isolette ever so slightly, she managed to dress Emily in it without disrupting any of her tubes, pipes, or sensors. Emily was fretting and protesting while she dressed her. "She does not want to wear clothes," Belinda said, laughing. My daughter, the nudist.

I found an institutional gray folding chair that I thought would be more stable than the fabled blue stool. Gently, Belinda scooped Emily out of the isolette. For a moment Emily was disconnected from her breathing tube so Belinda could reattach it outside the isolette. Belinda was an expert at this procedure. It went off without a hitch.

And then she was handing me my daughter.

The blanket Emily was swaddled in had little bunnies on it, just as I had imagined. She was wearing a knit cap, pink and blue stripes, so small it might have covered a golf club. Emily was wrinkling her forehead in what Belinda and I took to be dismay. If this seemed like the most natural moment in the world to me, it must have seemed strange and foreign to her.

She slipped into my left arm and I gazed at her in wonderment. All the books and experts insist that premature infants lack the ability to focus even on close objects, but I swear that she returned my stare. I found myself softly rocking her. It was a natural gesture, one I didn't even have to think about.

New babies have the most remarkable aroma, the scent of pure freshness. There is no fragrance like it in the world. Emily's whole short life had been spent in this hermetic environment, so she retained this magical bouquet. I hoped it would glue itself inside my nostrils so I could summon it up forever.

There I sat, mesmerized. Belinda had cautioned me that Emily should not be out of the isolette for very long—not, anyway, on this maiden voyage into the world. Holding Emily's breathing tube, she gave me a little sign. Not much longer, it said.

I bent down to give Emily her first kiss, planting it right in the middle of her forehead.

"This is called a kiss, and it's from Daddy and me," I told her.

Unaccustomed to this kind of expression of physical contact, Emily grimaced. Had she been able to talk, she probably would have squealed, "A kiss! Yuck!"

The small ring of spectators who had gathered around us laughed, but I refused to be dissuaded. This was an unreal moment for me. I was holding Emily, my child, and kissing her.

"This one is from Ethan, Sarah, and Grandma Jean," I said, and repeated the ritual.

And finally, a third kiss, "From everyone else in your whole world, baby Emily, because all your world loves you so very much."

Belinda rolled Emily into her own arms and swiftly returned her to the isolette. The hat, shirt, and blanket came off; the tubes were repositioned. Emily was lying on her back, looking, I thought, a little befuddled.

There were hugs from all the nurses. I looked up, and there was Mrs. Diaz, standing tentatively in the doorway. She hugged me, too.

"Esperanza," I managed to sputter through tears that were threatening to cause a flood.

"Esperanza, siempre," she agreed.

Never give up hope.

At home that night, I could not stop talking about how it felt to hold Emily, about what an incredibly encouraging moment this had been, about how sweet she smelled, about—

Fox stopped me when I got to the part about the kisses. Angry words and nasty notes were forgotten. He bent down and gave me a soft kiss on my forehead, just where I had kissed Emily.

"And this one is for Emily's mommy," he said. "From Emily's daddy."

NINE

After lunch one day, I returned to K9 to see two women I didn't recognize sitting on the legendary plastic couch. In a less generous frame of mind or in a less enlightened era, I would have thought of them as little old ladies, for all they were lacking was tennis shoes. Instead, I chided myself for ageism and assessed them as older women. As I smiled at them, I wondered idly whose grandmothers they were.

Both had recently had their hair done, all sprayed and stiff. One had white hair; the other had tinted hers to a chestnut color. They had long, thin faces, sharp noses, and exactly the same ectomorphic body type. Both were sitting in the same pose, hands crossed over large handbags—the kind you actually carried with your hands, not strapped across your chest in the manner of the veteran New York City subway rider. The one with the white hair was wearing a pink hospital smock, while the brunette had taken a yellow one. They were sitting so close together that their knees and shoulders touched. Things tended to get pretty absurd here in the strange theater of K9, and at any moment, they looked like they might break into a chorus of "We are Siamese, if you please. We are Siamese, if you don't please."

"We're the great-grandmothers," they declared in perfect unity.

"Baby Field," they said. I suppose I must have looked blank.

Speaking over my shoulder while I washed up at the sink, I allowed as how baby Field—Molly—was lucky to have two great-grandmothers, much less two who were willing and able to make the trek to the hospital. The one with the white hair said she had taken the subway, or the train, as she called it, in from Forest Hills, in Queens. The other had driven in from a suburb on Long Island. They expressed surprise that I would think it unusual to have great-grandparents.

"Doesn't your baby have any great-grandparents?" the brunette asked.

I dried my hands and forearms and told this nice older lady that this was a subject of great disappointment to my husband and me. I deeply wished that Emily could have met her great-grandmother—my grandmother. But not only did she not have great-grandparents, she did not even have two sets of grandparents. My husband's parents had been dead for many years, I said, and the two great-grandmothers shook their heads sadly. My own parents were very far away. We all agreed this was a shame.

Again it looked as if they had rehearsed the movement when the two women stood up at the same moment. They walked, naturally, in rhythm, as if each step had been choreographed. Clutching their handbags close to their chests, they joined me as we headed down the long hallway. The one with the brown hair suddenly whispered conspiratorially.

"We're not really the great-grandmothers," she said. She blurted the words out, then looked around to make sure no one had heard this confession.

"Well," she added, and gestured with her eyes toward her companion, "she is." The white-haired one beamed.

"I'm the great-aunt," the brown-haired one told me. They both smiled approvingly when I commented that no wonder they looked so much alike, obviously they were sisters. I was not quite sure why they had chosen to enlist me in their plot, but I decided to take it as a compliment. We all knew that great-aunts were not on the approved list of visitors here in K9. Once again, Carla and her family had managed to outsmart the system.

"We'll come visit your little baby," the real great-grandmother said. "We'll be her great-grandmothers."

The proscription on visitors was one of the drawbacks to life on K9. I understood the rule, and it made perfect sense. The place was small and quarters were cramped. Doctors and nurses did not need hordes of visitors making noise and clogging up what little space there was. Besides, these very small babies lacked effective immune systems, and so sanitation was vital. The hospital couldn't have crowds marching in and out, spreading who-knew-what kind of germs and bacteria. Besides, if the hospital hadn't put limits on who could and could not see the babies, people like Carla—and probably me, too, I realized—would have run tour buses down the long hall.

Now that my mother had gone back to California, Fox and I had no family to share Emily with. So I was thrilled when Kate Patterson, the fertility-shrink-turned-marriage-counselor, told me she would try to stop by the NICU. Kate was on staff at the hospital; in her white jacket, and with her official name tag, she could walk in at will.

"Dr. Patterson," she said with authority as she breezed past the receptionist's desk. Kate seemed to have been born with a stunning degree of self-assurance. Just try and challenge me, her body language announced.

But even Kate, this personification of worldly competence, was rendered humble by the sight of the tiny people who populated K9 and the NICU. I was sure that in her practice, Kate had learned to register no reaction when clients unloaded their deepest secrets on her. But when she first caught sight of Emily, I watched a transformation. Kate's face softened. Her eyes widened, and she broke into a smile I had never seen before. Even her voice changed.

"Elizabeth, she's magnificent," Kate said in a soft tone. "Look at her. Look at those tiny feet. Look at her hands and her ears. They're perfectly formed. They look like little pink shells."

In an instant, Kate's professional guard had dropped. All her weighty credentials had suddenly become irrelevant. She had gone from superpsychologist, well-known specialist in issues of infertility and sexual dysfunction, to universal mother. As per the canons of her calling, Kate had revealed little of herself during the several months when Fox and I had sporadically seen her. But I knew she was married and that she had children who were in college and graduate school. She was only a few years older than Fox.

"God," she said. "What a beautiful baby."

That comment made me laugh outright.

"I notice she's no longer a fetus," I said. For quite some time, Kate had refused to concede babyhood status to Emily. Her theory seemed to be that if something awful happened—that is, if Emily were to die—bonding with a fetus would prove less treacherous than bonding with a baby. For the first week or so of Emily's life, Kate had cautioned me against establishing too close a relationship with her. She tended in those early days to discuss Emily as a kind of abstraction. Apparently she could talk about a fetus in an almost cavalier fashion, but a baby was something else again.

"No, this is definitely a baby," she said.

Kate walked around so she could view Emily from every possible angle. She looked like someone inspecting a major work of sculpture, or perhaps an expensive new car.

Now it was Kate's turn to laugh, for she knew the advice she was about to give me was so ridiculous. "It's probably all right for you to start bonding with her now."

I told her I thought we were a little beyond that.

There was one nonfamily category of visitors that was permitted on K9, and that was clergy. Several times I had been present when a tired-looking priest, one of those Central Casting guys with the gray hair and jowls, had shown up to administer last rites to some baby who was not expected to make it. It was distressing when this happened, because the baby was about to die, and because the poor priest looked so beleaguered. Once I remember one of the priests coming in very late at night, when even the family of the baby in question had gone home. His clerical collar stood up above the regulation K9 smock. He looked very haggard.

Between Fox and me, organized religion had been a sort of pass-the-subject issue. Whereas I welcomed the sense of intergenerational community that came with church membership, Fox chafed at what he saw as rampant hypocrisy among many churchgoers. "How many people actually live by the tenets they espouse one morning a week?" he would ask, not entirely rhetorically.

Yet, for my part, I continued to cherish my sporadic correspondence with a dear friend who was an Episcopal priest in my old hometown of Santa Monica. Some years earlier, Malcolm Boyd had become a kind of celebrity when a collection of his poetry, *Are You Running With Me, Jesus?*, soared to best-seller lists. Before joining the priesthood he was a veteran of the film industry who had worked with Mary Pickford; he was a tireless political liberal who had been active in the civil rights movement; and he was one of the first prominent members of his church to come out of the closet. When I lived in Santa Monica, I loved going to Malcolm's church because it was such a curious combination of high Anglican ritual and leftist politics. We were always praying for countries I had never heard of, presumably because they hadn't existed the week before.

Malcolm called one day to say he would be in town to meet with his publisher. He knew Fox and I must be going through a rough time. Maybe I would like to have lunch?

I leapt at his invitation. Better yet, I said, let's meet for lunch near the hospital. That way, I told Malcolm, we could walk over to see Emily afterward. Malcolm was clergy. Finally, I thought, someone with whom I could share our beautiful little girl.

Malcolm is short and cherubic, with blue eyes that really do twinkle. It took him about thirty seconds to charm the nursing staff of K9. Leslie, a student of comparative religions, among other topics, had read Malcolm's book. I think she was only sorry that she didn't have a copy with her for him to autograph.

Very soon after Emily's birth, another old friend in Los Angeles had Federal Expressed me a copy of *The Book of Common Prayer.* "This may help," Lucinda wrote. I had stored it in the cupboard space beneath Emily's isolette, and sometimes read during long, lonely stretches in the NICU.

Malcolm was downright gleeful when I produced the book. "Let's read her some psalms!" he said.

He made a wise selection. The Psalms were about all I did remember from my brief exposure to religion as a child. My parents were an odd mixture of an ex-Catholic, Dad, and a fiercely agnostic Protestant, Mom. But thinking, that, much like horseback riding, good table manners, and a passable presence on the tennis court, every nice young lady ought to spend time in Sunday school, they sent me to one of those generic Protestant churches where we spent most of our time doing coloring books of the Bible. Since we were living in California, Jesus always looked like one of the Beach Boys, with blue eyes and flowing blond hair. Mary tended to have an Earth Mother quality, like someone who would shop at the natural foods co-op.

We were big on Christmas pageants—lots of gazing off into the horizon and proclaiming, "Hark! A star is risen in the East." And we did read and study the Psalms. We sat in a circle, and in clear children's voices recited these short sacred songs. Now, as Malcolm and I stood alongside Emily's isolette, he thumbed through the book to locate his favorites.

"How dear to me is your dwelling, O Lord of hosts," we read to this child dwelling in a clear plastic box. "My soul has a desire and longing for the courts of the Lord. My heart and flesh rejoice in the living God . . .

". . . Happy are they who dwell in your house, they will always be praising you. Happy are the people whose strength is in you."

Malcolm was captivated by Emily. All her tubes and equipment amazed him. He was particularly curious about the respogle tube that drained green fluid from her infected belly. But it was the baby who really entranced him. "A revelation," Malcolm said softly when he first looked at her. At first when we arrived she was asleep, but soon she was wide awake, tugging hard on her breathing tube. She seemed to be looking directly at Malcolm. While he was standing there, he swears that she smiled at him.

What happened next was not something we had planned. It was not, as Fox, feeling slighted, would later charge, part of some grand conspiracy to exclude him from decision-making about Emily or to impose my will over his. It was not, as Fox later felt, that I was acting as if Emily was only my baby, not his, too. But in the spirit of that moment, we decided to christen Emily. What this was about, we agreed, was less some statement of religious ritual than of introducing Emily to a broader community of souls.

Leslie brought Malcolm a jar of sterilized water—the same water that was used to suction the babies. What a shame the company that produced these little jars of hospital-approved water did not know what was going on. They could have added a whole new endorsement: "Approved for use as emergency holy water!"

Malcolm slipped his hand through Emily's porthole. This was something we were doing for Emily. In large measure it was a demonstration of our belief that she belonged not just to Fox and me, but to the world. Besides, as Malcolm said, Emily was a mirror of courage, and, "we have courage in God's presence."

Malcolm, Leslie, and I traded big hugs. We were only sorry we could not pick Emily up and pass her around for a hug, too. For now, we had to hope she knew just how much she was loved.

Not every baby on K9 was so lucky. One child, a little girl, had been visitorless the whole time that Fox, Emily, and I had been in residence. One day, the little girl, Carrie Lynne Smith, seemed to return my attention when I talked to her. She had such huge, empathetic brown eyes that I impulsively started to pop open her portholes to give her an affectionate stroke. Leslie saw me and stopped me before I got myself in big trouble.

"Elizabeth, don't. You really can't do that," she said. "If you touch a child other than your own, they'll throw you out of here forever."

It was relatively early on in our stay, and I didn't yet know all
the rules. My gesture was well-intentioned; Carrie Lynne just
looked like a little girl who needed some love. The expression that
she gave me seemed to cry out for interaction. Hug me, I thought
her big brown eyes were saying. Touch me. Treat me like a baby.

The strange thing was that her eyes could not have been
sending me such a message. Carrie Lynne was blind from birth.
She was also born mentally retarded. She had severe breathing
difficulties that the doctors said would plague her for life. There
was no hope, Leslie said, that any of these conditions might reverse
themselves.

Leslie explained that Carrie Lynne was suffering from something called Reger's syndrome. It was a rare chromosomal condition, she said—one of those awful things that most people have
never heard of. Unlike Down's syndrome, or some of the other
more familiar genetic abnormalities, Reger's was something one
would probably not even recognize if it showed up on an amnio
report. Carrie Lynne had inherited this vicious condition from her
mother.

"The mother is fifteen and a half," Leslie said. "Mentally
retarded. And blind."

By itself, each element seemed imponderable. Carrie Lynne
had already had two major eye operations. She would never see. At
the age that Carrie's mother had borne this child, I was still selling
Girl Scout cookies.

Taken together, Carrie's problems were overwhelming. When
I focused on them separately, I kept coming back to age. I was
again struck by the nagging reminder that I had waited far too
long to have a child. If I had started at Carrie's mother's age, my
child would now be twenty-five, and probably thinking about children of his or her own.

Carrie's grandmother was younger than I was, about thirty-
three, Leslie said. "Certainly no older than thirty-five." Carrie was
born in late January, two months before Emily. The grandmother
had been to see the baby once, several days after her birth. But
since then, no one from the family had visited Carrie, or even

called more than once or twice to find out how she was doing. The K9 nurses had called and called, urging the grandmother to visit and suggesting that she bring Carrie's mother in as well. But the grandmother said she couldn't make the trip to the hospital. The young mother was incapable of traveling to the hospital on her own. So Carrie stayed there by herself.

Well, if I couldn't touch Carrie, I could at least talk to her. I could try to offer her some kind of stimulation, let her listen to an adult voice. I thought she must be very lonely in there, in her little plastic habitat, all by herself, all the time.

Whatever the hospital had been feeding her must have worked, for by preemie standards, Carrie was kind of a tub. She had chunky little thighs, whereas Emily had legs that were lean and slender like a racehorse or, to be more blunt, skinny and brittle-looking. Carrie's face was full and soft. She had thick, healthy-looking black hair that curled in great cascades all over her head. Many of these premature infants seemed to come in odd hues. Where there was jaundice or kidney problems, the children were yellowish. Those in need of transfusions could look vampire-like in their paleness. The ones who had just had transfusions were rosy to the point of florid, as if they had overstayed their time in a tanning parlor. Very sick babies looked gray. But Carrie was a warm brown from head to toe. She was a beautiful, healthy-looking baby.

From a medical standpoint, Carrie Lynne was making good progress. But once she was discharged from the hospital, life ahead was questionable. "If the grandmother says she can take care of her, then there's not much we can do about it," Leslie said. From the point of view of the state, medical intervention was apparently appropriate, but moral intervention was not.

The next day, Belinda decided it was time to give Carrie Lynne a bath. As skillfully as she had lifted Emily out of her isolette, Belinda raised the lid on Carrie's see-through house. She carried on a running conversation with the baby while she scrubbed her plump little body, then shampooed her soft, curly hair.

The baby was tolerating the experience so well that Belinda decided Carrie could use some further stimulation. She raced to the supply area and returned with a K9-issued preemie outfit—little shorts and a T-shirt.

"Sorry that they're blue, Carrie, but that was all we had," Belinda told the child. "You don't care, do you?" Belinda put her nose right next to Carrie's while she spoke.

"Carrie, Carrie, you need some cuddles," Belinda was saying to the child. With Carrie still tied umbilically to her breathing apparatus, Belinda was bouncing her and talking to her softly.

Carrie Lynne should have been laughing. Wasn't this what every little child loved, to be caressed, hugged, held? Didn't every little girl long to be told she was beautiful and special?

But Carrie's face was contorted in a terrible grimace. Her cheeks were wet with tears. She was crying. But of course with a tube locked in her throat, there was no sound, not a sob or a whimper. Even when Belinda returned her to her isolette, Carrie's silent tears continued.

I was such a fixture in the NICU that when Dr. Friedman drifted in with his band of eager interns and residents, they would sometimes fail to notice me, and forget to tell me to leave. This little ritual always made me laugh, for they looked like insects in a swarm—like some weird exercise in human biology. There they were in paper shoes and pastel smocks atop blue hospital pajamas, hovering around Dr. Friedman, the chief insect. They traveled silently and en masse, peregrinating from station to station. Once they began their little synopsis of each patient's condition, I would take my cue to leave.

"Hold it, guys," I would tell them, for often they had overlooked my presence. This much I knew about hospital policy—that rules of confidentiality prohibited me or anyone else from being present during these medical rounds. I was not even permitted to listen in while Emily's condition was assessed.

But late at night, the rules tended to ease up. No one did rounds, but since babies were inclined to ignore the clock when it came to their delivery times, very often, new arrivals came in to the NICU at strange hours. Usually I had gone home by then. Fox and I generally tried to have dinner together, though often this did not transpire before nine or ten o'clock at night. One night when Fox was out of town, I was still at Emily's side at around eleven o'clock. A new baby—a twenty-seven-weeker—had been whisked up from the delivery floor. The child was splayed out on a warming table at the far side of the NICU.

For a lot of reasons, I tried to ignore the flurry that surrounded these new admissions. Even without knowing the parents, I tended to sympathize with their right to privacy. Also, I was beginning to realize that there were things I didn't want to know; that each time I learned about a new horror of prematurity, it became another potential terror for Emily.

On this night, the physician on duty in the NICU was Dr. Milo. He was a pediatric cardiologist whose Polish-sounding surname actually had about thirty-two syllables. For purposes of simplification, he used only the first two. Lean and lanky—a runner, I was told—Dr. Milo was joined tonight by a young woman doctor I didn't recognize. She barely reached Dr. Milo's chest, and had her hair pulled back in a cap, a sure sign that she had been in the delivery or operating room. The two of them were going through the standard procedure that accompanied every new admission to the NICU. With a checklist in front of them, they were marking off each detail of the child's anatomy. One would call out the parts; the other would note their presence or absence.

"Nose?"

"Check."

"Mouth?"

"Check."

"Eyes?"

"Two. Fused."

"Throat?"

"Ten."

"Birthmarks?"

"None."

And so it went, down the list. They were so efficient that they might have been quality control inspectors on a Detroit assembly line.

Except that even these marvels of medical proficiency could get silly from time to time. I had tuned out on whatever might have preceded their difference of opinion. But when their anatomical litany abruptly stopped, I realized that something was going on.

"Whaddya mean, no breast buds?" Dr. Milo was steaming at his colleague.

She stood her ground. "The kid's got no breast buds," she repeated.

"How can you say there are no breast buds?" Dr. Milo challenged. "What do you call those things right there? Those are obviously breast buds."

His associate was unswayed. "No breast buds," she said again.

Dr. Milo had an idea. He would call for an outside opinion.

"Get Mehren over here!" he demanded. "She's been here long enough to know as much about this as we do."

I looked up, and Dr. Milo was gesturing for me to come join them at the warming table. They looked exhausted, but were smiling anyway. I think this is what you call giddiness.

"Okay," Dr. Milo said sternly. "Take a look at this baby. Does she or does she not have breast buds?"

I stared at the child for a moment.

"What's a breast bud?" I asked.

"Exactly!" Dr. Milo's colleague said with a triumphant note. "She doesn't see them either. No breast buds, just like I told you."

"No, wait," I said. "I mean, I have no idea what I'm supposed to be looking for."

"A breast bud is the beginning of a breast," Dr. Milo said. "Breast buds—get it? Like the way a bud is the beginning of a flower?"

I looked carefully at this tiny female child. She was still boiled-lobster red. The babies who were stretched out on the warming table like this always reminded me of butterflies in a case. Around here, they were not much bigger, either.

Staring at her small chest, I thought I detected two minute dots.

"Those things?" I asked Dr. Milo.

"Aha!" he exclaimed. He nodded a bit too knowingly at his associate. If I had been her, I probably would have punched him out.

"Breast buds," he said. Case closed.

A few minutes later, Dr. Milo approached me at Emily's isolette. He and some other staff members were ordering out for Chinese food. Would I like something, he asked?

I wasn't hungry, it was late at night, and I didn't think I could face a plate of greasy carryout Chinese food. Still, I recognized this as an important ritual of acceptance. "Sure," I said, and reached into a shelf under Emily's isolette to retrieve my purse. "How much do you need?"

Of course within twenty-four hours, it was as if none of these late-night follies had taken place. The next time I saw Dr. Milo, striding down the hall in his burgundy Ben Franklin glasses, he looked right through me. He did not return what I intended only as a friendly smile. Here was another NICU regulation: Things that were silly by night were apparently not to be referred to by day.

But silly things did sometimes happen by day, such as the surprise birthday party the nurses organized for Felipe, the receptionist. Georgeanne slipped out during her morning break and took a cab to the Baskin & Robbins store ten blocks away.

"She better get the right one," Felipe muttered. Actually, Felipe had not only ordered the cake, he had orchestrated the entire event.

At lunchtime, the nurses gathered in the staff lounge. Off-limits to parents, this was the room where the nurses, and often the doctors as well, gathered for breaks and for meals. It opened right on the main hall, with no door. When you walked by, you couldn't help hearing bits of conversations, such as today, when Robin was trying to jam birthday candles into the frozen cake without breaking any of them. "Shit!" she said, then covered her mouth in mock embarrassment. "I mean, oh darn." Finally she was satisfied. "Go and get Felipe," she told Wanda, another nurse.

Felipe had a side business cutting hair for the nurses and interns. His own hair was an orangish sculpture that added two inches to his height. Felipe was theatrical to the core, and wanted to make sure he made the proper entrance. He stuck his head through the doorway. Satisfied that his audience was ready for him, he stepped back into the hall, then pranced into the staff lunchroom with a mixture of nonchalance and expectation.

"Surprise!" they all cheered.

Felipe stopped dead in his tracks.

"Oh, come on," he said, hands on his hips. "You can do better than that."

He sounded like a veteran drama coach instructing his cast in their roles. What he wanted, he said, was enthusiasm. Make it sound real, earnest, like it was coming from the heart.

Felipe returned to his entry position in the hallway. Again he sauntered into the lunchroom. This time the chorus was deafening.

"Surprise! Surprise! Surprise!"

Felipe grinned in appreciation.

"Much better," he said.

Then, reverting to his own role, he continued: "My goodness! A surprise birthday party! Why, you didn't have to do this! And look, an ice cream cake! Oh, chocolate! My very, very favorite . . ."

A little hint of comic relief snuck in, too, the day before Mother's Day. It seemed strange that on a Saturday, there would be so few visitors on K9, but the place was almost deserted. Very few parents were around, and no supervisors or bureaucratic paper-clip-counters either. There was so little to attend to that Robin, Emily's nurse that day, had turned the radio to a soft rock station.

For me it was a day of special jubilation. Incredibly, Emily had hit one thousand grams, and had added an extra sixty grams as well. The Broviac tube was working, and she was doing her job of gaining weight. Since the tube had been inserted, her size had almost doubled.

"My daughter, the overachiever," I told Robin while we crowed about Emily's accomplishment. She weighed more than a kilo now, the magical figure Dr. Wolf had established as the threshold for performing surgery. Emily's X-rays continued to offer encouragement. There seemed to be no indication of further blockage in her intestines. From time to time she had passed small amounts of blood with the tiny mucoid stools that were the product of her Hyperal diet. Dr. Rosenblatt kept telling me this was to be expected. Maybe Emily had a small internal abrasion, he said. He did not think it a worrisome sign.

On the contrary, Drs. Rosenblatt and Friedman continued to adhere to their theory that whatever damage had been caused by the NEC would be corrected by surgery. She was too active and alert to be desperately ill. A completely nonfunctional digestive system was the worst imaginable outcome of NEC. If that had happened to Emily, the doctors pointed out, how could she be gaining so much weight?

The place was relatively calm, for a change. I was feeling light-headed about Emily's big weight gain. The radio was filling the room with easy listening: Stevie Wonder, Christopher Cross, Dionne Warwicke—nothing that required any effort. There was even sunshine outside. Suddenly, Robin had a brainstorm.

"Emily needs a hair ribbon," she announced.

I agreed. She deserved some kind of big gold star for reaching and surpassing her weight goal. Besides, she needed to be reminded that she was a girl. A hair ribbon sounded like a great idea. There was just one problem. Emily's hair was thin, and often it was almost glued to her scalp by the safflower oil we continued to rub all over her body. It made her look sort of punk, like a baby who had already decided she preferred the shiny look of gel to the fluffy look of mousse. Next, I supposed, Emily would ask for a black leather jacket and multiple pierced ears. But what I couldn't figure out was how Robin proposed to make a ribbon stay tied.

"No problem," said Robin. "Watch this."

She went to a supply cabinet and returned with a pair of
scissors and one of the face masks the nurses used when working
with babies who required completely sterile conditions. The masks
tied on with little white bands, which Robin deftly snipped off. She
took one of the bands and tied it in a bow. Then, using medical
tape, she attached it to the side of Emily's head.

"Oh, it looks fantastic!" We both cheered. Robin ran to get
the Polaroid camera that was kept locked up in a cupboard on K9.
We snapped one picture, then another.

"Okay, ladies," Robin announced to all the female residents
of the NICU, "everybody gets ribbons today."

Soon Robin and I were mutilating the face masks, saving the
string and dumping the mouth covers in the trash. I tied the bows
and Robin taped them on the babies. Still in our goofy frame of
mind, we stepped back to admire our handiwork. I thought Carrie
Lynne looked the prettiest, because she had the most hair. But
Robin was partial to baby Valenzi, in the corner, a child who had
had been born with major heart and lung problems. Baby Valenzi
seemed to be getting stronger every day.

It was at that moment that baby Valenzi's father walked in.
Slight and balding, he was one of the few men who regularly
visited the NICU. He seldom spoke to anyone, not even to say
hello. But I always felt that he was kind of eavesdropping. I had
this sense that he was one of those gluttons for other people's
troubles. Certainly I had known plenty of women like that. The
mother of a girl I grew up with was like that, always ready to feed
on someone else's problems. And this man reminded me of her, the
village vat of communal woes. Maybe by filling up his own tank
with the ills of others, his own looked less menacing by comparison.

Baby Valenzi's father looked quizzically at his daughter's new
hair decoration.

"Everyone got ribbons," Robin said. Five minutes ago it
sounded hilarious. Now Robin's explanation sounded weak, almost
apologetic. With a withering glare directed jointly at Robin and
me, baby Valenzi's father removed his daughter's bow. Robin

shrugged and returned to her nursing duties. I noticed that she turned down the volume on the radio, too.

No matter. I thought Emily looked gorgeous. Now that she weighed more than two pounds, she looked enormous. I barely even saw all the tubes and pipes and sensors and monitors. It was true that her entire hand wrapped around just one knuckle of my finger. But I didn't notice that any more, either. I just marveled at the strength and sureness of her grip. I referred to this activity as "playing with Emily." Again, it was a matter of making the best of what we had.

That was what I was doing when Dr. Friedman walked in. He seemed to move on his own odd mode of energy. He burst from place to place, without using any visible means of locomotion. It was as if he were some sort of chemical reaction.

He may have augmented this impression by his tendency to begin a conversation with no preliminaries. Never "hello," or "how are you," or some other pleasantry. Dr. Friedman dived right in, right to the guts.

"Now that Emily is big enough for surgery, you know there is a possibility that what we will find in there is massive necrosis," Dr. Friedman said.

As usual, he was leaning against her isolette. I still had my hands through Emily's portholes. I was still in the playful frame of mind that had begun earlier in the day with Robin. I was not sure I had heard him right.

"Excuse me?" I said.

"Well, we haven't really talked about this. I mean, I know I've mentioned it to you and raised it as a possibility, but it isn't something we've discussed at any length. But you do have to be prepared for the fact that we may go in there and find rampant damage, necrosis, from the NEC. It doesn't happen often, but it does happen, and you should be aware that this is a possibility. Of course, there would be very little we could do for Emily if this did turn out to be the case."

There is an old expression, "to drop a bomb on someone." All of a sudden I understood the full impact of the phrase. I felt as if

Emily and I had just been targeted by Dr. Friedman's personal bomber.

As gently as I could, I extricated myself from Emily's grip and snapped her portholes shut.

"By 'in there,' I gather you mean her intestines," I said.

"Well, yes, of course. We're hoping Bob Wolf will be able to do this surgery soon—this week. We need to talk about this so we can know what you expect us to do if we do find extensive and irreparable necrosis."

There was, of course, no place to sit. I refused to join Dr. Friedman in using my daughter's isolette as a leaning post.

"What exactly are you asking me?"

"Well, we need to know your preference," Dr. Friedman said. "Whether you will want us to take extraordinary measures to save Emily if we do find that kind of damage." I watched him shift his weight from foot to foot as he prepared to launch into his medical lecture mode.

"In the event of massive necrosis, we may be faced with the situation of trying to piece together whatever small sections of her intestine there are that can still be salvaged. Now this, of course, is possible. We may be able to—"

I had to interrupt him.

"Dr. Friedman," I began. "Do you really think this is the time or the place for us to be having this conversation? I mean, it's the day before Mother's Day, I'm standing here, playing with my little girl, and you come over and dump this on me?"

I had noticed in the past that Dr. Friedman did not respond well to anything he took as a challenge to his authority.

"This is something that has to be discussed," he snapped. "It happens to be relatively quiet here, and I happen to have some time right now."

"Yes, and I happen to think that this is a subject that should be discussed jointly with my husband, Emily's father, don't you?"

"You seem to have some trouble getting him here," Dr. Friedman said. It was a low blow.

I suggested to him that perhaps we could eliminate personal

digs and approach this question in a professional fashion. "Let's make an actual appointment for sometime when the three of us can sit down together. Let's meet somewhere else, not in the NICU, where we're not leaning against Emily's isolette. Let's sit quietly so that you can explain what we can and can't expect from surgery, and let's all three of us go over the options."

Dr. Friedman said he would be off for the next few days, so we agreed to meet at eleven o'clock Wednesday morning. I suggested we meet at Dr. Friedman's office or somewhere else in the hospital, I was not sure where, but he seemed uncomfortable with this idea. We agreed instead to meet at the receptionist's desk.

Dr. Friedman turned to leave.

"Did you see Emily's hair ribbon?" I asked him.

He looked quickly in Emily's direction, but did not meet my eyes.

"It's very nice," he said. As quickly as he could, he left.

TEN

That Sunday was Mother's Day, and for once our dark little apartment was flooded with light. It streamed through the lace curtains, dancing on the walls in little sun-tracings. Our wrought-iron bed was squeezed into an alcove, with barely a centimeter to spare.

As part of our ritual in this made-for-one, now-inhabited-by-two living space, I had learned to step over Fox without disturbing him. I slept closest to the wall, and even in the best of times I slept far less than he did. I had always managed to function on a minimal amount of sleep. These were definitely not the best of times. In these stressful days I seemed to have pared even my normal minimum in half.

I was not quite sure why I was so enthusiastic about Mother's Day. It, like Father's Day, had always been a kind of antiholiday in our weird Berkeley household when I was growing up. It was a merchant's holiday, my father the cynic used to growl, "an invention of the greeting card companies." They never turned down the gifts or cards that Peter and I made in school. But our parents, who seldom agreed about much of anything, firmly adhered to their premise that children should not need one special day each year to acknowledge their mothers and fathers. Appreciation should be a year-round phenomenon, they maintained in lectures that often grew too lofty for their own good.

In principle they may have been correct. But today I almost felt like Ethan and Sarah on Easter morning, looking around for the goody baskets they regarded as their birthrights. It was Mother's Day, and for the first time ever, I was a mother. Fox and I had a child, a beautiful, alert, active little girl. At last I was officially entitled to celebrate this day.

I had done my best to shake off my unhappy conversation of the day before. "Friedman needs to see us both," I told Fox. "Wednesday morning." Fox pressed me for details, but all I told him was that he wanted to discuss Emily's upcoming surgery. I had almost convinced myself that that was all that would be happening.

So there I sat with the breast pump, now none-too-lovingly known as the milk machine. I had a cup of herb tea, and the Sunday paper spread out before me. While the machine tugged at my breasts, I could try to persuade myself that the events in the world were more compelling than the daily drama of our own lives.

"Good morning," Fox said when he stepped out of the bedroom. He was rumpled and unshaven. He held a large box behind him. He had a big smile because he knew that for once, he had actually managed to surprise me.

"This is from Emily and me," he said. "It's for you, for Mother's Day." He leaned over and kissed the top of my head. "Your first, the first of many."

The box contained a wonderful dress from one of my favorite stores. It was sea green, Fox's and my favorite color, with a delicate provincial print. "I thought it looked like something we would decorate with," Fox said. I loved the silly combination of smug and humble that always surfaced when Fox knew he had hit something right.

"Hold it up," Fox said. The machine was still pumping; I still had the plastic cone that sucked milk out clamped to one breast.

"Oh, sure." I was a disaster waiting to happen. If I held up the dress, I would probably either knock over the milk machine or spray Fox and most of the room with mother's milk.

Instead, he held it up and pirouetted, as if he were a fashion model. "Just my size," he said. It was an especially sweet gesture for him to have chosen something designed to make me feel soft and pretty. In truth, I still felt lumpy, and had been far too preoccupied with Emily and the events at the hospital to think about whether I had returned even remotely to my prepregnancy body shape or size. More than once I had envied Carla, and later Monique, for being able to put so much energy into personal appearance. Carla seemed to possess a limitless wardrobe, with textured stockings and color-coordinated footwear for every one of her hundreds of outfits. She always had a fresh manicure and sensibly must have followed the advice of the postpregnancy books that tell you to get a good haircut soon after the baby is born. As Beverlee had improved, Monique had, too. She wore dresses with lace collars and regularly took time to have her hair done. I was wearing the same clothes over and over, day in and day out. I just couldn't be bothered with organizing my closet or figuring out what did or did not fit.

Fox was proud of the dress he had selected. It was loose in the hips, where, he suspected, I was still broader than usual. "And it buttons up the front, to make it easy when you breast-feed," he explained. There was the evidence that Fox was thinking optimistically of the future. I would be able to wear this dress when we brought Emily home. Not if, but when.

As it happened, the dress was beautiful. But if it had been purple stripes with puce-colored polka dots I still would have wept with happiness.

Which I did. It was my first Mother's Day. I was finding out that I liked the sound and feel of that word, *mother*.

It was a particularly warm, sunny day. We decided to enjoy it by taking a long, leisurely stroll up Columbus Avenue. We walked hand in hand, like the good old days before we had fought so much, and cried so much, and feared so much. We walked slowly and window-shopped, even daring to look at the displays of some of the Upper West Side's ridiculously trendy kids' shops. Fox called them the Baby Brie set. Along with their Upper East Side cousins, these were the kids I saw each day in Central Park on my midday outings. The smallest ones rode in huge navy blue English perambulators, with giant wheels and folding hoods. As they outgrew these vehicles, they graduated to Aprica strollers. In cool weather these strollers were covered entirely with see-through plastic. It made the babies look prepackaged, as if their parents had gone to Saks and said, "We'll take that one."

Because it was Sunday, maybe especially because it was Mother's Day, these babies were out with their real parents. Usually when I saw them in the park, they were being pushed by dutiful nannies who looked like the United Nations played by an all-female cast. I imagined their mothers and fathers on Wall Street, making deals. The thought was alarming enough to make me return to Emily each day and promise we would get her out of Manhattan, whatever it took.

In this first warm day of spring and in our rare romantic frame of mind, Fox and I walked nearly all the way to the hospital. Usually I would have argued with him in favor of saving a few dollars by taking the bus, but today I happily climbed into a cab for the ride through the park. It was Mother's Day, and Fox and I had a little girl. Yes, she was in the hospital. But for once Fox and I were going to visit her together. In our own fractured and fragmented way, we felt like a family. I put my head against his shoulder—something I had not thought of doing for many weeks.

Emily was sound asleep when we arrived in the NICU. We gazed at her with a new sense of marvel. She weighed nearly two and a half pounds now, which sounded huge to us. Her whole body was longer and fuller. Her head had grown. Her belly was still distended, an indication of NEC. But to us she looked robust.

We stood in front of her in silence, and then Fox surprised me by leaning down.

"Emily," he said in the softest voice I had ever heard him use, "don't you think it's time to open your eyes for Daddy?"

At that moment her bright blue eyes rolled open.

"Unbelievable!" said Robin, who had witnessed this scene.

It was enough to persuade Robin that Daddy, too, should get to hold Emily. So what if it was Mother's Day? Daddy was here, and wasn't it about time he held his baby in his arms?

Fox was not so sure he liked this idea.

"We don't want to tire her out," he protested. "We don't want to do anything that will exhaust her. Elizabeth just held her the other day. Are you sure it's a good idea to take her out again so soon?"

Robin said she would not have suggested it if she thought it was a bad idea. If he wanted, Robin said we could page one of the doctors to double-check. But she didn't think that was necessary.

"The baby will be fine," said Belinda, who had been listening to this exchange with no small measure of amusement.

"Emily's strong," Belinda added. "She'll do fine. Besides, it's time she got to know her daddy."

Again I was struck by how adroitly the nurses could work with these small people in their strange plastic environments. Robin had Emily wearing a little T-shirt in minutes, all without disturbing any of her pipes, tubes or monitors. She wrapped her in a little receiving blanket, teddy bears this time, not bunnies. Then she stretched one of K9's famous blue-and-pink-striped stocking caps over Emily's head.

Sometimes it was hard to read the expressions of this child, to whom much in her small world must have seemed puzzling. Certainly this odd custom of being occasionally encased in cotton knit garments was cause for bafflement. Emily had not gone through the many daily changes of clothing that most children her age undergo. She had never even had a real bath. She had her forehead wrinkled while all this was going on. Even at this young age and this small stage, Emily did not strike me as the kind of kid to be confused by much of anything. She was very single-minded, focusing her energies on the job at hand—in this case, getting big and strong. But I had to think from her expression while Robin was dressing her that she was just a little perplexed by all this strange activity.

Robin found the Polaroid camera, too. This was a moment we wanted to record. We pushed the blue stool beside Emily's isolette. Fox sat in it awkwardly. He was not sure what he was supposed to say, or do.

"Just sit there," Robin told him.

Moments later she placed Emily in Fox's arms. He held her as I had, with a mixture of awe and love and terror. They looked at each other curiously. She was such a cause of wonderment, this tiny child who had fought so fiercely. But for the blue eyes, she was an absolute miniature of her father, or as Robin put it, "Fox in a dress." She had the same face; the same long, lean body; the same slender, elegant hands; the same second toe that protruded out beyond the big toe, a Butterfield trademark. Fox had been tentative with Emily until now. He had looked at her lovingly, held her hand, and stroked her back. But it seemed that he had taken Kate Patterson's advice to heart. Kate had warned against bonding with her, but had taken those words back the day she saw Emily. Holding his baby daughter, Fox seemed to be throwing Kate's counsel out the window, too.

He kissed the baby on her forehead. "I love you, baby Emily," he told her. "Daddy loves you."

We were both elated. But we were scared, too.

"There's blood in her tube," Fox told Robin. "That can't be a good sign."

It was true. The doctors had placed a tube down Emily's throat to drain the gunk from her infection. Usually it was filled with greenish fluids. Today it was filled with blood.

"It could mean a lot of things," Robin said. The most benign possibility was that the tube had begun to irritate a spot in her stomach, causing it to bleed. Another was that some small incident of bleeding had occurred somewhere in Emily's system. The third option was massive internal bleeding due to the NEC. "I think you should talk to Dr. Rosenblatt about it," Robin said.

But Robin was congenitally cheery. "It's probably something minor," she said. She flashed a big, optimistic smile. "Let's hope so." Then she shifted gears. She wanted to divert us from some potentially heavy discussion. You could see Robin, the middle child in a family of five girls, being the one who intervened. You could imagine the oldest sister screaming and the youngest one crying. Robin would be the one who would say, "Wait a minute, you guys, it's a beautiful day outside."

"I've got a great idea," Robin said. She pulled out the Polaroid camera, which had been sitting on top of an empty isolette.

"Pictures!" Robin announced. "It's picture time!"

She handed me the camera. I snapped picture after picture of Fox with Emily. Someday, I would sit with Emily and describe to her the first time her Daddy held her. I would tell her how his eyes filled up, and how our big brave Daddy Fox, the one who had faced battle and gunfire, was terrified that he would drop someone so small. I would tell her how he examined each feature of her face; how he gazed at her perfect, long, thin fingers. I would tell her how he gingerly kissed her, and I would tell her how baby Emily wrinkled her forehead when he did. I would probably tell her that Fox furrowed his brow in exactly the same way. Try as I might, I could never master that gesture.

Robin glanced up at the clock. "Okay, Mom, now it's your turn," she said to me. Very, very cautiously, Fox and I traded places. I felt the soft weight of Emily fill my arms. She looked up at me. For a moment our eyes locked. I felt so proud, so lucky to be the mother of Emily, our little Courage Girl.

Soon after we returned Emily to her isolette, Dr. Rosenblatt stopped by on his regular rounds. He read through Emily's nursing reports, then nodded a hello at Fox and me. I remembered once that a colleague of mine had told me he always wore bow ties because they made him laugh, because no one who wore a bow tie could keep a straight face. Dr. Rosenblatt was an exception. He looked very serious, almost grave. His plaid bow tie rose up above

his pink K9 smock. If it looked silly—which it did—Dr. Rosenblatt was completely unconcerned.

Fox told him he was worried about the blood in Emily's tube.
"I'm worried, too," Dr. Rosenblatt said. But Dr. Rosenblatt was
always worried. "I think if it were really serious, it would have
happened sooner," he said. That sounded reassuring to me. I knew
better than to expect bona fide hope from K9's resident pessimist.
But I was ready to grab on to anything even remotely positive. I
had to. I had to believe that the bleeding was nothing serious. I had
to believe that Emily would overcome this new hurdle, as she had
so many others. I had to hold on to the hope.

Fox and I wandered back to the family room to deposit our
smocks. There was LaTanya, sitting on the couch with a young
man in thick, heavy-framed glasses. He was slender and wore a
small mustache. His hair was cut short. He looked young. LaTanya
looked up with a smile. The edge had been taken off her. I had
never seen her look quite this soft.

"Elizabeth, this is—" I smiled at LaTanya. I knew who it
was. It had to be Jacques Louis's father.

"This is Ronald," LaTanya said. They were reading together
from an oversized paperback book with a pale yellow binding. It
was a prayer book.

"I'm so happy to meet you," I told Ronald. To LaTanya, I
said, "And this is—"

"Fox," she finished for me. LaTanya had never met Emily's
father, either.

"Fox," I went on, "this is LaTanya and Ronald. LaTanya is
Jacques Louis's mother. He's the little boy in the corner, the one
who weighed the same as Emily at birth." I talked about all these
people—the babies, the mothers, the nurses, the doctors—when I
came home from K9 at night. They were my world now. But I was
never sure how much of this was of interest to Fox, or how much
he was absorbing. Did it matter to him that Jacques Louis was a
twenty-five-weeker, too? Or that LaTanya had changed her hairdo?
Or that Ronald had finally shown up at K9?

LaTanya had her feet curled up under her on the green Naugahyde couch. Her head was on Ronald's shoulder.

"LaTanya's right," I told Ronald. "He looks just like you."

Ronald looked embarrassed, but smiled anyway. I turned to leave, because suddenly I felt I was intruding. Fox and I threw our gowns into the big bin.

"Hey," LaTanya called. "Hey, Elizabeth. Happy First Mother's Day."

I spun around to catch her huge grin. "And to you, too, LaTanya. And to you."

Emily's life rolled by in two-week rotations of the hospital training staff. We had been through Drs. Klein and Stein, our first and still favorite pediatric residents. Next came Dr. Ho. Now Emily was in the charge of Dr. Louise Meyers. Louise was a nonstop talker. In her first day on our case, she had managed to tell me every detail of her upcoming wedding at Tavern on the Green. Dr. Klein always made me laugh the way she wore her diamond engagement ring safety-pinned to her hospital scrubs. Dr. Meyers boasted an equally impressive piece of jewelry, a ring with a giant ruby and two diamonds. Often she twisted it idly while we were speaking. She obviously had no intention of wearing that ring anywhere but on the third finger of her left hand.

Right away, Dr. Meyers told me that she wanted me to call her Louise. She felt more comfortable that way, she said. That was a surprise, because so far, none of the other doctors had ventured such intimacy, pseudo or otherwise. Between the doctors and the nurses there seemed to be a real class distinction, in that the doctors called the nurses by their first names, but except in very unusual circumstances, the nurses were allowed no such informality with the physicians. Louise Meyers, however, seemed to be an exception.

Louise did not want to get chummy, exactly. But she did make it clear that she appreciated interaction with the parents of her patients. I told her about Dr. Stein's failure to call us when Emily first showed signs of an infection. As I had done more than once before, I tried to explain to Louise how frustrating it was to be a parent, in essence, by observation only. We NICU moms could only hover. We had none of the hands-on joys of mothers in the outside world, or even of mothers in the well-babies unit of K9. We didn't have their woes, either, but Lord knows, we had problems of our own. Louise nodded her head in what I took to be a sign of understanding. What I was trying to tell her was that I really needed to feel involved with whatever was happening with Emily. She smiled and told me that sounded reasonable enough.

"If anything happens and you're not here, I'll be sure and call you," Louise promised. "I want you to feel included in this process. I want you to be part of this team."

Louise looked sincere when she uttered those words. I actually believed her. When I found out later that she had authorized and overseen a transfusion on Emily without informing me, I went nuts. Absolutely crazy. I screamed. I yelled.

"How dare you do this?" I demanded. "What about our promise? How could you do a thing like this?"

"Ms. Mehren, it wasn't just a transfusion. It was a transfusion of platelets," Louise said. "You can't live without platelets. You die." I had been trying to locate Louise since I had found out about the transfusion. I finally reached her by telephone. I was standing in the hall of K9, screeching into the telephone with fury and indignation.

"Donor anonymous platelets," I snapped back. "Thanks a lot, Louise." I wasn't sure if the HIV virus could live in platelets. But I assumed that if the AIDS-causing virus was carried in the blood, it was also perfectly content to be transmitted in the platelets.

"There were no donor-specified platelets available, Ms. Mehren. When we need platelets, we use platelets." There was a new impatience to Louise's voice. I could imagine her spinning her big ring around her finger. I noticed also that we were no longer on a first-name basis.

"Louise," I began, then corrected myself—"Dr. Meyers. What about our agreement to discuss these measures before taking them? What happened to all your promises to call me? Why did I have to learn about this from reading Emily's chart, which I'm not even allowed to do anyway?"

Now her tone was steely. Her patience was forced. Emily's blood count had shown her platelet level to be dangerously low, Dr. Meyers, Louise, whoever she was, explained. She had to make a decision right then. She decided to transfuse. She knew I would agree in any case because the organ at greatest risk if Emily's blood platelets dropped that low was her brain.

"Her brain, Ms. Mehren, her brain," she said. "Her cranial sonograms so far have been encouraging, and I knew from talking to you that you would not want to compromise your daughter's brain."

She was correct, of course. Weakly, I told her so, but added that I wished she had called me anyway. Ms. Foreman, the head nurse, walked by. "You'll have to get off the telephone," Ms. Foreman said. "That's not for patient use." Dr. Meyers and I hung up.

Early the next morning, Dr. Meyers gingerly approached me while I was standing at Emily's isolette.

"I realize I was wrong not to call you, Elizabeth," she said, apparently reverting to our old buddy-buddy mode. "But I stand by my decision. I had to transfuse those platelets. There wasn't any choice. I just couldn't jeopardize Emily now—not when she's doing so well."

Ronald's visit continued to provide a kind of spillover joy for LaTanya. Her reputation on K9 was not great. She often argued with the doctors and nurses. They found her contentious, at best. But since Ronald's visit, LaTanya showed a new sense of tranquillity.

"So, what did you think of him?" LaTanya demanded. I was standing beside Emily's isolette, watching my baby sleep. LaTanya began her conversation without so much as a hello or any kind of introduction. That's the kind of friends we were these days.

"He seemed very nice." Based on my three minutes' acquaintance with Ronald, it seemed foolish to engage in any greater kind of personality assessment.

"Yeah, and he's smart," LaTanya said. There was a note of defensiveness in her voice. I recognized it because this is something all women seem to do at one point or another: We boost up our men in the eyes of our peers. Feminism notwithstanding, we turn into unpaid PR people when we think they're under attack. Last week, before he had visited the hospital, LaTanya would have been the first to describe Ronald as a jerk, although she might have used a less complimentary noun. Now he was Einstein. More than once in this extended sojourn on K9 I had heard myself do the same for Fox.

"Yes," I agreed, "but you're smarter. Jacques Louis is his mother's kid. I wouldn't let Emily marry him if he wasn't."

Then LaTanya disclosed the other reason for her attitude transplant. Jacques Louis was doing so much better that the doctors had said he could probably be moved next door, to the healthier babies' nursery, before the end of the week.

"Emily'll be over there, too, soon," she said. "I know she will."

That same day, Mrs. Diaz got the news that Charles was well enough to transfer next door, too.

Charles did look much better. His stomach was no longer swollen and bright yellow. He was still not the most active kid in the unit, but neither was he the wan beach ball I had seen for so many weeks. For days on end Charles had barely opened his eyes. When he did, they looked almost lifeless. Now he seemed much more responsive, and much stronger.

"Mucho mas fuerte," I told his mother, hoping that was the right phrase.

It must have been close, because Mrs. Diaz beamed. She rattled something off, which when she slowed down and stuck to the present tense seemed to translate to "and you will be there soon, too." Or words to that effect.

I remembered how happy I had felt for Mrs. Diaz the day she had first held Charles. I felt that way again today as I thought about how far her sickly little child had come. He was only moving next door, a matter of a few feet. But it represented a huge journey in so many ways. Charles had been in this spot in the NICU for two months, almost to the day. Most of the nurses had assumed at first that he would not leave the NICU alive. Charles was a true miracle kid. The doctors could take credit if they wanted. But it seemed to me that most of the recognition should go to Charles himself, to his parents, and to their unswerving faith in a power far greater than any of these machines their baby was hooked up to.

"Esperanza y patienza," Mrs. Diaz reminded me. For all the times we had traded our little code phrase, I had never heard her speak it with such enthusiasm.

She was smiling broadly when Charles's isolette was wheeled to the nursery next door. When he left, the spot beside Emily seemed very empty.

Early that evening there was another alarming complication. Emily began passing frank blood through her rectum.

"Oh, my God," Christine said. "She looks like she's having her period."

My baby was just six weeks old. Her face was contorted in what looked to me like real pain. I knew that if she did not have all that equipment in her windpipe, we would probably be able to hear her crying.

"That's not funny," I chided Christine.

With her military demeanor and her supervisor's mentality, Christine was not normally given to wisecracks or inappropriate remarks.

"I didn't mean it to be funny," she said. "That's what it looks like."

There was no official explanation for this surge of blood. Dr. Meyers was off duty; Dr. Rosenblatt was on call, but not on the floor. It fell to Dr. Milo, the pediatric cardiologist, to look at the baby. He admitted he had no idea what was causing her hemorrhaging.

"It probably will stop on its own," Dr. Milo said. "We'll just have to watch it."

This was the kind of emergency that made me terrified to

leave Emily's side, even for a moment. I'm not sure what I thought I could do for her, but I knew I had to be there. Lurking fairly close to the front of my brain was the constant fear that the worst could happen at any moment, that Emily might die and I would not be there when it happened. Late at night when I called K9 for information about Emily, and early in the morning when I telephoned before leaving the house, I unconsciously braced myself for the bad news. When the nurse on duty patiently told me that things were fine, that Emily had had an uneventful evening or night, I could then exhale.

Logically, of course, I knew that this made no sense at all. But logic wasn't the issue. Being with Emily was.

Whatever diffidence or aloofness I might have felt from Christine in the past melted as I sat beside Emily in the throes of this latest crisis. In short order I was revising my earlier opinion of her. She was no autocrat; she was a real person, who sensibly hid her own vulnerabilities behind a mask of competence. She was thirty-six. Every day, she grappled with the issues of when and how to have children.

"Not whether," Christine said. "That's never been a question. I've always known I wanted children."

"Even with all the grief and sadness you watch around here every day? Even with the terribly sick babies you see coming in here?" It seemed to me that witnessing these daily tragedies would make many sane people afraid of having children. In my own flippantly confident way, I had never imagined the real risks and complications of prematurity when I was carrying Emily. It was not so much that I assumed blithely or blindly that everything would go right, just that I didn't know how many things there were that could go wrong—or how wrong those same things really could go.

"I'm not unrealistic about it," Christine said. "I certainly appreciate how much of this is out of our hands. I also know that for every tragedy there's a miracle. I do see a lot of grief, a lot of tragedy. That's true. But I also see a lot of hope, and a lot of happiness, too."

So here was the dilemma. It was a variation of what Leslie and I had talked about, a small departure from what sent Robin to bars and parties every Friday and Saturday night, an echo of the conversations I had had with friends on more occasions than I could count. We all had good jobs, much better, for the most part, than anything our mothers could have hoped for. But what we really wanted was family. Family meant a husband. But most of all, it meant children. Behind her brusqueness, this was the most important thing in Christine's life. Even as she thought of entering a doctoral program or switching to teaching nursing, this question of how to make a family was playing at center stage.

It was clear that up until now, I had done a masterful job of misjudging Christine. Here I thought that the supervisor with the blue eyeglass frames was a dictator. But she was one of us. Same problems, same priorities, same predicament.

"You probably ought to think about going home pretty soon," Christine said. "The bleeding seems to have stanched itself."

It was eleven o'clock and Christine's shift was ending soon. "You're working double-time," she said. Her tone was friendly, even jocular. I could tell that she did not want to leave with me just sitting there.

"I really think she's going to be okay tonight," she said gently. "Whatever it was has passed."

I put a kiss on my fingertips and rubbed it on Emily's forehead. "This is for you, baby Emily," I told my child through her porthole, "from your mommy and daddy and from Christine, because we all love you very much."

Christine gave me a softer smile than I had ever seen from her as I walked down the hall to get my coat. I knew that what I had just told Emily was true.

Leaving K9, I stopped at the reception desk to sign out, a matter of protocol that I often forgot. Because I frequently neglected to record my "out" time, anyone checking the sign-in sheet —not that anyone ever did—would have had to conclude that I was residing in the hospital. This was not far from the truth.

As I leaned on the desk, I noticed a cupboard directly behind it was standing wide open. Taped to the inside of the door was a large manila envelope. "DEATH CERTIFICATES," it read in huge block print. I wished that whoever was running this desk had had the sensitivity to close the cupboard.

As much as it was possible for him to do so, Dr. Friedman looked almost relaxed when he came to meet us in the NICU on Wednesday morning. He had been off for three consecutive days, a major luxury in NICU-ville. I was happy to see him looking less wired. Perhaps, he wished he could have said the same for me.

Fox and I were standing by Emily's isolette, our usual K9 perch.

"We need to go somewhere else," Dr. Friedman began. He may have looked relaxed, but his awkwardness when he said this reminded me how lacking he was in social graces.

But Dr. Friedman faltered when I suggested we go down to the cafeteria for a cup of coffee. He wanted to be in a place where he could leave, not someplace where we all might have to leave together. He had not invited us to his office, which seemed to me the logical place to have any kind of important or borderline-intimate discussion.

"I really don't have time for that," he said. "Let's just go down the hall."

Fortunately, "down the hall" turned out not to mean the family room. I think I would have walked out if he had led us in there. Instead, he turned into one of the unused nurseries. It was the place where nursing mothers sat to use the milk pump.

The empty isolettes gave the room an eerie quality. They might have been for babies who had not yet arrived on K9. Or, they might have been for babies who had died there. In either case, they made me uncomfortable.

Emily's surgery had been tentatively scheduled for the next day, Dr. Friedman told us. Dr. Wolf would meet with us later today, and so would a pediatric anesthesiologist. "He's one of the best," Dr. Friedman promised. It was impossible to say exactly when the operation would take place because so many procedures were scheduled, and there was no way to predict how long any of them would take. But it certainly would not happen before ten in the morning, and probably not before early afternoon—maybe even later. Dr. Wolf would review the details of the operation with us. Dr. Friedman added that we also couldn't be sure how long Emily's surgery would take. It all depended on what they found once they got in there.

Which brought Dr. Friedman to the delicate part of this discussion.

"I know how relieved you are that Emily has responded so well to the Broviac tube and to the nutrition," he said. "We're all pleased that she has grown so well and that she has reached a point where this operation can be performed."

Dr. Friedman said he was fairly confident that things would go smoothly. As he had said all along, he suspected that he and the surgical team would find and correct an abdominal blockage caused by the NEC.

"But we do have to talk about the possibility that we'll find something much more serious," he said. With this preamble, I felt every muscle in my body tighten. I resisted the urge to begin chewing on my lower lip, a nervous habit that dates to early childhood. Fox was staring directly at Dr. Friedman as he spoke, measuring each word. When Dr. Friedman began this portion of his speech, Fox leaned across and squeezed my hand. This conversation aroused our deepest sense of dread.

"I don't think it's likely," Dr. Friedman said. "The X-rays have given us no information to suggest that this is what we will find, and Emily has responded too well, too consistently, for us to suspect this is really what we will encounter, but there is always the possibility that when we open Emily up, we will find massive necrosis."

Massively necrotic tissue would mean that the NEC had killed Emily's intestinal tract.

"In that case, there would be nothing that the surgeons, or any of us, could do."

Dr. Friedman paused, just for a moment. He obviously wanted this news to sink in. It did.

"Should that be the case, we will need some direction from you, Emily's parents," Dr. Friedman said.

It was possible, he said, that Emily could be kept alive for an indefinite period with no intestine, or with a minimum of intestine. "But what you have to understand is that what we are talking about is the most compromised, the most partial of existences imaginable." Emily would never leave the sterile world of her isolette. Even if she did grow larger, which was doubtful, she would have to remain in a sterile, closed-off world. Her growth would be compromised. She would never walk, she would never be allowed outside the hospital, she might or might not talk. Her neurological and psychological development would be questionable. Occasionally, Fox and I might get to hold her. We would never get to take her home. She would never go to school. She would have no friends or playmates. Her world would be limited to the sterile confines of the hospital.

Even this scenario presumed that she could actually survive with feeding tubes and a heavy protocol of drugs to ward off infection. It was just as likely that she could succumb at any moment to some unforeseen bacteria, or that her body would rebel against the effort of staying alive under such extenuating circumstances.

"Intestines do not regenerate. They do not grow back," Dr. Friedman said. "Unfortunately, they are not something we can transplant, either—and there's no indication that we will be able to in the foreseeable future. So it's not as if we could keep her alive until a transplant became possible. I'm not sure that that's ever going to happen."

There was another pause. Fox and I could not meet each other's eyes. Both of us gazed at the floor.

"So we need to know what kind of measures you would like us to take," Dr. Friedman said. "If we do find massive necrosis, we need to know how far you want us to go to save Emily."

Fox was rocking softly in his chair. I knew he had to be

recalling similar conversations he had had with his mother's doctor, when she was dying of cancer, and with his father's physician, as his body was overtaken by heart disease. Now it was his daughter, a child who had never had the chance to live even the cut-short lives of his parents.

"I think we need to talk about the element of suffering," he said. Fox's words were slow, like a metronome on low.

"That's a decision you two will have to make," Dr. Friedman said. "Some people would find it acceptable to have their child live indefinitely in the kind of environment I've described. I know how I would feel if it were my child, but it really doesn't matter what I think. It only matters what you two think, and what you want for your child.

"As for suffering," Dr. Friedman said, "we can do a great deal to reduce pain. But of course we can't promise that Emily's existence under these conditions would be pain-free."

What kept coming back to me was the desperate plea I had issued to Sandy, my obstetrician, while I was in labor with Emily. Sandy had said then that Emily would be too small to survive the birth process. I remembered begging her then not to take extraordinary measures, not to force Emily to lead a fraction of a life. Now Fox and I had had Emily for seven magic weeks. We had held her in our arms. We had indulged in the fantasies of taking her home, of making a family with her, our beautiful baby girl. But was it any more reasonable now for us to ask her to commit to a life of pure compromise?

"If you do find massive necrosis," I asked him, "and if you do bring her upstairs and hook her up to a million machines, is there any possibility that she will recover, that you will find some cure for her condition?"

Dr. Friedman shook his head. "You don't ever want to say that anything is completely impossible. Let's just say it's so unlikely as to be unimaginable."

"I don't think either one of us wants to doom this child to some kind of technological nightmare life," I heard myself saying. "We brought her into the world to love her, to share joy with her, to give her a real life—" In spite of myself, I felt tears spilling down my cheeks. It was getting hard to talk. "We brought her into the world to let her tickle her toes in the sea, and to chase bunnies, and to laugh—"

In the dark, difficult moments immediately before and after Emily's birth, Fox and I had talked about this doomsday what-if. We had agreed early on that we did not want our child to be merely a bionic monument to the wonders of science and technology. We knew that many babies who were very, very premature and very, very sick did survive, but with no hope for any kind of normal, productive, pleasurable, or painless existence. Even before we knew anything about K9, or the NICU, or prematurity, we would have said without a moment's hesitation that these babies are persons, and that as persons, they have the basic human right to die. Now that we had spent so much time around these very tiny people, now that, with Emily, we had experienced the phenomenon of prematurity firsthand, we were probably more convinced of that than ever.

Fox and I knew we did not want our baby to be some human lab experiment. We knew we did not want to demean her. We knew that neither of us could ask her to lead a life that we ourselves would not find tenable.

Fox finally spoke for both of us. "If when you undertake the surgery on Emily, you do find this worst-possible-case scenario, nothing but dead tissue—a situation that sounds to me like it's inoperable anyway—then I think both Elizabeth and I would agree it's best to let nature take over. At that point I don't think we should try to impose our scientific or medical wills on what seems fated to happen anyway."

"You're saying we should do our best," Dr. Friedman said, "but if there's nothing we can do—"

Fox and I nodded in assent. I was glad Fox had had the courage to speak. Though I concurred entirely, those words would have been very difficult for me to say.

Abruptly Dr. Friedman brightened. His face took on the hundred-watt quality that I remembered from our first visit, down in the postpartum recovery area, nearly seven weeks ago.

"Well then, that's that," he said. "Let's hope this whole conversation will prove unnecessary. I'm hopeful that it will."

He got up to leave, and to our amazement, extended his hand in an uncharacteristic gesture of—what? Friendship? Cordiality? Partnership?

"One caveat, Dr. Friedman, please, before you leave."

Dr. Friedman gave me a look that said he dreaded whatever I was about to say. While we sometimes talked about cooking or current American fiction or fitness or whatever, our relationship had been prickly. He knew me to be outspoken and demanding. I think he had wanted to leave this meeting on a positive note. Now what does she want? is what I'm sure he was wondering.

"It seems to me that as humans, we have the right not to expect to suffer permanent, intractable pain," I began. "It seems to me we can expect not to have our dying prolonged. This is my little girl, Dr. Friedman. This is our baby. Just please promise me that whatever happens, Emily will endure no pain or suffering."

"Well, you know we can't make any promises," Dr. Friedman said. "But we will do our best. We physicians are supposed to try and relieve pain, as you know, not inflict it."

"Yes, but what I'm saying is that if the worst does happen, and if we do, as Fox put it, 'let nature take over'—that is, if we do let death come to Emily on its own terms—then please promise me she'll have no pain, not for one single moment."

"We can do our best," he said. And then he smiled that quick smile that had come to be so familiar. "And we'll hope that none of this will be necessary."

ELEVEN

Emily had never seemed so attentive or so aware as when we arrived at the hospital that Thursday morning. Her eyes were wide open, and they scanned every inch of her hospital world. She seemed to stare sharply at Fox, and to cast an equally acute gaze at me. From the beginning, Emily had been what we called a wiggly girl, a kid who flipped and flopped in spite of all the tubes and paraphernalia that should have weighed her down. Today she was turning her head every which way and following the action around her like a little radarscope.

"It's as if she knows something's about to happen," Fox said. "As if she doesn't want to miss a thing."

She had gotten big enough to manage a preemie pacifier, a miniature version of the kind made for larger babies. Because they are never encouraged to suck, either on a breast or on a bottle, some very premature infants fail to develop the sucking reflex. But Emily was gumming that pacifier with a vengeance. It was obviously a new source of pleasure, and there was no way she was going to part with it.

If Emily seemed filled with some new kind of energy, Fox and I were trying hard to temper our anxiety with optimism. It seemed that all the K9 nurses knew that today was Emily's day for surgery. Many stopped by to give us little pep talks, or simply to smile at Emily and wish her luck. The sense of community among this disparate collection of humanity had never felt stronger.

As luck would have it, Leslie was not scheduled to work today. This was as disappointing for her as it was for Fox and me, because at this point, she seemed as close to Emily as we were. I knew Leslie was skilled at avoiding excessive emotional involvement in her work. If not, how could she have survived more than a decade of K9's joys and heartaches? But I was also certain that she had meant it when she had said she came to love these babies as if they were her own. I had heard that theme from too many of the NICU nurses not to believe it was true—and I had seen it in action myself, over and over.

Late Wednesday afternoon, Leslie and I had had a long talk about the implications of this procedure, and what to expect from it.

"I know you've got to have some mixed feelings about this," Leslie said.

She was right. We were happy because this much-anticipated day had finally come. But we were also terrified, because if it didn't work out, we knew this was the end of the line.

Leslie repeated what by now had become the standard line on Emily. She said she had talked extensively to Drs. Rosenblatt and Friedman. She felt confident that Emily would breeze through the surgery itself, and the odds were good that the surgery would correct whatever damage the NEC had caused. Soon we would be moving next door or across the hall, she predicted.

"Really, if you look at what's likely to happen, the worst situation is probably that she'll end up with a colostomy," Leslie said. "Big deal. I'll teach you how to change the bags, no problem."

By midsummer, not long after Emily's original due date, we would probably have her at the Glades, Leslie said. "And don't forget, you'll need a nurse. I'm coming with you!"

Leslie and I had been together for almost two months now.

Our relationship was tinged with a special kind of intensity, and also a real sense of intimacy. Most of all, there was a bridge of trust between us.

"Leslie, there's something we need to discuss," I told her. "It's all well and good for everyone to be talking about what a trooper Emily is and what a brilliant surgeon Dr. Wolf is. It's great to hear the doctors say they think things are going to go well in surgery tomorrow. But if they get in there and it's a complete mess inside Emily, then we have to go back to our original promise. Promise me you'll let me know exactly what's happening, and promise me that you won't sugarcoat any of it. I don't know how long we have this child—"

"Nobody ever knows that about their child, Elizabeth," Leslie said.

"I know, Leslie, I know. What I'm saying is, if things look bad, if it looks like . . . like Emily's going to die, please tell me. Do not spare any details thinking you're doing me some big favor. You're not. I need to know, no matter how bad the news may be."

Leslie's voice was somber. "That's never been a question, Elizabeth," she said. "I told you from the beginning that I would be honest with you. I told you that if I thought you should be worried, I'd let you know."

"And do you think we should be worried now?"

She thought for a moment before she answered.

"I think you probably have cause for worry," Leslie said. "And if I were in your position, I'm sure I'd be scared to death. But I think there's an equally good chance that things will come out fine."

We'd also met with the pediatric anesthesiologist, a softspoken man with the unfortunate name of Aiche. He was slender and bearded and relatively young, certainly no more than thirty-five. Yes, he assured me, he had administered anesthesia to babies of Emily's size. It was creepy to think about "putting these babies to sleep" (a term that even Dr. Aiche said made him cringe), but the science was so sophisticated that doctors seldom experienced major

difficulties. I think both Fox and I let our brains glaze over while
Dr. Aiche described the particular combination of preparations he
intended to use on Emily. We didn't really care what they used, just
as long as she felt no discomfort, and as long as we could be
assured that the operation would proceed smoothly. But we listened carefully when Dr. Aiche explained that once Emily returned
from the surgical arena, she would be in a rigid, nonresponsive
state. "She'll almost look as if she's dead," he said. It was not
exactly the news we wanted to hear. This condition would result
from a drug called Pavulon, which acts as a temporary paralytic
agent. Dr. Aiche said that Pavulon functioned very much like cu-
rare. From Latin American history courses I remembered that this
was the poison that Indians in the Amazon area had for centuries
applied to arrow tips to immobilize their prey.

"We just don't want you to be surprised," Dr. Aiche cautioned
us.

Blessedly, my own direct experience with surgery had been
limited. But I remembered reading that some doctors like to operate with music in the background. For some reason it became
important to me to be able to picture the place where our daughter
would be while all this was going on. We of course would not be
permitted into the room where the operation was taking place. Dr.
Friedman had said we would not even be allowed to wait outside in
the hallway. As we had come to be increasingly aware, hospitals—
this big-city hospital, anyway—were places where business took
place. Accommodating family members was generally not part of
that business.

"Tell me what the operating room looks like," I asked Dr.
Aiche.

He looked surprised. Apparently this was not on his list of
most-frequently-asked questions.

"It's a large room in the basement, the lower floor, of the
adjacent building," he said. "It's very, very bright, with white walls.
Emily will be on a table in the middle of the room."

I tried to picture this two-and-one-half-pound person on a
full-sized operating gurney. With all those grown-ups hovering

over her, surgeons with their big, adult-sized hands, Emily would seem microscopic.

"Do you have music?"

Dr. Aiche did not know quite how to respond to that one.

"I beg your pardon?" he said.

"Well, I've heard that sometimes surgery is performed to music. Do you guys do that?"

Dr. Aiche said that sometimes he did take tapes in with him. He had his own preference for certain gentle jazz medleys, either that or music from the Baroque era.

"Good," I said. "Emily likes Mozart."

Dr. Aiche looked at me quizzically.

"Mozart, right."

"And Bach," I said. "I think she likes Bach, too. But no jazz, please."

Dr. Aiche was probably figuring at this point that the tension had really gotten to us. Was it possible, he must have been thinking, to Pavulon the parents?

"Right," he said. "No jazz."

Dr. Wolf and his latest assistant, a man we suspected did double duty as a cigar store Indian, also came by on Wednesday afternoon so we could sign the papers authorizing surgery. This time I let Fox do the honors.

From Dr. Wolf we learned that Emily's was the last operation scheduled for the day. If, as he projected, the earlier procedures went smoothly, he foresaw taking Emily early in the afternoon, maybe even as early as midday. With his fingertip, he demonstrated how the incision would be made in Emily's abdomen. Dr. Wolf was cool and unruffled while he described this first essential step in the surgery. But I had to fight to stay calm. The mere thought of carving up this beautiful, tiny child was enough to give me the shakes.

"Elizabeth, it's got to be done," Fox said, noticing my discomfort.

Dr. Wolf paused for a moment. "It's hard, isn't it, when it's your child?" he said. This lapse into humanitarianism surprised me. "I probably wouldn't want to think about doing this on my kid, either."

He expected that the whole operation would be over within an hour, two at the most.

"She'll do fine," he said. With his arms still folded across his chest, the cigar store Indian shook his head in agreement.

And Wednesday we learned also that Kate Patterson had been in touch with Dr. Friedman. Early that evening, she called us at the hospital from her car phone to tell us she had discussed the details of Emily's surgery with Friedman. I suspected that what she had really talked about was how Emily's parents would react to her surgery. On the other hand, I knew Kate was concerned about what happened to our baby. Ever since her visit to Emily, the baby had become real to her as well. The timing on all this was not the most opportune. Kate herself was leaving for England early Thursday morning.

"You won't be able to reach me if things do go wrong," she said. "But from what I understand from Dr. Friedman, that's not likely. He really sounds positive about this."

I told Kate that he hadn't sounded so positive at our meeting that morning, where he had gone step-by-step through the most horrible possibilities.

"Yes, he told me you didn't react well to that conversation," Kate said. "But he had to enumerate every single possible outcome," she said. "That's his professional responsibility. He had to make sure he understood your wishes. My sense is that he really doesn't think any of that will be necessary."

"Did you tell him that if things don't turn out well, I'll be a complete basket case?" I asked Kate.

"I didn't tell him that because I don't think that's what will happen," she said. "I think you'll handle whatever outcome there is."

Kate was too sensible to engage in idle praise. I hoped her optimism was not misplaced, either.

• • •

By midday on Thursday, the only word we had from the operating arena was that things had backed up. Even the most routine of procedures had taken longer than anyone expected. In the time that Dr. Wolf had expected to complete four or five surgeries, he had barely made it to three.

"So do you think they'll end up postponing us to another day?" I asked Robin.

"I doubt it," she said. "They really do try to stick to the schedule down there. I think they'll take Emily, but it won't be until later this afternoon."

To our amazement, Emily had not dozed off for one moment since we arrived that morning. It is not at all uncommon for premature babies to sleep as much as twenty hours a day. Certainly we were accustomed to watching her sleep for hours at a time. Today she was almost watchful.

"She knows something's up," Robin said, echoing Fox's earlier comment.

If Leslie could not be there, I was glad that Robin had been assigned to us. Her quick sense of humor and cheerfulness helped lighten an atmosphere that otherwise seemed pretty leaden. She knew to give Fox and me a lot of space, but also a lot of support. I had to hand it to her, she was doing both with commendable skill.

Before Robin took her break for lunch, she did some further checking. There was still at least one child scheduled for surgery before Emily, she said, and maybe even two. She felt certain that Emily would not be summoned to the surgical area while she was at lunch. "And I think it would probably be good for you to get something to eat, too. This is obviously going to be a long day, and you're going to need all the strength you can get."

"How much time do we have?" Fox asked.

"A couple of hours, anyway," Robin said. "Really, do yourself a favor. Take a break. Nothing's going to happen now. Emily's doing fine, and you need to pay a little attention to yourselves."

The sun was out, and so were the trees and flowers in the

park. I had read that there were lilac groves, but I had never seen
them. "Maybe today's the day for the lilacs," I told Fox.

We grabbed a bag lunch and headed toward Central Park.
Sure enough, as we approached 105th Street, we saw an amazing
garden, exploding with lilac trees in every possible hue. The aroma
was intoxicating. There was a bride, posing for pictures in wedding
gown, veil, and satin slippers. A woman who must have been her
older sister stood close by, occasionally refreshing the bride's lip
gloss or blusher. Several small children leapfrogged around the
lilac trees, and the usual parade of nannies with perambulators
marched along the narrow gravel pathways. Fox and I found a
small stone bench, one of the few that was vacant. With all this life
and vitality and fresh blossoms erupting around us, we ate our
lunch in near silence.

By some private accord, we detoured through the park on our
way back. The activity around us, all those children, provided some
perverse comfort. Couples were entwined on rocks, and families
were spread out on blankets. A big plastic ball drifted across the
walkway, and from not very far away we could hear the sounds of a
softball game in progress.

We were not far from the hospital when we heard a familiar
voice.

"Elizabeth? Fox?" We turned to see Leslie, barely recognizable in her civvies. She was reading a book, and sitting on a bench
where she could look up and see K9. Leslie saw the surprise in our
faces.

"I just had to be near her today," she said.

I sat down beside her. "Any news?" she asked. "Has anything
happened?"

We shook our heads and explained that Dr. Wolf's entire
surgical schedule had gotten backed up.

"That happens," Leslie said. "He's smart, but even he doesn't
know what he's going to find when he starts operating."

We told her that it now looked unlikely that they would take
Emily before late this afternoon—four or five o'clock.

"You two must be a wreck," Leslie said. "I'm not doing so

well myself, and I'm in the business." Her eyes drifted from Fox's face to mine, and back again. "You should get back there," she said. "I'll call later to find out what happened." She lifted her hands up. Her fingers were crossed.

"Oh, Leslie, I'm so scared—" I could feel myself about to start crying again. Fox put his arm around me and guided me back across the street toward the hospital.

It was well after four o'clock when Dr. Friedman finally showed up in his green surgical scrubs. They were rolled up at the cuff like a little boy's too-long jeans. "This was all they had in the supply room," Dr. Friedman said. He sounded almost sheepish. "I think they were made for Wilt Chamberlain."

Once again, Dr. Friedman reminded us that we were welcome to wait in the family room if we wanted, but there was no place for us to sit, or even stand, downstairs in the other building where the surgery would take place.

"It's going to be a couple of hours," he said. "If I were you, I'd get out of here. Go for a walk, do something. Go home for a while. We can call you as soon as we bring Emily back here. You'll be here in ten minutes."

"What I'd really like to do is go for a run," Fox said.

"That's a great idea," Friedman concurred. "Work off some of that tension. You've been standing around here all day. There's nothing you can do for Emily right now, and going for a run would be something really good you could do for yourselves. Take a shower afterward, it's just what you need."

"You'll call us the minute you have any information?" I asked him.

Friedman gave us that smile. "Yes," he said. "We'll call."

"I mean, the absolute minute," I persisted.

Dr. Friedman looked at Fox. "She never gives up, does she?" Then he turned to me. "I said we'll call. We'll call. Don't worry."

Robin promised that she would escort Emily to the operating room. "You can ride down in the elevator with her if you want," she said. "But I really don't see any point. I'll be with her. I'll talk to her. And she knows you're there in spirit."

Emily was still sucking eagerly on her pacifier. One at a time, Fox and I put our hands through her portholes and let her grip a finger.

"We love you so much, brave baby Emily," I told her. "You're such a model of courage. I couldn't do this, and look at you—you're doing great."

We promised her we would be there as soon as she came back upstairs to K9. We told her we loved her. We wished her luck. And then we watched them roll her isolette down the hall and into the elevator.

Fox and I hardly spoke while we chugged our way around the reservoir in Central Park. I couldn't really believe we were doing this, jogging while Rome burned, as it were. But what else were we going to do? We couldn't focus our attention on anything long enough to read or to conduct a relatively intelligent conversation with anyone, even each other. We didn't feel like eating. And neither one of us was the kind who anesthetized ourselves with drugs or alcohol. In this case, that may have been a pity.

Both of us had on shorts and T-shirts. I was also wearing the special, industrial-strength athletic bra I had bought to protect my breasts, still tender from nursing. It wrapped around me like something from a medieval torture catalog. Right now, the pain felt good.

Emily was in the operating arena at that very moment. I hoped to God that things were going well.

Back at our apartment, I had just showered and dried my hair when the telephone rang. I was scared to answer it.

"You get it," I yelled at Fox. I backed away from the phone as if it were a poisonous snake.

I knew from his voice that it was the hospital.

"You can't tell us anything?" he said.

I began to cry uncontrollably. Fox looked at me grimly.

"That was Robin. They want us over there, right away. They said they can't tell us anything on the phone."

"That means the news is bad, Fox. You know they would have told us if things were all right."

"Let's just go," he said.

It was almost 8 P.M. when the elevator let us out on the ninth floor. Emily had been wheeled off almost four hours earlier. Friedman and Wolf were leaning against the receptionist's desk when we arrived. Robin was there, too. She looked awful. Her eyes were drained and her mascara had run down her cheeks. I knew from looking at her what they were about to tell us.

"I'm afraid it couldn't be much worse," Dr. Wolf said.

"Wait, Bob, let's go in here," Dr. Friedman said. As usual on K9, there were people walking up and down the hall, only pausing long enough to give us looks for blocking traffic. Dr. Friedman led the way back behind the reception area, into the so-called doctors' lounge. It was a small room, maybe seven feet by nine feet, with the familiar high-school-style metal lockers lining two walls. Used surgical scrub outfits, standard issue for residents and interns, lay in clumps on the floor and the couch. Empty coffee cups and soft-drink containers were lying around, and also a half-eaten box of Ritz crackers. The wall decorations included photographs from a social occasion that must have been some kind of physicians' follies. They featured doctors in diapers, doing the cancan.

"We just weren't prepared for this, either," Dr. Wolf said. He had changed from his scrubs into a blue blazer. He, too, looked drawn. "Her entire intestinal tract was wracked with necrosis. Just destroyed. There was almost no tissue left alive, nothing to work with. We tried to piece it together, but there was not enough viable tissue to make it work. There's almost nothing left in there."

In spite of myself, I had begun to sob and shake. I wanted to hear every word these doctors had to say. I wanted to remember every syllable. More than ever before, I realized that whatever they told me now was what I would have to hold on to. As I had done at Emily's birth, I needed to memorize this scene, to freeze it in my brain forever. But I had begun to sob loudly.

I hadn't seen him come in, but now I noticed that Dr. Milo was part of this group as well. He was sitting on a desk opposite the couch, staring at me as I cried. What was he doing in here, anyway? There was always one kid in elementary school who stared at the kid who had hurt himself on the playground, eyes open wide and mouth even wider. That little future rubbernecker never had any words of comfort, or offers of aid or succor. This was Dr. Milo now. Hadn't his mother taught him that it was impolite to ogle someone at a time like this?

"As you know, this wasn't what we expected," Dr. Friedman said.

"When could this have happened?" Fox asked. "When did all this damage take place? Is this the result of failing to diagnose the infection immediately?"

"We don't know any of those answers," Dr. Friedman said. "As soon as we suspected the presence of the NEC, of the infection, we placed Emily on antibiotics. That should have stopped the course right then, and presumably it did. We took X-rays day after day, and none of this damage showed."

"I don't understand," Fox said. "How could she have seemed so healthy if she was this sick?"

"How could she have been growing?" I asked. "How could she have had bowel movements?"

"With this kind of damage to her system, it's true, she shouldn't have been responding as well as she has," Dr. Wolf said. "She shouldn't have accepted the feedings this well. She shouldn't have grown and gained weight as well as she did. She shouldn't have been as responsive as she has been all along. There should have been more external signs of the damage. She should have seemed sicker.

"We spent a lot of time in there. That's why the surgery took so long," Dr. Wolf continued. "We really tried to connect her bowel back together. If we could have, we would have. But there were just very, very small segments of live tissue, not enough to sew together. We tried, but it just wasn't possible."

His tone was matter-of-fact, but the way he presented this information, Dr. Wolf sounded almost apologetic. He, too, was leaning against the desk, arms folded across his chest.

"It was the second big shock of the day for me," Dr. Wolf said. "Just before Emily, I operated on a child, a two-year-old, whose cancer we believed to be in remission. We were expecting a very routine procedure. Instead we found cancer cells everywhere, in most of the child's vital organs.

"I had to come out and tell that child's parents that instead of having the healthy little boy they thought they had, their child will be dead within months."

"I'm sorry to hear you've had such a bad day, Dr. Wolf," I said. "Of course, this hasn't exactly been a tea party for us."

"Elizabeth," Fox said. He hated it when my saber tongue aimed at anyone, but especially at what he saw as hapless victims.

"No, she's right," Dr. Wolf said. "I shouldn't have brought it up. That child's tragedy has nothing to do with yours. I feel bad for his parents, and I feel bad for you. These moments are always awkward. I don't quite know what to say, except that I'm very surprised and I'm deeply sorry that it turned out this way. That's all, I'm sorry."

There was a silence. Dr. Milo was still staring. At least his mouth was closed; otherwise, he probably would have been reduced to drooling by now. Dr. Wolf had his arms clasped tight over his chest, and his eyes fixed on the ancient linoleum tile floor. Dr. Friedman became a kind of board chairman by default, returning to the business at hand.

"So I assume your next question would be, what can we do now?" Dr. Friedman said.

"What is there to do?" I said. My voice was whiny, and I hated it. "What can we do? She's going to die."

"Elizabeth—" Fox said.

"Fox, she can't live without an intestine. No one can. We know that."

"What we can do," Dr. Friedman said, "is try to make her as comfortable as possible."

"When will this happen?" Fox asked. "I mean, how long do you think she has?"

"That's impossible to say," Dr. Friedman said. "But usually in a situation like this, death comes within twenty-four to forty-eight hours. For your sakes, I hope it's merciful and swift."

"For our sakes?" I said. "What about Emily?"

"For all of your sakes," Dr. Friedman said.

The longer it took, the more difficult it would be, and the harder to watch, Dr. Friedman said.

"She may become bloated, edematous. Her color will change, until she is either gray or almost translucent. Eventually it will be too hard for her to open her eyes. You'll see her breathing with greater and greater effort. This kind of thing is not pretty to watch."

"What about your promise?" I demanded. I hated the tone that had crept into my voice.

"Emily is on morphine," Dr. Friedman said. "It's being administered intravenously. We'll keep her on it as long as necessary."

"How will you know if she's in pain?" I asked.

"We'll try to keep her on a sufficient dose so that won't happen," Dr. Friedman said.

He paused. "This is about waiting now. It's about waiting and trying to make her as comfortable as possible."

Dr. Wolf cleared his throat. "When you see Emily, you'll see a stoma, an ostomy. There's a bag to collect waste outside her stomach. It's all we could do. There simply wasn't enough intestine left to do anything else."

"And there wasn't enough to do a real colostomy?" I asked. "She wouldn't be able to get by with what you did?"

Dr. Wolf shook his head.

"No. I just didn't want you to be surprised when you see her."

"Don't forget that she's on Pavulon, too," Dr. Friedman said.

"Right," I said. "Dr. Aiche warned us. She'll look like she's dead. It'll be good practice."

"Elizabeth—" Fox said. His voice was full of rebuke.

We all filed out of that awful little room. On the way out, Dr. Friedman stopped for just a moment. It sounded like he was about to spit something out.

"Sorry," he said.

We looked at him in amazement because we had never expected to hear that word from him. Technology may have been his long suit, but compassion was not.

"Thanks," Fox said.

I nodded my head in accord. "Thank you."

But several minutes later, after Fox and I had scrubbed up and donned our hospital gowns, we walked by the staff lounge on the way down the hall to the NICU. As always, the door was wide open. Dr. Friedman was sitting at the table, eating a sandwich and, it appeared, telling jokes. His head was thrown back and he was convulsed in laughter. It was as if nothing had ever happened this evening, as if our terrible conversation had never taken place.

I supposed then that this is what had to happen. Doctors have to learn to steel themselves to what the rest of us regard as tragedy. To survive in a field where death intervened when it chose, Dr. Friedman and his ilk probably had to construct a kind of emotional moat between themselves and their patients. They could hide behind technological armor. They could point to the machines as signs of progress, perhaps even of conquest. All those advances were dazzling. The whole notion of defensive medicine, all those fancy tests and procedures, was worthy of some small measure of wonderment. But what we really wanted to hear was something much more basic. What we wanted to hear were the words it was clear that this well-trained, highly competent physician was incapable of uttering. What we wanted to hear was, "I care."

It made sense that in a way, death was the mortal enemy of these ostensible purveyors of health. Maybe that was why they had chosen the field in the first place, to do battle with their own mortality. That kind of mind frame would explain why the patients who did "well," those who recovered swiftly, were rewarded with figurative gold stars from their doctors. A patient who fared poorly, like Emily, was a sign of defeat.

No one wanted to look failure in the eye. I could understand that. But still, I wished that Dr. Friedman weren't laughing quite so hard, not quite so soon.

Among the nurses, the word about Emily traveled quickly. There were quiet condolences, "I just heard, I'm so sorry." And there were expressions of amazement—"Not Emily, we never thought this would happen to Emily." Robin's work shift was officially over by more than an hour, but she had waited for us.

"I can't believe this," she said. "I just had to tell you how sorry I am."

As the doctors had predicted, the Pavulon did make Emily look paralyzed. She was rigid and immobile. I began to weep the moment I saw her.

Fox was weeping, too. No matter how hard we had tried to brace ourselves for this eventuality, we were unprepared. Nothing could have readied us for this sight of our baby and the knowledge that she would soon be dead.

She was too drugged even for us to touch her. We knew she would not respond. But I had read somewhere that even under the influence of Pavulon, postsurgical patients can hear.

"Emily, it's Mom," I told her through her porthole. "Mom and Dad. We love you very much. And we're so proud of you, so proud of how brave you are. We're so lucky to be your Mom and Dad."

"You're our Courage Girl," Fox said in a thin, strained voice.

We were both crying. It was difficult for us to speak.

"Emily, you're a real model for us," I told her. "I don't think either of us could go through what you've been through, not with your dignity."

At that point I collapsed in tears onto Fox's chest. "She's incredible," I said through sobs. "She just keeps holding on. How does she do it?"

We sat with her for several hours, sometimes talking to her, sometimes just gazing at her with a sense of marvel. We barely saw the tubes or the ugly plastic doughnut, the waste bag, now hooked up to her belly. To us, Emily was still so beautiful, and so very, very brave.

Her vital signs were surprisingly stable. Her heartbeat held firm, but in Dr. Milo's view, this could not possibly last. My instinct was to sit with her for as long as it took, not to leave the hospital, or even K9, for so much as one minute of what remained of my daughter's life. But Fox refused to accept Dr. Milo's pessimism. "This kid's a fighter," he kept reminding me. "I don't know where she got it, but this kid's got some amazing strength." Late at night, and even then, only after we had badgered Dr. Milo into a promise that he would call if Emily's heartbeat took so much as the slightest dip, Fox persuaded me that we should go home and try to get a little sleep.

"She's going to need us for the next couple of days," he said. I hoped he was right.

At home, Fox and I were too tired to return any of the phone calls that were waiting for us. He foraged for something remotely edible in the refrigerator, and poured us both a drink. We knew we needed something to numb us, but the only thing we had with alcohol in it was the awful malt liquor I had been urged to drink to up my breast-milk production.

"I guess we won't be needing this anymore," I said. We were sitting on the bed now, facing each other, only a few feet away. There was a loft sleeping area above us, so the bed was almost like being in a cave. Since what we wanted most of all was to steal Emily from the hospital and hide from the rest of the world, the little tight space felt safe. If only we had her with us, I thought. If only, if only.

"Will you take the milk machine back?" I asked Fox. "I don't think I can face those women again." I was surprised that I would think of such a mundane consideration at a time like this. But that's what happens. Faced with the imponderable, you zero in on

what small tasks of daily life you can manage. It's a wonder I
didn't start vacuuming, or run out to do the wash.

"Sure," Fox said. "I'll do it tomorrow."

At any moment, I expected the phone to ring. I felt certain
that Dr. Milo would call and tell us to get over there right away. I
had changed into sweatpants, not a nightgown, so that if I had to, I
could race out in a moment.

"Where do you suppose she gets her courage?" I asked.

"She's had it since that very first second, since she came out
screaming." Fox had not been there, and so he had never heard his
daughter's first fierce cries. I knew this was something he continued to anguish about. He felt he had let both Emily and me down
by not being there. And now it was clear he had missed his one
chance to hear his baby daughter.

"That wasn't just courage, that was defiance," I reminded
him.

"We know where she gets that," he said, and gave me a sharp
but loving look.

We both felt so adrift. Combined, we had nearly ninety years
of life on the planet. Nothing had prepared us for what was happening to us, to all three of us, now.

"There has to be some way to make sense of it," Fox said.

I agreed, but how do you make sense of the loss of a life with
so much promise? How do you explain a spirit like hers, strong and
proud and brave, snuffed out before it had had a chance to blaze at
full strength?

"That's the one thing we won't lose," Fox said. "Her spirit.
They can take everything else away from us, but that we've got
forever."

We talked like that for a long time, hours, I think. We
brought up old business, garbage between us that suddenly seemed
unimaginably petty and foolish. Fox's jealousy, my rigidity. The
stupid, ridiculous demands we made on each other. The terrible
sense that somehow one of us was responsible for what had hap-

pened with Emily, or that maybe we both were. In the context of a child who had set such a stalwart example, our own concerns seemed like adenoidal whinings.

Fox and I were huddled in the sleeping alcove, sitting shoulder to shoulder. While he talked, I used my finger to outline the pattern of our quilt. From time to time I tasted a tear as it dripped down my face.

"I've been afraid of this all along," Fox said.

"The NEC?"

"Oh, no," said Fox. "I mean, yes, maybe. It could have been the NEC. It could have been anything. I never doubted Emily's strength or valor. I've just been so afraid we'd lose her."

"You didn't think she'd make it?"

"It's not that I didn't think she would make it. If anybody could have made it, it was Emily. I just thought the perils were too great."

"But, Fox, you saw those kids going home from K9 day after day." I realized as I said it that this was not quite true. Fox had not been there day after day, and maybe now I was beginning to understand why. "You heard the miracle stories about kids who were much worse off than Emily—kids who made it, kids who went home."

"I trusted Emily's courage," Fox said. "I've never questioned that. But the fear never went away. The possibility of this kind of ending was always too real to ignore."

From Fox—from any man, probably—that was a huge admission. I stopped drawing flowers on the quilt and leaned over to put my face next to his.

"We all did the best we could," Fox said. "You did it your way, and I did it mine."

"And Emily did it her way."

"Yes," Fox said. "Emily did it her way. And hers was the very best."

Through the lace curtains, the sky was just growing light when Fox and I made a solemn pledge to each other. We might not have her in our arms, but we would forever hold Emily in our hearts. She would be there for us, a beacon and an angel. In return, we would try with every measure of our beings to live up to the model she had set for us. We would try to marshal her courage and dignity. Emily would be there to remind us of what truly mattered. With her as our guide, we would try to weed out the trivia that so often bogged us down and came between us. Emily had held on through remarkable impediments. We would try to do the same.

Emily was a very small girl. But her legacy was enormous. We promised her, and ourselves, that her life would not have been lived in vain.

Fox and I held each other close. Then, for the first time in many, many weeks, we began to make love.

For a moment we both hesitated. Without acknowledging it directly, I think we both wondered if this act would somehow be disloyal, or even blasphemous. Was it vulgar to engage in an act of love when our child might at any moment be taking her last breaths?

Again, without speaking, we reached the same conclusion. It was love, after all, that had brought Emily into the world.

So we did make love, tenderly and with the passion of emotions worn bare. And far from being a sacrilege, by the early morning light, our intimacy felt sacred.

TWELVE

Just after 6 A.M. I slipped into the living room to call the hospital. Exhaustion had clobbered both Fox and me. Mercifully, he was still asleep.

"She's holding on," said Claire, the night nurse. "Everything's steady."

So much for Dr. Milo's dire, she'll-be-dead-before-daybreak prognostications. I threw on the clothes I had worn the day before. I still felt proud of Emily, this child who through mere perseverance could blast holes in the confident omniscience of an entire profession. "Assume nothing," Emily was teaching Fox and me. Assume nothing, and take nothing, not one idle moment, not one fleeting breath, not one small squeeze of a tiny hand, for granted.

"See you at K9," I scribbled in a note to Fox. "I love you."

Emily had dazzled us with her fortitude. "Medicine can't explain this," Dr. Wolf said when we pressed him about how Emily could have fooled so many experts for so many weeks. Among the many tragedies of what was unfolding in these dark and final hours was that the world was losing a kid of strong determination, a kid whose system was obviously made of steel.

My own system felt more like Jell-O. I had reverted to a kind of automatic pilot. I probably brushed my teeth, but who really knows, for sure, or cares? I dressed with no concern for my appearance, only a sense that clothes were a necessary appurtenance in the outside world. Did I wash my hair? Who remembers?

On Central Park West I waited and waited for a cab. Every taxi in the world that day sped past me, headed downtown. Even the awful gypsy cabs, clunkers with their mufflers dangling and meters that ran (or failed to) according to their drivers' whims, seemed to be avoiding me. At last, impatient, I settled for a bus. "Good morning!" the driver said cheerfully. It was the day's first real evidence that I was actually alive, not just some impostor ghost. I happened to catch sight of someone's newspaper on the bus, and realized for the first time that it was Friday the thirteenth. Another of God's hilarious practical jokes.

The night before, Fox and I had made the few telephone calls we felt were mandatory. We called my family and the close friends who had offered to serve as conduits to everyone else. Here at the hospital, there was no need to make such efforts. The way Felipe averted his eyes at the K9 reception desk told me he knew exactly what had happened in Emily's surgery. His gaze met mine for just the slightest moment as I walked through the heavy double doors. Then suddenly he swirled on his swivel chair and busied himself with paperwork. Avoidance seemed like a reasonable enough response. What, after all, could he or anyone else possibly say?

But just outside the NICU, Leslie was waiting for me.

"I heard," was all she said. She folded me in her arms. I was so glad she was there, and told her so. She had called the hospital the night before and learned the results of Emily's surgery. She had used the whole evening to cry and to process the information that she had feared, but that even she had never really expected. The smile she wore now was not about happiness or good cheer. It was about affection and support.

"You're going to have to help me," I said.

"Anything," she said. "You know that."

I told her I didn't think I could face the phonies or the curiosity-seekers. I did not want rubberneckers staring at my child like the remnants of a roadside wreck. K9 was a strange place. These tiny babies and their oversized parents mirrored many of the best and worst qualities of the outside world. I knew there were people there, LaTanya and Mrs. Diaz among them, who would feel genuine sadness over what was happening to Emily. But I knew that others would feel the sense of relief people often experience when something terrible happens to someone else.

"It's already happened," Leslie told me. Stopping off at the hospital on the way to work, the father of baby Valenzi had demanded to know why Emily was wearing a colostomy bag, what had happened that had made this necessary.

"I got real bureaucratic and asked him what his relationship to the family was," Leslie said, knowing full well that he had none. "He got all flustered and told me he was the mother of baby Valenzi. I told him I doubted very strongly that he was the baby's mother, and he got even more embarrassed. I also told him he knew perfectly well that we were not at liberty to disclose details about the condition of other patients."

This was one of the many times when I truly loved Leslie, when the ex-schoolteacher came out in her. She could dress anyone down, and practically have that person standing in the corner thinking over what he or she had just done wrong. It had happened to me just once, and had elevated my respect for Leslie enormously. At this moment, it was a relief to know I had such a formidable ally.

Together, Leslie and I approached Emily's isolette. Emily, though sedated, raised her eyelids at the sound of my voice.

"Emily, baby, it's Mom," I said, and slipped a hand through her porthole. She grabbed for my finger instantly, and gripped it with her fierce python hold. Her bright blue eyes were focused directly on me.

Blood had collected in the doughnut-shaped bag that now clung to her stomach. Emily rocked her head slightly. Her shoulders twisted and she seemed restless. She looked paler than she had even last night. Her vital signs, however, continued to hold steady.

"Oh, God, Leslie, I think she's in pain."

"She can't be," Leslie insisted. "She had morphine less than two hours ago."

But Emily seemed fussy and uncomfortable to me. If I didn't know better, I would have sworn she was asking me for help.

Still breathing steadily, still displaying even levels of oxygen saturation and a sturdy heartbeat, Emily had drifted off to sleep by the time Sandy Baumgartner stopped by to see us at midmorning. I wondered how the obstetrical practice had gotten the word about Emily so quickly. I guessed that Dr. Friedman had called these three women who had figured so closely in this tiny child's life saga.

"Actually, we called him," Sandy said when I asked. They had been following this case very closely.

From time to time in these last two months I had seen Sandy around the hospital. Once, late at night, I bumped into her partner, Cindy Rubin, in the cafeteria. She did a double take and said she barely recognized me "because you know, when you don't expect to see someone in a particular place, it's hard to place them." Jane Gerstner and I had run into each other several times, too, usually when she was hurrying off to some seminar or to visit an obstetrical patient.

But here was Sandy, just stopping by. I remembered those big eyes, the expression of astonishment when Emily was born alive and fighting. I remembered the tone of surprise in her voice in the delivery room when she marveled, "She's big!"

Now Sandy was taking the conversation in another direction entirely.

"Do you know what you'll do?" she asked me.

I looked at her blankly.

"Where you'll bury her, I mean," Sandy said.

It seemed so stark, that question, but it also seemed caring. I knew that in the broad scheme of her own life, it couldn't possibly make any difference to Sandy where we buried Emily. From someone else, at some other time, the question might have seemed coarse and insensitive. But in a strange way now, it seemed intimate. It was a question even many close friends could not have brought themselves to pose. Here in the bright, brutal light of the NICU, it felt comforting to have Sandy ask. No, I did not want to think about burying my baby. I did not want her to die and I did not want to dig a hole for her and put her in the earth. But I did want someone to care. Just at that moment, it seemed that Sandy was asking because she did care.

"At the Glades," I said. "Our summer house. In a little grove in the woods, between her grandmother and grandfather. Under a holly tree." It was the first time I had thought it out so clearly. I was surprised that it came out in such an organized sequence.

"That's nice," said Sandy, who must have known that one word that did not apply to the subject of burying one's baby was "nice."

"You'll want to have her near you," she added.

"I think I want to be near her," I agreed. "I think I have to."

Later, after Sandy had left, it occurred to me that I knew nothing about the logistics of death. What do you do? How do you claim the body? Do they force you to have an autopsy? How do you transport it afterward? Where do you take it? Do you have to pay to get it out of the hospital? New York has taxes on everything else. Do they put some kind of toll on dead bodies? Do children get a discount?

"Talk to Dr. Friedman," Leslie suggested when I bombarded her with these questions. "But I'm going to tell you. I don't think it's going to be as soon as everyone else is saying. I think Emily is going to surprise people. I just don't think she's ready to go."

It was midday when Fox came by. As usual, he rummaged through the pile of gowns to find a yellow one, and as usual, while he washed up in the family room, he managed to spray Hibiclens, the surgically approved hand-washing solution, all over the wall behind the sink. I watched the thick pink goop drip down a surface that hadn't been painted for years. Maybe this was where Jackson Pollock had picked up his inspiration.

"I returned the milk machine," Fox said as he dried his arms

off. He was still patting himself dry up to the elbow, the way the
instructions on the wall said to do.

"You were right," he said. "They yelled at me for getting it
dusty."

"Did you tell them why you were returning it?" I asked.

"Yes, but I don't think they even listened, or heard. They just
started in about how they had every right to charge me extra. I
walked out. I didn't need to hear that."

I told Fox we needed to find out how death operated in this
big-city hospital. He agreed; we both knew that this was information we might need at any moment. He said that if it would make
it easier for me, he would try to find Friedman and talk to him.

But before we could locate our doctor, we nearly collided
with Iris Brick, the social worker, chugging down the hall at an
alarming pace. Iris had lost her vacation sunburn, but her great
girth still made her look like Gibraltar on wheels. At first she gave
us a pleasant but perfunctory smile. "Don't bother me," it said.
"I'm busy, and whatever it is, I don't want to talk about it." When
she realized that we were blocking her way, and that we obviously
had something to speak to her about, she ground to a halt. One
hand held the clipboard I now suspected she took to bed with her
each night, and the other came to rest on her hip. It was a definite
gesture of impatience.

"Yes," she said.

"Iris, maybe you heard about Emily," I began.

"Yes, I did," she said. The annoyance had moved from her hip
to her voice. We waited for some expression of sympathy or compassion, maybe something like "What a shame," or "We're so sorry
things turned out this way." Iris said nothing.

Fox took over. "What we were wondering is, what do you do
when a person dies here? How do you take care of what are euphe-
mistically known as 'the arrangements'?"

With her hand still clenched firmly on her hip, Iris looked
from Fox to me and then back again. She spoke in a tone that
suggested that a pair of idiots in full costume had just shown up at
her house the day after Halloween.

"You call your funeral director, of course," Iris said. She might have been suggesting that we call our dentist or our hairdresser. Didn't every family have a funeral director at the ready? Iris seemed to be suggesting.

"Well, that's not really someone we've needed since we've been in New York," Fox said. His own voice was extraordinarily calm. I knew this was a control technique he employed when he was really about to lose it.

"Does the hospital have some kind of a list of references?" Fox asked.

"No," Iris said. "No, we don't keep any kind of a list. We can't possibly be making recommendations for something like that. But there is Frank Campbell over on Madison. Don't they have a branch on the West Side?"

Fox said he would look into it, and Iris pushed on past us. From the hospital's official channels, that was the beginning and end of anything resembling grief counseling. Now we remembered why we had started calling her the antisocial worker.

Back in the NICU, I looked up in horror to see the Siamese twins, the great-grandmothers, headed in our direction. Their shoulders actually looked like they were connected while they walked from the well-baby nursery across the hall toward Emily's isolette. As usual, they were wearing print dresses and giant grins.

"We came over to see your little baby," the gray-haired great-grandmother, the real one, said.

I had lodged myself in the doorway, with my arms thrust out spider-style to block passage.

"Not a good idea, not a good idea," I said. "She's very sick."

"Oh, what a shame," the great-grandmother said. "Here, we'll cheer her up."

They were craning over my shoulders when Leslie intervened.

"I'm terribly sorry," she said in her crisp bureaucratic voice. "No one is allowed to see patients in the intensive care unit except immediate family."

"We've been in there plenty of times," the brunette great-grandmother, the pretend one, protested.

Leslie's voice turned very stern and authoritative.

"Well, then, you've been in violation of hospital policy. I'll overlook it this time, but if I hear that you've been in here again, I'll have to report you. Now, please, leave the Butterfields alone."

Chastened, the great-grandmothers scurried back across the hall.

Late in the afternoon, Fox left. His stamina was failing him, and he knew he still had phone calls to make about "the arrangements." He promised to return if anything changed, even slightly. Obviously Fox had more confidence in the New York City transit system than I did.

All I could do was sit there. Leslie's shift ended and Linda took over. Linda, another longtime NICU veteran, had always struck me as completely cool and unflappable. She was the kind of person you would like to have along in case you happened to run into a tidal wave. Today I noticed that her eyes were glassy. This was hard for her, too.

As with all the babies in the NICU, sheets of specifications about her care and "meds," or medications, were taped to Emily's isolette. Since early Thursday evening, just after her surgery, the information about Emily had included a "D.N.R." order, for "do not resuscitate." This particular instruction came out of the very difficult discussion Fox and I had had with Dr. Friedman before our daughter's surgery. If things turned out for the worst, we said, never believing they actually would, we wanted only minimal intervention. Basically, what we asked for was pain relief. Beyond that we felt that nature should be allowed to take what we hoped would be a swift and merciful course.

Leslie was among the NICU staffers who fully concurred with this decision. "There isn't any other choice," she agreed when I told her about our talk with Friedman. I saw now that Linda, too, must have shared the same view. I knew that not all the nurses did. Several were deeply religious, and saw our position as heathen, or as some kind of threat. Several believed it was amoral, maybe even criminal, to "let a child die." Even if the child showed no hope for an even minimal existence, these nurses maintained that maximum measures should be taken to prolong its life. Lifesaving was their mission. I suspected that Carolyn Foreman, the icewater-for-blood chief nurse of K9, was one of those. But to my surprise, Carolyn had let it be known that no one who disagreed with the decision Fox and I had expressed would be assigned to work with Emily in her final days.

Whereas Leslie often chatted, Linda went about her work quietly. When she did speak, it was in soft, subdued tones. The result was that I could focus solely on Emily—just sit there, thinking of her, hoping she knew how much I loved her. Until Linda wordlessly stuffed a tissue into my hand, I did not realize there were tears falling down my cheeks.

Just before midnight, a pair of newcomers arrived in the NICU. They were twins, "O'Brien A and B," as they were labeled, a girl and a boy, born a few days short of twenty-seven weeks of gestation. The girl was born vaginally, I heard the doctor who was examining them say. But the boy had a more difficult delivery, and finally came via a cesarean section. From across the room I recognized that both bore the peculiar florid hue of so many preterm infants. They were no larger than boiled lobsters, and from a distance, that is what they looked like.

Soon after they were examined, a pediatrician I did not recognize was escorting the father and both sets of grandparents into the NICU for a kind of Cook's tour. This made five adults—six, if you counted the doctor, a major violation of K9's two-adults-per-baby rule. Probably I was just cranky. Here they were, celebrating the beginning of two lives while Fox and I were watching one end. But having such a crowd in there at that hour made me mad.

Their presence did not irk me as much as the pep talk the doctor proceeded to administer. To hear him tell it, the children were all but guaranteed the rosiest of futures. The boy would be a football star, a rocket scientist, a rock musician, anything he wanted. The girl would be a beauty queen, a rocket scientist, a rock musician, anything she wanted. Well, yes, the boy was showing a little trouble with his lungs, but this was perfectly normal among these very small babies. No problem, the doctor assured his tour group. The little girl might have had some cranial bleeding, but this happened, too. I could not believe my ears. I had been in the NICU almost two months, long enough to know that with such small humans, nothing was guaranteed, one way or the other. Things changed suddenly, and often, and usually not for the better. Where had this doctor parked his reality quotient?

The babies' father looked totally dazed. He was short, with curly brown hair that trailed down over the back of his collar, and a thick mustache. He was wearing high-top athletic shoes with the laces untied and dragging behind him. One grandmother looked buoyant; the other wore a smile that seemed tentative and apprehensive. The two grandfathers seemed overwhelmed by what they were hearing and seeing.

"They sure are small," I heard one of them say. It occurred to me he was probably talking not just about his own two grandchildren, but about all the residents of the NICU.

The doctor completed his speech. Much of it sounded reminiscent of the Prematurity 1A overview that Friedman had delivered to Fox and me. It felt like centuries since we had heard that introductory lecture. In just under two months we had learned a lot more than we ever could have imagined, and a lot more than we ever really wanted.

But unlike this physician, Friedman had never been so encouraging about Emily's chances for survival. From day one, Friedman's best guess for Emily had been fifty-fifty. This guy was all but promising not only success, but superachievement.

"Any questions?" he asked.

The buoyant grandma spoke up.

"When do they get to come home?" she asked.

The doctor replied in a glad-you-asked-that kind of tone. "As soon as possible," he said. "We know you're eager to have them at home, and we want to get them to you as soon as we can."

The twins' relatives trundled out, stopping to peer into several nearby isolettes on their way out. "They sure are small," I heard the grandfather say once again. Sitting with my sick—no, with my dying—child, I was still stunned by the doctor's Little Harry Sunshine discourse. Did he think he was doing the family a favor by sounding so sanguine?

There was a lot of activity around the warming table that held the boy twin. Snippets of muffled conversations from the residents suggested that the boy's respiratory system was a mess. The radio was tuned to soft rock, Arlo Guthrie's "City of New Orleans." By early morning, the male twin was dead.

But Emily was still holding on. Her oxygen saturation levels were high, not a good sign. Her little heart, on the other hand, was relentless. It kept ticking away steadily. Her eyelids were heavier, but still she lifted them at the sound of familiar voices. If she was going anywhere, it wasn't voluntarily.

I'd finally stumbled home sometime around two that morning. I started to tell Fox about the twins, about their grandparents; the father with his long, dragging shoelaces; and the doctor who had already issued the twins their college diplomas, cum laude. But Fox was too preoccupied to be amused by my nightly installment of "Days and Nights in K9," our personal family soap opera. He was worried about Emily. He was upset that I was taking taxis around New York by myself at that hour. And while jogging in Central Park that night, he'd lost his wedding ring.

"I don't know how it could have happened," he said. "It's always been loose, and it must have just fallen off." He was speaking very quickly, uncharacteristic for Fox, and his voice was higher than usual. This level of strain was obviously about something much bigger than his wedding ring.

"I went back with a flashlight and retraced my route, step by step," he said. I tried to imagine Fox scouring the area around the reservoir in the pitch dark. All I could think of were hordes of muggers lurking in the bushes, wondering what the hell this guy in the shorts and sweatshirt was up to. "I looked everywhere," he said. "It's just gone."

He was pacing the length of the living room. "I told them when we bought it that it was too big, but they kept telling me it was better to have it loose." I remembered the day we'd ordered his ring from an old-line jeweler in Boston. Fox had never worn a wedding ring before, but this time, he said he really wanted to. He said he liked looking down and seeing the slim band of gold on his left hand. He saw it as tangible evidence of the force of his commitment to this marriage.

"I can't believe I lost it," he said.

So that was what this was all about, loss. We were staring it straight in the face with Emily, the most unimaginable loss there was. No one we knew could cope with it. And we, who had no choice, were not doing much better. Here we were, swinging along on the entitlement tree. But suddenly the limb we were clinging to was cracking right off. No one had prepared us for this. No one had given us loss lessons. In all those years of training as winners, as people who could achieve and attain and obtain, no one had figured on something like this.

Maybe that was why our phone had been strangely silent these last twenty-four hours. Some friends were respecting our terrible sadness and our need for sanctuary, but others couldn't cope with what was happening to Emily and to us. If all hell could explode in our faces, how could they feel safe or immune?

Emily's fate was out of our control. I tried to console Fox by focusing on what small matters we could manage. "Look, don't worry about it. It's just a wedding ring, a little piece of gold. We can call the jewelry store tomorrow. We'll get another one."

"But it was engraved," he said. He was almost in tears. I knew it was not the ring he was crying about it.

"So we'll have it engraved again," I told him. "Big deal. We can always get another ring."

But we knew we could never get another Emily.

• • •

Leslie was so very gentle that next day. As much as she could, she let me help with Emily. I could not administer medication, but in almost every other procedure, she let me participate. She urged me to touch Emily and to continue talking to her. Leslie saw nothing at all bizarre about these long, maternal colloquies with a child too sedated to know which end was up. From time to time Leslie put her hand on my shoulder to shore me up. No one could have taught her that in nursing school.

As Friedman had predicted, Emily was beginning to show signs of edema. Also as he had predicted, it was not pretty. She was beginning to inflate, a pale balloon of a child. Retaining liquids like that was stretching her skin. I told Leslie I was worried that the baby would abrade herself on the coarse hospital linen. Leslie nodded, and after a while, she briefly disappeared. When she returned, she was carrying a roll of lamb's wool.

"Here," she said. "I ordered this for Emily."

Very carefully, we lifted our frail, sick baby and stretched her out on the soft wool padding. Immediately I broke into tears, because now more than ever, Emily looked like a tiny naked angel floating on a cloud.

"She'll be more comfortable," Leslie said.

The way the nursing rotation had been set up, Leslie would be off for the next two days. She reminded me of this late in the afternoon, as her shift was about to end.

"I want a little time with my Emil-lee-lee," she said. "Just the two of us. I have some things I need to tell her."

I turned my back and left them together. I knew that Leslie was saying good-bye.

"It's all right," she said a few minutes later. "I'm done. You can come back now."

Yes, she had needed to bid Emily her own private farewell, Leslie said.

"But you know what?" she said. "I don't think it's over. I think she'll still be here when I come back on Tuesday."

Leslie said she couldn't pinpoint what it was about Emily that made her feel this way. It was nothing medical, for on that front, the prognosis was terrible.

"I don't know what it is," she said. "She's held on longer, done better, than any adult I've ever seen. I think maybe it's that she's just too young. She's just not ready to let go."

Late in the afternoon, Dr. Wolf came by. He looked drawn and discouraged. I was surprised. I would never have pegged him as someone who took each case so personally. Watching Friedman laugh and carry on just moments after Emily's surgery had reminded me about the extra layer of emotional callousing that doctors are forced to develop. Wolf had seemed so arrogant, so sure of himself as a surgeon, that it had been easy to throw him in with the rest of them.

"It's untenable," Dr. Wolf was saying as he peered into Emily's isolette. "Yes, that really is the only word for it, untenable."

There was no moral justification for this kind of an outcome. "No explanation," Wolf said. He shook his head.

"We try to treat each patient as if he or she were our own child, because that's the highest level of care we could give," he told me. I was grateful for this insight, and wished he had given me this information before he had operated on Emily. It couldn't have altered the result, but it might have changed the way Fox and I felt about some of these physicians.

"It's an awful thing to say," I began, carefully, because I knew I was about to skate on brittle ethical ice, "but in some ways, it almost would have been better for everyone—certainly for Emily —if she had never made it out of the surgery."

Wolf and I were both looking at Emily. We were studiously avoiding each other's eyes. "There's no question," he agreed. "You're absolutely right. There's no possible excuse for putting her through this kind of prolonged death. It's terribly unfair to her." Then he looked up from Emily and for a moment gazed straight at me. "And also to you and your husband.

"Certainly it would have been more right," Dr. Wolf said, "if we can use such a word, if Emily had failed to make it through the surgery.

"Unfortunately," he said, "I'm not prepared to act as executioner."

His words sounded harsh. Once again I was struck by the terrible dilemmas presented by the sweeping changes in technology, and in how medicine is actually practiced. The responsibility of Dr. Wolf and his fellow physicians here on K9 to their dying patients had in no way changed. What was different, thanks to technology, was their power to intervene, sometimes cruelly, in the process of dying. I wondered if these doctors did not sometimes stop to wonder if they had not been sucked too unquestioningly into the vortex of this technological revolution. Did they stop to think each time they made a life and death decision? Did they think of what they would do for their own sick child?

Dr. Wolf was writing something on Emily's file. At the least sign of discomfort, he promised, Emily's morphine would be increased.

"Take away the pain," he said. "That's the least we can do."

But in the view of some of the nurses, apparently, there was much more they could do. Late at night, Emily once again began to writhe in what had to be pain. Christine was standing beside me, watching the meter record a change in Emily's heart rate. It seemed to me that her heartbeat became more erratic as the morphine wore off. But according to the doctors, the dosage was much too high for that to be happening.

"I think you're right," Christine told me. "I think this kid's in pain."

Four years at Berkeley in the drug-filled 1960s and I had never so much as smoked a marijuana joint. I don't think I was really a goody two-shoes, just a coward, and someone who deeply feared losing control in the face of mind-altering chemicals. In the years since college I had steered equally clear of anything stronger, as I liked to joke, than Dom Perignon. Drugs terrified me. But in

the upside-down world of the NICU, here I was, demanding drugs
for my own child.

"Christine, she needs more morphine," I said. "We can't let
her be in this kind of pain."

To my surprise, Christine marched right over to Dr. Milo, the
doctor on duty. Since his prophecy that Emily would not survive
the night after surgery, Dr. Milo had done little more than nod at
Fox or me. The same physician who had invited me to share in
Chinese food one night and who had asked me to intervene in the
great breast-bud debate now swerved his eyes away from Emily's
station when we were sitting there.

"Carl, this little girl is in pain," I heard Christine tell him.

Dr. Milo repeated that this was impossible. The dosage had
been adjusted by quantity and frequency, he said, waving Christine
away.

Christine stood her ground. "Carl, are you a pediatric cardiologist, or what? Emily's heart is holding just fine, then suddenly it
jumps from here to Queens and back. She's writhing. Her face is
contorted. This kid's not in pain?"

In an impatient tone, Dr. Milo told Christine that the consequences of a morphine overdose could be disastrous. I wondered
just how much more disastrous it could be than anything else
Emily was facing. He said he did not want to be responsible for
that particular disaster. Besides, Emily had had morphine just two
hours ago. It was not possible, said Dr. Milo, that she could be
needing more. Dr. Milo buried himself in a file folder.

I loved Christine for what she said next. She raised her voice
just a notch and squared off so that Dr. Milo could not possibly
ignore her. "Carl, this kid's defied us on everything else," she said.
"Why do you expect her to be any different now?"

Dr. Milo looked up. Christine had gotten to him.

He paused for a moment, then said, finally, "Go ahead, give
her the morphine."

Christine unlocked the drug cabinet and prepared a fresh
dose. But even with the hypodermic needle in her hand, she stood
close to me, as if she wanted a confidential conference.

"Listen, you don't have to agree to this," she began. "You may think it's crazy. But there's something I'd like to try on Emily."

I wondered just how much crazier anything could be compared to what was going on around us. Death was crazy, at least when it came to this child who hadn't even gotten a real chance at life. More than ever, I felt the mad dizziness of Alice's rabbit hole. But none, alas, of the mad merriment.

"I'd like to try some alternative medicine," Christine said. "What I'm proposing is something called healing hands."

Now this was craziness I could, as they used to say in my native habitat, relate to. California may not have invented the notions of conservation and maximization of energy, but we in the Golden State had certainly perfected it. My own mother had tried some variant of healing hands for her chronic rheumatoid arthritis. Just about everyone I knew in California advocated treatments such as therapeutic massage or even Rolfing, where the negative energy was supposedly pounded out of you. Healing hands, however, added a spiritual dimension, Christine said. The idea was to summon forth a higher kind of energy and direct it to the ailing person. As she and I agreed, there was no guarantee that healing hands would help Emily. But it couldn't hurt to try.

Christine took several deep, long breaths. She rubbed her hands together, almost as if she were washing them, but without soap or water. Then she took several more breaths, also long and deep. When she felt ready, she slipped her hands through the portholes of Emily's isolette. She held her hands directly over Emily, palms facing toward her naked body. Breathing very, very slowly, Christine closed her eyes.

She stood like that for close to fifteen minutes. Her hands held steady; so did Emily's heart. I noticed how utterly serene Christine's face looked. Finally she opened her eyes, then very gently, very slowly, removed her hands from the isolette.

"I'd like your permission to try that again," she said.

"Why would you need my permission?" I asked. "Of course, please, try it again anytime. You have my permission. I'm honored that you would even want to try this."

Christine smiled, but her eyes looked weepy. "There's something I have to tell you," she said. "Last night I dreamed of Emily as a five-year-old. She had blond hair and huge blue eyes. I woke up really believing it was her, really believing I had seen her. If there was anything I could do, any way I could make that happen—"

Shoulder upon shoulder, Christine and I stood and wept together.

In the morning I learned through the NICU grapevine that cranial sonograms of the surviving O'Brien twin had revealed severe bleeding. This augured poorly for little Alexa, as her parents had named her. One grandmother had been in frequent residence. She had stuffed a giant toy rabbit into Alexa's isolette. It was bright pink, and dwarfed the baby it was intended to amuse.

"We're going to have to rest this outside her isolette," Joyce, Alexa's nurse, told the grandmother. The grandmother protested, but Joyce explained that the huge animal blocked access to the baby. Grudgingly, the grandmother accepted this explanation. Alexa's isolette was against the wall and directly behind Emily's, so that when the grandmother and I were both sitting, our backs nearly touched. The grandmother had a loud, gravelly voice. She and Joyce discovered that both were avid opera fanatics. They shared a love for Puccini. And there, in the middle of the NICU, the grandmother began singing the love song from *Madame Butterfly*. If her spoken voice sounded like a rusty drainpipe, the grandmother's singing voice was impossibly pure and sweet.

Her high, clear voice seemed to encircle this room full of tiny people in small plastic boxes. What a strange, absurd theater this was. I remembered the story of Butterfly, looked again at Emily, and began to weep silently. I hardly noticed when Edna, one of Emily's first nurses in the NICU, quietly approached me.

"Mrs. Mehren," she said, still using the name that belonged rightly to my mother.

"Mrs. Mehren, I passed my road test."

I looked up at Edna. The grandmother was still singing behind us.

"For my driver's license," Edna said. "I passed my test. I'm a licensed driver in New York now."

Once again the contrasts seemed overwhelming: driver's license . . . death . . . opera . . . adoring grandmothers and giant pink bunnies. Where were we? What was happening?

I offered Edna my congratulations.

Just then Dr. Milo bounded into the NICU. He was trailed by a retinue of even younger doctors—interns, I assumed. Dr. Milo hadn't shaved and looked, as Georgeanne, the wisecracking nurse, told him, "like something out of 'Miami Vice.'"

"Hey, wait a minute," Dr. Milo said, rifling through the mound of papers he was carrying. "Where's O'Brien B?"

"O'Brien B died, Carl, get with it," said Georgeanne.

The younger doctors laughed uproariously, and so did Dr. Milo.

Later, after the opera-singing grandmother had left, Alexa's mother was wheeled into the NICU. She must have been in her mid-twenties, a gentle-looking woman with perfect ivory skin and soft brown hair. She wore a lacy white nightgown and a worried look on her face. Her husband hovered in the hallway. I noticed that his shoelaces were still untied.

The mother told Joyce that from her hospital bed, she had been making plans for the boy twin's funeral. They discussed the details in quiet, calm tones. The funeral service would be in their parish church in Brooklyn. She had chosen a coffin by phone. The mother gazed at her surviving child, and abruptly changed the subject.

"When I bring her home," she said to Joyce, "is it better to put her in a crib or a bassinet?"

It was her choice of adverbs that chilled me. I had to hope that this new mother was displaying optimism, not presumptiveness, in asking what to do "when" she brought her baby home. I wanted to gently share with her the lessons I had learned from Emily: Take lots of deep breaths, pray, hope every moment that your child will live a full, happy, and healthy life. Promise her that you will always, always try to do what is best, and right, for her. But never assume anything. Never think that you can script the outcome. A bassinet or a crib? How about a shoe box or a laundry basket? If you do get to carry this child home, first consider yourself blessed. Then worry about where the kid will sleep.

But of course I knew I had no right to say any of it. She would discover her own truths from her own child, as all mothers do. I smiled at Emily, pale and bloated. I wished our own learning together could go on forever.

Over the weekend it was especially quiet in the NICU. Under the circumstances, this comparative tranquility seemed like a gift. There were fewer people to avoid, fewer people to offer explanations to. Emily's condition remained grimly stable. Defiantly, her heart just kept on pounding. Leslie was off, and Robin was giving me my distance. Dr. Rosenblatt took me by surprise when he pulled a chair over and sat down beside me.

Objectively, it probably made sense for physicians like Dr. Rosenblatt to spend less time with patients like Emily, who would not recover. He had a limited amount of time and energy. From a cool, cost-benefit perspective, it undoubtedly served everyone better for him to invest his time, energy, and professional skills in those he could bring back to health.

But I was in no mood to be so charitable or detached. I looked across at Dr. Rosenblatt. I had nothing to say. I wondered just how he would begin a conversation with me.

How he began it, at first, was with a joyless gaze. Finally, in a low voice, he said, "I'm sorry."

I was awful to him, I admit it. But there was no way I was going to let him off the hook. I was mad at the whole profession, all of institutionalized medicine. There, sitting next to me, was one of its emissaries.

"Why, Dr. Rosenblatt," I said in what I knew was a horrible, sickly sweet, sarcastic tone, "what a surprise. I didn't think you were speaking to Emily and Fox and me anymore."

Had someone spoken to me like that, I probably would have gotten up and left. Dr. Rosenblatt would have had every right to. Instead he took a breath, and in a heavy voice, began to speak. It was as if every word were carefully weighed, as if he wanted to make sure he was saying exactly what he meant to say.

"People who go into intensive care work like success," he said. He drew another breath. "We don't do well when we don't get it."

I was amazed. It seemed to me that this was as close to, if not an apology, certainly an expression of sympathy, as we were going to get.

His intentions may have been good, but his logic seemed so skewed. It was not the time or the place for a debate or a colloquy, but I wished I could urge Dr. Rosenblatt to examine his thinking. If "success" meant keeping every patient alive, then Dr. Rosenblatt was doomed to lose every case. Sooner or later, with or without his medical genius or anyone else's here on K9, every one of these kids was going to die.

But maybe this whole notion of "success" helped explain why so often—as had obviously happened between me and Dr. Rosenblatt—the doctor-patient relationship breaks down over how much time the doctor is willing to give a dying patient, like Emily, and her family. Maybe in the doctor's view, as the patient got sicker, she in fact merited less of the physician's time, because even the physician cannot stand what is happening.

"People don't know what to say when things go wrong," Dr. Rosenblatt continued. "Nobody does. Not the doctors, not anyone."

Another pause. Now it felt as if Dr. Rosenblatt were speaking from somewhere deep inside himself.

"The hard part for parents in an intensive care situation is turning over control. Parents feel powerless," he said. "They have to let other people, the doctors, make the decisions.

"Well, that's how we feel now, too. What's happened to Emily is out of our control. And we're used to having that control."

From this tightly wrapped man it seemed an extraordinary confession. I knew that doctors, to conduct their business, must become inured to death. Many people in our comfortable, privileged society can escape with only the narrowest knowledge of death or horrific illness. But doctors must deal with it every day. It seemed to me that Dr. Rosenblatt had just opened a very small vent in his armor.

Didn't we patients, we family members, set these physicians up to be knights of healing? If they thrived on the adulation that came when a desperately ill person was returned to health, weren't we nonphysicians acting as unwitting co-conspirators to that hunger for unquestioning praise and gratitude? We want and need our doctors to be superheroes, men and women who will ride in on their white technological steeds and valorously save the day. Many of those who choose this profession are all too eager to fill that role.

But there ensues a vicious circle, an insidious mutual seduction: Because we who seek healing see our doctors in this unrealistically heroic light, they are easily, even eagerly, seduced by the adulation. When something goes wrong, when the trust and near-idolization begin to wane, it is truly like the end of an affair. Everything tastes vaguely tinny. The lovemaking, or in this case, medicine-making, isn't very good any more. All of a sudden you notice mortal failings—that someone like Dr. Rosenblatt is not just pleasingly plump, he's fat. It's an unrealistic set of expectations to place on any professional relationship. But there we were, Dr. Rosenblatt and I, living examples of how we had all bought into it.

There was not a lot I could say. I nodded at Dr. Rosenblatt. "Right," I said. "Thanks."

Moments later, I heard Dr. Rosenblatt using the NICU telephone. His voice sounded different now, lighter and softer. It took just a minute to realize that he was speaking to his own child.

"Remember," I heard him say, "if you get hungry, there's a

bagel in that plastic bag in the counter." He listened briefly, then said into the telephone, "I love you, and I'll see you tonight."

For a long, hard moment those words tugged on my heart, for I knew I would never have such a conversation with my own sweet child.

In the afternoon, while Fox and I were sitting with Emily, Cindy Rubin came by.

"Big day in labor and delivery?" I asked her.

Cindy shook her head. "I'm not even working today," she said. "I just came by to see you two." She corrected herself. "You three."

Cindy looked at Emily, not clinically, but with what seemed to me like concern and caring in her eyes. She sat there for a while; we traded small talk—the weather. Her work schedule. Fox's travails at the *New York Times.* Then Cindy shifted the subject.

"Every year I take three months and go to work in Guatemala," she said. "It's the only way I can survive Fifth Avenue."

This came as a surprise. I had only seen Cindy in the context of a physician practicing in a high-rent district, with patients who showed up for appointments in designer maternity clothes. Cindy explained that ever since she was in medical school, she had been working with a tribe of Indians in central Guatemala. "They're very isolated," she said. The tribespeople spoke an Indian dialect, and Cindy, who spoke Spanish, worked through an interpreter.

"You see these people with real problems, I mean life-and-death problems. It makes it hard to keep a straight face when a patient in New York screams and yells when she has vaginal itch."

But Cindy did not just want to discuss her Manhattan practice. She had brought up her work in Guatemala for a reason. Sometimes, she said, when a member of the tribe becomes terribly ill, the family consents to take the ailing person to a hospital in the nearest city.

"But when it's obvious that there's no hope, when medicine can't save the person, the family members take him out of the

hospital and back to their village. I've watched them take the tubes
out of a baby, then carry the child back to its home in the village.

"You see, they believe a person should die among family,"
Cindy said. "They think hospitals are unnatural. They believe they
should be there to encircle the dying person, and that the last thing
the person sees should be his home and his family.

"And if the person can't be saved, you know what? I think
they're right."

I told Cindy it was all I could do not to remove Emily from
her tubes and her machines and spirit her away.

Cindy looked me squarely in the eye. "You don't know how
much I wish I could help you with that," she said.

That evening, Marjorie, the grande dame of NICU nurses,
began reminiscing about how things had changed in her twenty-
five years of neonatal care. Marjorie was in her fifties, with her
fingernails painted dusty rose and filed in perfect ovals. Marjorie
was of the generation that probably began smoking in high school.
When she returned from breaks, Marjorie's breath betrayed what
she had been doing.

"I remember when it used to take all morning to mix up a
batch of Hyperal," Marjorie said, referring to the nutritional supplement given to these babies. "The nurses had to do it all. It was
so complicated, if you forgot what you had put in, you had to
throw it out and start all over."

Those were the days before respirators, Marjorie said, the days
when nurses had to stand around and "bag" the babies to help
them breathe. "You stood and pumped and pumped until your
hands got tired," Marjorie said.

When respirators were finally introduced, she remembered,
they were scaled to adults.

"These units are wonderful," Marjorie said. For emphasis she
thumped an empty isolette.

Marjorie said the abortions were probably the saddest cases
she had dealt with over the years. "You get them all the time, more
often than you would like," she said. "Aborted fetuses who sur-

vive." Sometimes the mothers had lied about the duration of their pregnancies; others may not have known how far along they were; and sometimes, Marjorie said, physicians had their own reasons for performing late-term abortions. Generally these terminations were performed via saline injections into the uterus. Some hearty fetuses actually managed to survive. When I saw how strong Emily was, at just one day into her twenty-fifth week of gestation, I could understand this.

"I had one as large as five pounds," Marjorie said. "You can imagine how late that had to have been."

She recalled one parent who sued—or tried to, anyway—because the baby had survived the abortion. And then there was the nurse Marjorie knew who became so attached to the survivor of a late-term abortion that she followed the baby all the way through to a foundling hospital, and finally through the process of adoption. When the child finally was adopted, the nurse sent the new parents flowers.

Marjorie told these stories with no hint of judgment in her voice. It was all part of a life's work, she seemed to be saying. They were like war stories, and I loved listening to them. I realized how much I would miss these stories; how much, in a strange way, I would miss Leslie and Marjorie and Christine and so many of the others.

THIRTEEN

Deirdre Klein, the resident who had been present at Emily's delivery, looked nervous and uncomfortable when she approached Fox and me. It was Monday. Emily's refusal to die had the doctors completely confounded.

"Hi," she said. She was wearing running shoes, and she was shifting from foot to foot. She looked at the floor.

"I don't know what to say that will make any of us feel any better," Dr. Klein said. She looked up. "I'm here today, if that helps at all."

Leslie said at least three nurses had stopped her that morning to say that when they saw Fox or me, they walked the other way.

I told her that this fed into a fear that I suspected I shared with many people who were dying or seriously ill: that those around them would disinvest emotionally because there was no future to the relationship. It seemed to me that that was what some of the doctors had done, and certainly some of the K9 parents. Carla and her husband, for example, had actually spun in their tracks when they saw Fox and me headed down the hall of K9.

But Leslie said it was much less complicated. There was no

great psychological conspiracy going on here, she said. "They just don't know what to say."

What to say, that was the question. Friends and family were at a loss. Doctors and nurses had no words. Mrs. Diaz, my old partner in hope and patience, had simply taken my hand in hers. No words. And none was needed. LaTanya Cooke, celebrating Jacques Louis's much-awaited promotion to the well-baby nursery, threw her arms around me and held me so close that her tears dripped down my cheeks. She pulled away slowly, and as she backed up out of the NICU, she gave a shy wave, just like a little girl, then ran forward and hugged me once again. We had shared so much, LaTanya and I. And we knew our sharing was about to end.

Leslie knew how much I wanted to hold Emily. She knew I wanted to clutch her close to my chest, to stroke her, to tell her we loved her, and to thank her for being so brave. So at midmorning, she carefully opened Emily's isolette. All her tubes and devices were still attached, and Emily had more than doubled in size from edema. Her labia had puffed up fiercely. Her head had so increased in size that her hair, a pale golden brown, barely stretched around it. From lying in one position she had a small bedsore on the side of her head. An "owie," one would have said to an older child. I wanted to kiss her and tell her the kiss would make it well. But of course I knew it would not.

Emily, our little angel, was stretched out on her cloud of cotton fleece. It sat atop a mattress covered with a pink, lavender, and aqua striped blanket. Little bunnies and elephants cavorted between the stripes. Leslie edged the mattress out so I could lean over to touch her whole body. It looked as if Emily were on a tray coming out of an oven, as if she were a platter of cookies or a TV dinner.

Emily was wiggling her toes. I watched her struggle to open her eyes. Her skin was so thin now it was translucent. I could see her eyes moving and trying to force the lids open, but the effort was too great. They remained closed.

With Leslie's permission, I kissed Emily's forehead. Over and over I kissed her, from me, from Daddy, from Grandma, from Grandpa, from everyone I could think of. Her skin should have been papery, Leslie said, but it felt soft, like butter that has been left in a sunny window. She tasted so clean and pure—not at all the way I imagined incipient death would taste. Maybe this is not how death tastes, I thought. Maybe this is what heaven tastes like.

I looked up to see Dr. Wolf standing nearby.

"This really isn't fair," I said. "This shouldn't be happening, and it shouldn't be happening here. Fox and I should have Emily at home with us. Not here, with all these machines and strangers."

Why couldn't I just take her home? I demanded. Why couldn't I be like the tribal people in Central America that Cindy had told me about? Was this kind of an ignominious death proof of how advanced medicine had become in our society?

Dr. Wolf waited until I had finished my outburst. He folded his arms and gave me a somber expression.

"It may just be that in our country, we're too advanced for our own good," Dr. Wolf said.

"Let me know if there's anything I can do, anything you want," Leslie said, gently rubbing my back after Dr. Wolf had left.

I appreciated her compassion, but still I lashed out at her. "I want her to be well again," I said. "I want her to be whole and healthy. I want to take her home. I want to dip her toes in the sea."

Leslie smiled helplessly at me. I noticed that she had removed the resuscitation bag from Emily's isolette, lest any falsely well-intentioned samaritan be tempted to use it.

Leslie leaned against the pole next to Emily's isolette. I had put my hand through the porthole. With an almost fearsome force, Emily was gripping my finger. It seemed at the minimum a metaphorical statement: Please Mom, I don't want to let go.

"She exhausts me," Leslie said. "Not because I have to do so much for her. She exhausts me because I don't have that kind of energy. I don't know where she gets it. I don't know how she does it."

That was how Fox found us, poised in front of Emily, word-lessly marveling. Traffic had tied him up, he said. "Yesterday it was an AIDS parade, all the way up and down Central Park West. Today it was just traffic. I don't know which is worse."

Fox found a stool and pulled it next to me. He, too, slipped a hand through the isolette. Emily gripped it immediately. We stayed in these positions, immobile, a weird, high-tech version of a Henry Moore family grouping, until Leslie cleared her throat behind us.

"I'm off in a few minutes," she said. "But there's something you might want to think about. You might just want to talk to Emily. You might want to give her permission to go. It sounds strange, I know, but she may be waiting for that. She may need to hear it from you."

Smiling thinly, Leslie turned to leave.

"Just a minute," Fox said. He looked at Leslie but did not let go of Emily's grip.

"Thank you," he said.

Late that afternoon, Fox and I took a short walk in the park. It was a spectacular, sunny day, with flowers in bloom everywhere we looked. As always in Central Park, there were musicians every-where, too. Their drumbeats made me nervous. They sounded too much like overamplified heart monitors.

Just for a moment, Fox and I sat down on a small grassy knoll. Nearby, a huge family was having a picnic. They were laughing and shouting in Spanish. Small children were tossing balls and dripping mustard from fresh-cooked hot dogs. Just on the other side of us, two homeless people were sleeping in black plastic garbage bags. In this setting, with very little discussion, Fox and I decided to heed Leslie's advice.

The NICU was almost empty when we got back, an almost rare event that seemed fortuitous. Fox leaned close to Emily's isolette, opened a porthole, and began to speak to her.

"Emily, baby, this is Daddy," he said. "It's Daddy and I love you. Very, very much. And Mommy loves you. She loves you more than you could ever imagine. You're her world, Emily. She loves you so much. We both do.

"Emily, we've never seen anyone fight as hard as you've fought. You've made us so proud. You're amazing, Emily. You just don't give up. You've shown those doctors. You've shown them how wrong they were when they said you wouldn't make it, when they said you wouldn't survive birth, when they said you'd never make it to this stage. You've given us time with you, Emily, and we're so very grateful. You've let us come to know you, a person, our daughter, who will always live in our hearts. My God, Emily, we're so very lucky to be your parents.

"Emily, you've taught us about courage. We never knew what courage was until we knew you. We know now that courage means nothing until it is tested. You've shown us dignity, genuine dignity. You've given us so much.

"But Emily, listen carefully. It's all right for you to lay down your burden. You don't have to fight anymore. You don't have to keep struggling. If you want to go, Emily, it's all right. It's okay to cross over the bridge."

Fox's voice was cracking. He was sobbing while he spoke. Very quickly, we each slipped a hand into Emily's isolette. She grabbed them, and held on, and held on.

It was our last morning—I knew it almost the second I walked through the heavy wooden doors of K9.

It was May 17, a Tuesday. It was Emily's fifty-third day of life.

"I've called Fox," Leslie said. "He's on his way over."

"This is it, right?"

Leslie nodded. "I think so, yes."

Emily's heart was arrhythmic; her saturation levels appalling. She was turning a dusky color. There was not much time left.

We assumed our familiar positions, Fox and I. Bulbous and bloated, her chin nearly touching her chest and her eyes shrunken to tiny slits, Emily still could squeeze our fingers. Leslie was administering morphine every hour. Our routine was so well choreographed that she could inject the drug while Emily continued to clutch our hands.

Clearing his throat, Dr. Wolf announced his presence. As always, he was accompanied by his resident of the day. This one was particularly stolid, with arms crossed protectively in front of him. His name was Dr. Alcott. He looked like the little boy who was trying to dress right in order to please the teacher. Like Dr. Wolf, he was wearing pleated pants with his Metpath beeper strapped on; like Dr. Wolf, he wore a white shirt and a safe, striped silk tie.

Dr. Wolf peered at Emily. He looked at us, at a loss for words for the first time since I had known him. Stress plays strange games, and I found myself trying to help him out. A little innocuous conversation, I must have thought. That's what we need right now. For no reason at all, I heard myself asking if he had ever finished that book on the Civil War.

"Oh, no," he said. "I got busy, life got crazy. I mean, I'm sure I'll get back to it—"

"Well, didn't you want to know how it ended?" I asked.

All of us, even the stolid resident who had never so much as cracked a smile, laughed in spite of ourselves. It broke the tension a little. But Dr. Wolf's smile was short-lived.

"This is so sad," he said. "So difficult for everyone."

"Most of all Emily," I said.

"Most of all Emily," he agreed.

Just after ten, Dr. Friedman entered the NICU. It was the first time I had seen him since Friday. Today he was flanked by two women I did not recognize, both wearing street clothes and expressions of professional curiosity. "This is Twin A," Dr. Friedman said, stopping in front of Alexa's isolette. "Born vaginally, two days shy of twenty-seven weeks. Twin B, born by cesarean, expired. 'A' shows indications of severe cranial bleeding." Dr. Friedman was wearing his lizard smile. He had risen to the role of perfect host, or lord of the manor showing off the family estate. His two guests nodded with interest as he offered more details about the O'Brien twins, then moved on to baby Smith.

"Reger's syndrome," he began. He described the particulars of Carrie Lynne's case, noting that her mother was just fifteen. He talked about Carrie Lynne's tracheotomy and her blindness. He made no mention of her aloneness in life. Maybe he saw nothing medically significant in the fact that in five months of life in the hospital, Carrie Lynne had not had a single visitor.

To my horror, I realized that Dr. Friedman and his companions were headed toward Emily.

"Now this female infant was born at twenty-five weeks," Dr. Friedman began. "Ruptured amniotic sac—"

I couldn't believe it. Our child was in her final hours, maybe her final minutes, and Dr. Friedman was turning her into a laboratory exhibit.

"For God's sake, Dr. Friedman, have you no sensitivity at all?" I exploded.

Friedman looked stunned. He was not accustomed to being challenged, certainly not publicly. Just because he had donned his armor that morning did not mean he was intending to do battle— not this kind of battle, anyway.

"What is this, a house tour? And we're the interesting furniture? Are you moonlighting as a museum docent?" My voice was quite loud, louder than I would have wished. I did not want to sound like I was out of control, but I was close. "What is going on here?" I demanded. "Is it too much to ask for us to have a little privacy with our dying daughter?"

Dr. Friedman began herding his guests into the hallway. I could hear him muttering something about "inappropriate reactions" and "emotionally distraught."

"You bet I'm emotionally distraught," I called after him. "My child's about to die. Don't you think that would make most people emotionally distraught? And by the way, has anyone ever talked to you about inappropriate medical reactions? You don't think maybe you're being a little callous toward a dying child and her family?"

Dr. Friedman stuck his head back in the door. His eyes had narrowed and his mouth was tight.

"I'm in charge of this unit, and I have a job to do," he snapped. "I'll do it as I see fit. I don't need you to tell me how to do it."

Emily died at 10:53 that morning. Fox and I were holding her hands. We felt her writhe, and then we felt her stop moving. We knew it was over. We knew her heart could go no further.

"That's it," Leslie said when the monitor went flat.

Lovingly, Leslie wrapped her in the blanket with the bunnies. Because there was no place else to go, we sat with her in the awful doctors' lounge, the one with the dirty coffee cups everywhere, the used surgical scrubs balled up on the floor, and the pictures of doctors in diapers taped to the wall. Leslie stood guard outside. From time to time I heard her menace potential intruders: "Don't go in there. The Butterfields are in there. Leave them alone, please."

This was when I rocked her, when I held her the way I had promised to hold her. I talked to her, clutched her, stroked her, and kissed her. I had never seen such a beautiful child.

Fox took her from me and held her tight. It occurred to me that he had never heard her cry, and that now there would be no chance. He touched his nose to her head and took a long, deep whiff. "I never want to forget this," he said. "I never want to forget the way she smells."

Fox held her close to him and studied her carefully. "You know what?" he said. "She feels bigger, heavier." He smiled with what I took to be paternal pride. "She feels just like a real baby."

There were tears in his eyes. In an odd way the three of us felt for the first time like a real family. Now I held her again.

"Of course she feels like a real baby," I said. "She is a real baby. She's a beautiful baby. She's our baby."

On the way out, Dr. Friedman handed us a death certificate. I knew it had come from the manila envelope taped to the cupboard just behind the receptionist's desk. I had spent weeks trying not to see that envelope.

Dr. Friedman seemed unable to make eye contact with us. "I'm sorry it ended this way," he said. He gave a half a lizard smile.

For the past couple of days an isolette had been parked just outside K9. It was covered with a pink hospital gown, like a shroud. I knew it was waiting for Emily. On the way out, I tried not to look at it.

We buried her on a Sunday. Just as we had planned, we chose a spot for her between Fox's parents, under the holly tree. We made a strange procession, Fox and I, Ethan, Sarah, and my mother, trekking through the woods with spades and shovels, and with Emily's ashes in a small urn. It was cloudy and cool, and in an odd maternal gesture, I had wrapped the urn in a pastel baby blanket. My mother thought this made perfect sense. "You don't want her to get cold," she said.

When we arrived at the clearing where the holly tree stands, my mother reached for the blanket-wrapped package. "Please," she said. "Let me hold the baby."

Ethan and Fox set to digging with shovels, while Sarah worked the soil with a spade. The spacing of Emily's grave seemed important to Ethan.

"Grandma's here, and Grandpa, and now Emily," Ethan said to me. "And someday you and Dad will be here, then Sarah and me. And someday"—he seemed to brighten at this thought—"someday the whole place will be nothing but Butterfields."

My mother was still holding Emily close while we all said good-bye. I'd written a small service for Emily. It was a letter to her, really, thanking her for her courage and dignity, and promising that she would remain in our lives forever. Fox read a poem, Edgar Allan Poe's "Annabel Lee." Only with apologies to Poe, we changed it to "Emily-lee." We all recited the Twenty-third Psalm. Then, together at her funeral, we sang the song I'd promised Emily I would play at her wedding. There in the woods, we all joined hands and sang to Emily, "You are my sunshine, my only sunshine. . . ."

Our arms were linked as we walked back down the path. My mother had slung the baby blanket over her shoulder like a shawl.

Two days after we buried Emily, my mother and I returned to her grave site to plant flowers. The sky seemed clear enough until we knelt with our spades and trowels at Emily's spot between her grandparents. I had bought huge quantities of forget-me-nots, a flower I have always loved for its gentle modesty and for its sweet name. The pots were strewn around us and Mother and I were elbow-deep in soil. Suddenly the sky darkened above us. When we looked up, we saw that the rest of the sky was still clear, as if some cosmic meteorologist had drawn a circle directly over our little clearing in the woods. There were very few tricks that nature could pull on us at this point. We were not surprised to feel raindrops.

My mother squinted a moment as she looked upward, toward heaven.

"It's the baby," she said. "She's crying."

We planted the flowers in silence, pleased when Emily was covered with a lush blanket of delicate blue blossoms. Arm in arm, we walked down the path through the woods, toward the sea. Now the clouds vanished. On the hill by our house we saw a rainbow. We knew it was Emily, smiling.

EPILOGUE

The emptiness after Emily died was indescribable. Part of me had gone with her, and part of me and Fox together. I remember reading that Mary Todd Lincoln filled the White House with ghostly moans after her son Will died. So it was for me. I cried in bed. I cried in the kitchen. I cried while jogging. I cried in the car. I visited her grave a lot. I cried there, too, of course.

I wanted to die myself. It seemed the least I could do for this small child.

Fox was disconsolate. He had lost his baby daughter. And now it seemed he had lost his wife as well. Our fuses were short with each other. To avoid domestic conflagrations, we avoided each other. "Some marriage," Fox said, more than once. He was right.

We learned that the vocabulary of grief is very small. We heard the same safe bromides from people, over and over. "Well," they'd say, revealing their ignorance, "at least she didn't suffer." Or, "It's probably better this way. Who knows what limitations she might have had if she'd lived?" Or, "Someone so small was never meant to live." Or, "Isn't modern technology amazing? Years ago she would have died at birth." Or, "At least you had her as long as you did." Or, "We know just how you feel. We had a miscarriage once." I cringed each time I heard one of these remarks. No doubt they were well-intentioned. But did these people have any idea how stupid, how useless, and sometimes how cruel these comments could be?

The one that hurt the most was the one we heard the most. "Don't worry," these people would say. "You'll have another one." Once, not long after Emily died, I did lose control when a woman said this to me. She was my age, she had four children, and she should have known better. Nevertheless, she did not deserve it when I railed at her. "Children are not replaceable parts," I barked. "Do you think Emily is like a disposable razor? Do you think you can just throw her out and pick up a new one, and everything will be fine?"

The woman was mortified. So was I. I knew Emily could never be replaced. I missed her with every molecule in my being. But the truth was, I did want another child.

It felt disloyal to Emily even to think this, so I tried not to. For his part, Fox felt torn. He knew how desperately I wanted to be a mother. But he was terrified. What if something were to go wrong again? What would happen to us then?

One day Fox steeled himself. We were sitting on our deck, reading the Sunday paper. "Maybe we should think about adopting a child," he said.

Fox knew I was a champion of this subject. In high school, I worked for an adoption agency. I cheered each time a friend was able to adopt a baby. When you want a child, who cares about the origins? I'd always said. Just get a baby and love it as much as you possibly can.

But now, with my feelings so tender, I exploded. I felt as if my skin had been acid-washed away, as if my ganglia were exposed. I roared at Fox with the fury of every woman who has craved a biological child: "Oh, so I can't have my own. So you want me to take the booby prize?"

Fox chose not to bring the subject up again.

In the meantime, we made major changes in our lives. Emily's death did make us want to circle our family wagons. We moved to

New England to be closer to Ethan and Sarah. We bought a house. We got a dog. I learned to steer past the diaper and baby food sections of suburban supermarkets. I learned not to see the other women pushing their laughing, bouncing babies.

Time passed. If the ache of Emily's death did not heal, it did dull a little. We lived in a place where we had no history. When people asked, as they always did, "And do you and Fox have children?" I fought the urge to say, "Yes, but she's dead." Instead I would try to smile and say, "Fox has two terrific kids." When people who knew about Emily would say, "Well, maybe you'll have another one," I no longer raged out loud. "Maybe," I would say. "Who knows?"

Emily's first birthday fell on Easter Sunday. Among the traditional holidays, this celebration of new life, this feast of resurrection, has always been my favorite.

Winter had lingered late. There was still some snow and ice on the ground. We walked carefully up the small hill to the three-hundred-year-old church in our town. The time came for congregants to offer individual prayers. I stood and the strength of my voice surprised me. "Pray for Emily," I said. "Our beautiful baby girl. Born one year ago, she lived just fifty-three days."

We drove out to the Glades and left flowers for Emily. That night, we toasted her with champagne. I baked a birthday cake. We blew out her single candle.

Not long after that, I made an announcement.

"Fox," I said, and was surprised when the words came out so steady, "I think I'm ready to adopt a child now."

Fox was stunned. He thought maybe he had heard me wrong. He was also scared. My mind had been so closed to this subject when he brought it up. What accounted for this shift? And what if an attempt to adopt ended badly? What would happen then?

We talked it out. We talked endlessly. It felt good. This was the first time in many, many months that we had talked so openly. The pain of losing Emily wasn't fading, but the anger was.

We decided to work through a friend in California who ran

an independent adoption program. It was based on the principle of complete openness. Everyone involved would know everyone else, and the birth parents would be encouraged to remain in contact after the adoption. We knew how it felt to lose a child. We liked the idea of continued contact a lot.

But there was still a lingering voice in the back of my brain. Try it one more time, it said. Give a biological baby one more shot.

We consulted a new specialist. He told us the odds were not great. He armed us with a new raft of chemicals and a new set of instructions. This time I felt very clear-headed. The desperation I had felt in New York was gone. With the adoption procedure in progress, I knew we would get a baby, either way.

The new doctor was a white-haired Scotsman. His voice had a lovely burr. His office was filled with fertility symbols from around the world. Medicine can do so much, he said. But most of it is in the hands of the gods.

I made them do the pregnancy test twice. That's how disbelieving I was when it came back positive.

The pregnancy was tense. At any moment I expected the worst. I refused to buy maternity clothes—why bother, when things were only going to go wrong anyway?—and just wore big sweaters. So successfully did I practice denial that when a well-meaning person asked, "And when are you due?" the question I heard was "And what do you do?" "I'm a journalist," I replied.

My obstetrician specialized in high-risk pregnancies. He warned that I had a 50 percent chance of having this baby early, too. We did a lot of finger-crossing. Each week was a new milestone. Fox, my doctor, and I all breathed easier once we passed the twenty-fifth week.

Three weeks before the new baby was due, my friend Melissa held a baby shower for me. The date happened to be Emily's second birthday. It was a coincidence to Melissa. But to me it was a kind of signal from heaven. I felt we were celebrating for Emily, as well.

Sam Butterfield surprised everybody when he came full-term. He emerged with a sharp cry, just like another Butterfield baby. He is healthy and strong. Sam smiles a lot, and has a deep belly laugh that brings smiles to everyone near him.

Each day with Sam is a joy. We feel blessed by this child. We try hard to heed the lessons of his sister. We try hard not to take one moment for granted.

Sam and I like to take long walks together. We look at the trees, the birds, the flowers. Someday I am certain that we will look up and see a rainbow. "That's your sister," I will tell Sam. "That's Emily."